THE PROBLEM OF BURKE'S
POLITICAL PHILOSOPHY

Oxford University Press, Ely House, London W. 1

GLASGOW NEW YORK TORONTO MELBOURNE WELLINGTON
CAPE TOWN SALISBURY IBADAN NAIROBI LUSAKA ADDIS ABABA
BOMBAY CALCUTTA MADRAS KARACHI LAHORE DACCA
KUALA LUMPUR HONG KONG TOKYO

THE PROBLEM OF BURKE'S POLITICAL PHILOSOPHY

BY

BURLEIGH TAYLOR WILKINS

CLARENDON PRESS
OXFORD
1967

© *Oxford University Press* 1967

PRINTED IN GREAT BRITAIN BY
JOHN WRIGHT AND SONS LTD., AT THE STONEBRIDGE PRESS, BRISTOL

To

C. F. COWGILL

PREFACE

IN recent years Burke commentators have been especially concerned with the problem of whether Edmund Burke should be considered a natural law theorist, and it is this problem to which the present study is addressed. Unfortunately this problem has often been discussed in a partisan and polemical spirit which, while it has served to reactivate our interest in Burke's political philosophy, has tended to overemphasize Burke's relevance to the political problems of our day and to pass over in haste some of the internal difficulties in Burke's thought which have stood in the way of a general acceptance by scholars of the thesis that Burke was committed to the natural law. Such difficulties are most in evidence in what Burke has to say on the topics of human nature and natural rights, and it is these topics which I have, therefore, considered in some detail. In this study I have tried to fuse historical accuracy (a proper regard for the philosophical and historical traditions in which Burke operated) with philosophical analysis (a treatment of some of the logical difficulties that the natural law interpretation of Burke encounters). While the honour of being the first to advance the thesis that Burke believed in the natural law lies elsewhere, the more modest honour which I hope might be conferred upon this book is that, by virtue of taking seriously the major objections to the natural law reading of Burke and by proposing solutions to some of the philosophical difficulties in Burke's thought, it may perhaps make the natural law reading of Burke more acceptable to the scholarly community.

There is no standard edition of Burke's writings, although the definitive edition of his letters is well underway. Of various editions of the *Works* I prefer the Boston edition which I have used throughout. I hope that readers will excuse the Americanized spellings in my quotations from this edition.

I am indebted to Princeton University and to Rice University for financial aid in this study, to Professor Gregory Vlastos for some helpful comments and queries concerning the natural law, and to my wife for her assistance and patience in the preparation of this manuscript.

CONTENTS

PART ONE
BURKE AND
THE NATURAL LAW

I

BURKE AND THE HISTORIANS

THERE is nearly unanimous agreement concerning the importance of Edmund Burke (1729–1797) in the three areas of literature, politics, and, more recently, social and political philosophy. Yet the dimensions of Burke's achievements are not agreed upon. In literature the high praise of William Hazlitt, Thomas De Quincey, Matthew Arnold, and Leslie Stephen points to a permanent and richly deserved place not yet fully accorded Burke in either politics or political philosophy. Even here, however, the judgements that Burke was to English prose what Shakespeare was to English poetry or that he was the greatest prose writer of the eighteenth century may seem excessive. Unfortunately, Burke's writings give evidence of that 'rapid torrent of an impetuous and overbearing eloquence' which he detected—and disliked—in the writings of Lord Bolingbroke.[1] Indeed, it may be this impetuous and overbearing eloquence which is, in part, responsible for the peculiarly heated nature of the controversies still surrounding Burke's achievements in politics and political thought.

[1] Edmund Burke, Preface to *A Vindication of Natural Society*, *The Works of the Right Honorable Edmund Burke*, 12 vols. (Boston, 1865), I, 7. Burke's eloquence also has at times the effect of obscuring his meaning. David Hume's opinion of Burke's *Speech on Conciliation with America*, as reported by Boswell, is revealing: he found it to have 'a great deal of flower, a great deal of leaf, and a little fruit'. James Boswell quoted by Donald Cross Bryant, *Edmund Burke and His Literary Friends* (St. Louis, 1939), 224. But then, of course, Hume was an acquaintance and not a friend.

The older, nineteenth-century view of Burke's place in domestic politics as a defender of the English Constitution and Parliament against the conspiracies and wrong-doings of George III has been placed in jeopardy because of the doubts cast by Sir Lewis Namier and others upon the very premiss of George's misconduct. Was Burke's reason betrayed by his impetuous eloquence into overstating the case of the Rockingham Whigs against George III when he claimed that great principles were at stake in what was really an unprincipled (and pre-ideological) contest for power ? Perhaps Burke's impetuous—and overbearing—eloquence helps account for Namier's impassioned de-nunciation (in the name of a modern, sophisticated historio-graphy) of Burke's 'fertile, disordered, and malignant imagination'.[1]

In the field of international politics, how long is Burke's reputation as a remarkably prescient person who foresaw accurately—and from the very beginning—the course the French Revolution was to follow, likely to endure the charges made by Alfred Cobban and others concerning Burke's relative ignorance of French affairs and his mis-understanding, amounting almost to a wilful refusal to understand, of the causes of the Revolution ?[2] If these charges are correct, then Burke may survive as a prophet but his reputation as a man capable of making accurate, conditional predictions seems unlikely to outlast our know-ledge of his ignorance of those very conditions upon which

---

[1] *Personalities and Powers* (London, 1955), 21. Namier makes this charge in connexion with Burke's allegation of a 'double cabinet', a device whereby the King was said to have created a second, unofficial cabinet as a means of under-mining the power of the Cabinet and hence of Parliament; but it represents his overall estimate of Burke. Namier looked upon Burke's belief that George III conspired against the rights of Parliament as wholly mythical: 'In reality the constitutional practice of George III differed little from that of George I and George II.' Namier, op. cit., 43.

[2] Alfred Cobban, *Edmund Burke and the Revolt against the Eighteenth Century* (London, 2nd edition, 1960), 120–1: 'He falls back on the absurd expedient of assuming the Revolution to be the result of a conspiracy. . . . In addition to this fundamental error, he was persistently and almost ludicrously wrong in his detailed estimate of the state of French affairs.'

his predictions would seem to have depended for their success. However, Thomas W. Copeland's intriguing argument that Thomas Paine, unaware of Burke's true feelings about conditions in France and knowing Burke only as a friend of the American Revolution, revealed to Burke in advance the plans of the leaders of the French Revolution and thus turned Burke against the Revolution at an early date, might adversely affect even Burke's prophetic standing.[1] Burke's insight into the course of French affairs may, after all, have been in large part a lucky break and not evidence of an unusual grasp of political realities.

Within the imperial structure, Burke is known, rightly, as a champion, first, of the American colonies and, second, of the people of India. Yet on both these fronts his reputation as a statesman who saw deeply, and correctly, into the needs of his times is being subjected to grave doubts. Carl Cone and Charles R. Ritcheson, for example, seriously doubt the adequacy of Burke's plans for the conciliation of the American colonies. Cone writes: 'His proposals would not have satisfied the Americans in 1775. . . . To the Americans, rights were more important than they were to Burke. . . .'[2] Ritcheson remarks that what was needed in the American crisis was 'a genius who could cast in a new mold both the imperial and the domestic political scheme of things'.[3] Obviously, both Ritcheson and Cone doubt that Burke, adhering as he did to the traditional conception of Empire and failing to anticipate the idea of a Commonwealth, was such a genius. On the Indian question, historians have looked with new sympathy upon the efforts

---

[1] Thomas W. Copeland, 'Burke, Paine, and Jefferson', *Our Eminent Friend Edmund Burke* (New Haven, 1949), 146–89; J. T. Boulton, 'An Unpublished Letter from Paine to Burke', *Durham University Journal*, XLIII (1951), 49–55. Before Copeland, two of Burke's biographers, James Prior and Robert Bisset, had called attention to Paine's personal relations with Burke and to Paine's revelations to Burke concerning the plans of the French revolutionaries; but Copeland was the first scholar to establish the veracity and the details of this story.

[2] *Burke and the Nature of Politics, The Age of the American Revolution* (Lexington, 1957), 284.

[3] *British Politics and the American Revolution* (Norman, 1954), 190.

of Warren Hastings and with new suspicions upon both the motives and policies behind Burke's impeachment proceedings against Hastings. G. M. Trevelyan's judgement that Burke was wrong in his analysis of the Indian situation and in his apparent assumption that the Indians would willingly accept British domination (if only it were just) seems likely to continue to gain acceptance.[1]

It is not my purpose to try to resolve these problems, which belong to two species: (1) the extent to which Burke's analysis of contemporary affairs was factual rather than fantastic; (2) the extent to which Burke's proposed solutions to the political problems of his day were workable and statesmanlike. Even if, as is doubtful in the light of current debates among historians, the criticisms of Namier and others completely destroy in time Burke's reputation as a man extraordinarily aware of the political and historical processes of his day, a considerable part of Burke's reputation as a political thinker might still survive. Admittedly, it would be an odd, and for Burke personally an intolerably paradoxical, survival: he who professed to despise theory and to prefer 'fact' would be proved to be right in theory and wrong in fact.[2] But for some it might add to the significance of Burke as a political philosopher if one could pry him loose to some extent from debates about eighteenth-century political events.

Concerning the question of Burke's value as a political philosopher as distinct from the questions of his worth as a political commentator and actor, one can, I think, proceed fruitfully by the following strategy: accept Burke's factual premises as if they were true and see whether the conclusions he derived from these premises in conjunction with his ethical premises are at all illuminating in political philosophy. In other words, we need not proceed, as many contemporary political theorists have, on the basis of

---

[1] *History of England* (New York, 1952), III, 125.

[2] One of Burke's favourite maxims was 'It is . . . not uncommon to be wrong in theory and right in practice: and we are happy that it is so' (*Works*, I, 128).

debatable history, to ascribe to Burke an unusual wisdom concerning the political realities of his day and to claim that this shows the profundity of his political philosophy. As Burke was not a systematic thinker, by far the largest part of the present undertaking will be an historical construction or interpretation—an exercise in the history of ideas.

First, I shall consider a little more fully whether, if Namier and other critics of Burke carry the day, Burke might still be regarded as deserving independent consideration as a political philosopher or whether, deprived of his historical underpinnings, he might fall to the ground as a philosopher. J. H. Plumb's characterization of Burke as the 'servant philosopher' of the Whig oligarchy[1] and Sir Philip Magnus's interpretation of Burke's ideas as 'rationalizations' of his interests[2] suggest that Burke's autonomy as a philosopher is in jeopardy and that only political historians (and possibly psychologists) need concern themselves with this, somewhat unsavoury, subject. One must admit that, if it is at all relevant to mention Hegel's connexion with the Prussian state, it is still more relevant to mention Burke's connexion with the English state, his long and distinguished career as a member of Parliament, his role as a kind of party manager for the Rockingham Whigs, and his indebtedness—including financial indebtedness—to Lord Rockingham. (But service need not be confused with subservience.)

Burke was in short a deeply committed man, a fact which no charges of 'insincerity' and 'Irish adventurer' can upset. He was deeply committed to the institutions of his adopted country, to the Christian religion, to the Whig party, and, despite the embarrassments this sometimes caused him, to all the members of his family. Burke was a committed person, perhaps to a degree unusual even for a political philosopher; and he, admittedly, shared in those

[1] *England in the Eighteenth Century* (London, 1950), 187.
[2] *Edmund Burke A Life* (London, 1939), *passim*.

virtues and vices usually found in the make-up of such a person. No one can, however, honestly deny the philosophical quality of Burke's *Reflections on the Revolution in France* or of his *An Appeal from the New to the Old Whigs*. No criteria can be produced which would demote these works from the ranks of philosophy which would not also affect adversely Plato's *Republic* or Aristotle's *Politics*. (That Burke was not merely a political philosopher is shown by his *A Philosophical Inquiry into the Origin of Our Ideas of the Sublime and Beautiful*, a work which, while it may have been good enough to have influenced Kant, also struck Kant as being too 'psychological'.[1] Kant's criticism, along with the title of Burke's work, indicates that the *Inquiry into the Origin of* . . . belongs, in large measure, to the empiricist tradition.)

In a famous letter to Norman Malcolm, written in 1944, Wittgenstein wrote: 'I know that it's difficult to think *well* about "certainty", "probability", "perception", etc. But it is, if possible, still more difficult to think or *try* to think, really honestly about your life and other peoples lives. And the trouble is that thinking about these things is *not thrilling*, but often downright nasty. And when it's nasty then it's most important. . . .'[2] This seems to say that philosophers have a duty to inquire into first principles and basic commitments regardless of the nastiness of the undertaking, including, I suppose, the nastiness of the personal and social consequences of the undertaking. With some justice, Burke may be said to have shirked this responsibility: personally, he was serene and unquestioning in his Christian faith and political principles, and determined to remain so. From the letters of his undergraduate days[3]

---

[1] See Barrows Dunham, *A Study in Kant's Aesthetics* (Lancaster, 1934), xii, and J. T. Boulton's Introduction to Burke's *A Philosophical Enquiry into the Origin of Our Ideas of the Sublime and Beautiful* (London, 1958), cxxv-cxxvii.

[2] Norman Malcolm, *Ludwig Wittgenstein, A Memoir* (London, 1958), 39.

[3] See Arthur P. I. Samuels, *The Early Life, Correspondence, and Writings of the Rt. Hon. Edmund Burke* (Cambridge, 1923), 20–159. One of Burke's fellow-students at Trinity College, Dublin, characterized Burke as being 'damd absolute' on one occasion. Samuels, op. cit., 239.

onward there is about Burke an increasing air of certainty amounting at times to dogmatism and an air of satisfaction with the merits of his convictions amounting occasionally to smugness. In political debate his frequent reluctance to discuss first principles is notorious,[1] though, as I shall try to show, somewhat misunderstood. Part of his condemnation of the French revolutionaries and their English sympathizers is that *they* were willing to discuss first principles regardless of the consequences: 'It has been the misfortune (not as these gentlemen think it, the glory) of this age, that everything is to be discussed, as if the Constitution of our country were to be always a subject rather of altercation than enjoyment.'[2] Burke, to be sure, was willing to probe deeply into the claims to virtue made by others, to try to turn, for example, Rousseau's claims to virtue into 'rationalizations' of Rousseau's vanity.[3] But he would not perform this 'nasty' kind of analysis upon conventional virtue or upon the established institutions of his adopted country. Which shows only that he was not an especially brave philosopher. Earlier in the above-mentioned letter to Malcolm, Wittgenstein asked: '. . . what is the use of studying philosophy if all that it does for you is to enable you to talk with some plausibility about some abstruse questions of logic, etc., and if it does not improve your thinking about the important questions of every day life. . . .' This is as Burkian an utterance as one can find in contemporary philosophy; and it is a question which Burke asked so often, in, roughly, the same critical spirit in which Wittgenstein asked it, that some people to this day persist in denying that so outspoken a critic of philosophy could himself be a serious philosopher.

---

[1] Burke's *Speech on the Petition of the Unitarians* (1792), *Works*, VII, 49, contains the following typical reflection: 'The foundations on which obedience to government is founded are not to be constantly discussed. That we are here supposes the discussion already made and the dispute settled.'

[2] *Reflections on the Revolution in France* (1790), *Works*, III, 352.

[3] See, 'The Nature of Rousseau', by the present author, *The Journal of Politics*, XXI (November 1959), 663–84.

2

Those who have doubted that Burke was a philosopher[1] might find some delight in the fact that commentators have long persisted in linking Burke's name with schools or modes of thought which are ordinarily considered antithetical. Burke has been labelled both a utilitarian and a natural law theorist, a Lockian and a foe of both Locke's empiricism and of his political liberalism, a Humian and an enemy of Humian scepticism, a disciple of Montesquieu and one who departed from Montesquieu's most important teachings, and, finally, the most outspoken enemy of Rousseau's doctrines and—by one author at least—a man who shared certain fundamental ideas about morality and the state with Rousseau. Such basic disagreement among commentators provides *prima facie* reason to suppose either that Burke failed to make clear his position on crucial questions or else that his position on these questions was inconsistent. Historically, the charge of inconsistency is a very old one which Burke himself went to great, if unsuccessful, lengths to silence in his *An Appeal from the New to the Old Whigs*. It was with good reason that Burke made such efforts for, generally, critics who have emphasized his alleged inconsistencies have done so to convince us of his utter or near worthlessness, while those critics who argue for the consistency of Burke's principles have at the same time proclaimed the value and/or relevance of these principles (whatever they are alleged to be). I know of no commentator who has urged that Burke was both consistent and consistently bad, or wrong-headed, in his political philosophy.

The questions as to where Burke's philosophical loyalties lay and as to whether Burke's doctrines were consistent are, while interrelated, capable of separation for purposes of

---

[1] This company includes Karl Marx (who called Burke an 'execrable political cant-monger': *Das Kapital*, I, part iv, chap. xxxi, note), Jeremy Bentham (who looked upon Burke as 'a madman, an incendiary, a caster of verbal filth': quoted by R. H. Murray, *Studies in the English Social and Political Thinkers of the Nineteenth Century* (Cambridge, 1929), I, 67), and, more recently, Robert M. Hutchins ('But he is not a seeker after truth; he is not a philosopher': 'The Theory of Oligarchy: Edmund Burke', *The Thomist*, V (1943), 78).

analysis. I discuss the question of Burke's relations to other philosophers chiefly in Part One not so much as a means of answering it definitively as of showing its complexity and suggesting how it might be answered. The history of ideas may emphasize either this problem of correspondence and relationship or the problem of the coherence of a man's thought; and, with the exception of my discussion of Burke and Blackstone (Part Three) where I have, I think, something to contribute to the question of correspondence or relationship, my emphasis will be upon the second question. Given the present status of Burke scholarship, I consider the question of coherence and internal consistency to be the more fundamental. Once we have decided what Burke really thought about questions such as the basis of duties and rights, the relation of justice to utility, &c., then it would, in principle, be comparatively easy to lay these doctrines of his alongside, for example, those of the utilitarians and the natural law theorists and to decide where the greater resemblances lie. Therefore, while references to Hume, Locke, and Rousseau are sometimes essential in interpreting passages in Burke my emphasis will be upon restricting such references chiefly to this purpose. And if, as critics from Charles James Fox to Robert M. Hutchins and Morton Auerbach have charged, Burke's political thought is riddled with basic—and elementary—inconsistencies, then it seems pointless to go on comparing the *whole* of Burke's thought with that of various eminent political theorists. He would be, as his detractors have insisted, only another case of a politician projecting a deceptive image of philosophical depth and coherence. He would rightly become the exclusive property of political historians, some of whom have claimed him all along. For it is, I think, generally agreed that pithy maxims and occasional insights do not add up to a political philosopher—or to anything else of consequence.[1]

[1] But there is a recent edition of Burke's maxims. See Timothy Sheehan, *Reflections with Edmund Burke* (New York, 1960), for Burke on Blame, Blessing, Blessings, Books, Bread, Bribery, &c.

At this point in Burke studies when the archives have but recently been opened and the publication of his correspondence in the new, definitive edition is still in the process of completion, and when nothing resembling the definitive intellectual biography of Burke has risen to take the place of various specialized studies (of which this is but another), it would seem that marking the resemblances and differences between Burke and other philosophers is a tentative business, better justified on the heuristic level as an aid to our understanding certain internal problems in Burke's thought than on the historical level as a means of measuring Burke's exact place in the history of ideas and of systems of thought. The following pages are conceived primarily in the heuristic sense indicated above.

While contradictory positions have been ascribed to Burke, they have not all been ascribed to him at the same time. Historiography shows that Burke interpretation has been, to a distressing degree, a function of the ideologies of different historical periods. In the nineteenth and early twentieth centuries when utilitarianism was a vital force Burke was depicted as being by and large a utilitarian and a foe of the natural law; more recently, in conjunction with the revival of interest in the natural law, there has emerged a much revised portrait of Burke in which he now figures as a foe of utilitarianism and a champion of the natural law. Some harsh words have been said concerning the ineptitude of previous students of Burke; the earlier misconceptions of Burke reveal, according to the revisionists, shallowness or shabby scholarship on the part of 'liberal', 'positivistic', 'utilitarian', and 'secular' scholars.[1] So far has the pendulum swung away from the utilitarian reading of Burke that one should try to understand why such a reading ever held sway.

[1] See Peter J. Stanlis, *Edmund Burke and the Natural Law* (Ann Arbor, 1958), where he speaks of 'the addiction to theory and the limited moral imagination of Burke's utilitarian and positivist critics' (33) and '. . . the various errors of omissions, irrelevant intrusions, false distinctions, misinterpretations, and contradictions which run through the evaluations of Burke's utilitarian and positivist critics' (34).

There is in Burke a cluster of concepts which lends some initial credence to the view of Burke as a kind of utilitarian: *utility*, *expediency*, and *convenience*, to give the most obvious and the most frequent. To be sure, these are often offset by concepts such as *justice*, *equity*, *law of nature*, and *natural right*; but if deciding upon the main thrust of a political philosopher's thought were a simple matter of the statistical frequency with which certain concepts are employed the utilitarian reading of Burke would still predominate. On this reading, Burke's religious faith, while generally acknowledged, served to show not that Burke was not a utilitarian but that he was a theological utilitarian;[1] and if his faith still proved troublesome it could be noted either that Burke had a 'mystical' streak or else an extremely practical one: perhaps his was but an eloquent version of that hat-doffing toward the Deity which one expects of politicians. Then, too, those places where Burke speaks most clearly the language of justice and natural law were often quite obscure ones. For example, his *Tract on the Popery Laws*, written probably during the autumn of 1761, was not published in his lifetime; and his part in the impeachment proceedings against Warren Hastings, while hardly obscure, was often made noteworthy by violent temper and vituperative language more than by his appeals to justice and right. *God*, *justice*, and *right* have perhaps the appearance of strategic afterthoughts in *some* of Burke's utterances, and a sensitive modern historian still finds it apropos to question 'whether we can always place full credence in Burke's remarks'.[2] It must be admitted that

[1] Leslie Stephen, *English Thought in the Eighteenth Century* (London, 1881), II, 219–52. C. E. Vaughan also pointed out that Burke's doctrine of expediency 'comes charged with the strongest sanctions of duty and religion'. *Studies in the History of Political Philosophy Before and After Rousseau* (Manchester, 1939), II, 37.

[2] Carl B. Cone, 'The Burke Revival', *The Burke Newsletter*, III (1961–2), 82. But this question can be used in either of two ways: to question the extent of Burke's commitment to natural law, or to question his emphasis upon expediency. It could, for instance, be argued that Burke when appearing before the House of Commons spoke the language of expediency and practicality to please his listeners and that his true feelings about natural law and natural right would be

when Burke occupies the centre of the political stage and is at the height of his parliamentary influence and reputation, he most often speaks the language of expediency. *Expedient* remains the word for Burke's famous speeches during the period of the American Revolution: the *Speech on American Taxation* and the *Speech on Conciliation with America*.

Burke's estimate of the importance of the principle of utility is easily demonstrated: he speaks of how men 'make fictions of law and presumptions of law (*presumptiones juris et de jure*) according to their ideas of utility . . .';[1] and he mentions with approval 'those principles of cogent expediency to which all just governments owe their birth and on which they justify their continuance'.[2] One commentator has suggested that for Burke the word *expedience* 'had hardly the meaning of utility',[3] but this is not supported by the texts. 'Expediency', Burke writes, 'is that which is good for the community, and good for every individual in it.'[4] Utility, he insists, must be understood in the sense not of partial or limited utility but 'of general and public utility . . . any other utility may be the utility of a robber, but cannot be that of a citizen.'[5]

If Burke had been a utilitarian, he would in all likelihood have been a rule utilitarian and not an act utilitarian (more like Locke, if Locke had been a utilitarian, than like Bentham). This is indicated by his emphasis upon the importance of moral and legal rules as means of habituating men to virtue and obedience and by his placing the burden of proof *always* upon those who would make exceptions to such rules. (There are, of course, other kinds of rules, and

obscured by the press of day-to-day business in the House and by Burke's desire to be an effective figure there. I, therefore, think it wise to assume that an author or speaker means what he says in the absence of overwhelming evidence to the contrary.

[1] *Report on the Lords' Journal* (1794), *Works*, XI, 93.
[2] *Reflections on the Revolution in France*, *Works*, III, 451.
[3] George Sabine, *A History of Political Theory* (New York, 1950), 616.
[4] *Speech on Reform of Representation of the Commons in Parliament* (1782), *Works*, VII, 98.　　　　[5] *Tract on the Popery Laws*, *Works*, VI, 323.

in the case of rules of practical conduct Burke would have the burden of proof fall not upon the exception makers but upon those who claim infallibility and universality for their rules.) By expediency and utility Burke means the good of the community; he takes a long-range and comprehensive view of expediency and utility. It is a habit of Burke's to take up and relish words such as *expediency*, *utility*, and even *prejudice*, and to use these words usually without any acknowledgement of their sometimes dubious associations. It is a kind of deliberate provocativeness on Burke's part, an unphilosophical refusal to acknowledge all the senses of a term; and he has been severely punished for this by those critics who have (unjustly) branded him an immoralist for his endorsement of expediency and an obscurantist for his approval of prejudice.

While the reading of Burke as a utilitarian (either *in toto* or in large part) has influenced scholars for generations, it is difficult now to see in Burke's deference to the principle of utility sufficient warrant for this construction.[1] Even the quotations from Burke that I have given above do not commit us to such a reading if they are taken in context. In that passage of the *Tract on the Popery Laws* where he discusses utility he also discusses equity, and he writes that 'All human laws are, properly speaking, only declaratory; they may alter the mode and application, but have no power over the substance of original justice.'[2] Even the passage in which he speaks of how men make fictions and presumptions of law according to their ideas of utility admits 'there is some restraint' upon the employment of these fictions and presumptions in courts of law.[3] *Cogent* expediency must differ to some degree from simple expediency, and Burke's emphasis upon the test of the cogency or reasonableness of a law deserves mention.

[1] For a discussion of this earlier construction by Henry Buckle, John Morley, and William Lecky, see Stanlis, op. cit., 29–34. Vaughan, MacCunn, and Sabine are also cited by Stanlis as supporters of this view, despite their own considerable qualifications.

[2] *Works*, VI, 323.   [3] *Works*, XI, 93.

Whether a law is expedient in the reasonable sense must, if we take Burke seriously concerning the independence of original justice from declaratory human laws, refer to the problem of whether the human law in question affects only the mode and application of original justice. This poses the further problem of Burke's conception of original justice, whether it is more proper to emphasize the origins of this justice in the Divine Will or to emphasize its harmony with our nature. It seems permissible to say, without glossing over the difficulties this involves, that for Burke the ultimate source of original justice is in the Creator and the intermediate source (which may be treated as ultimate in certain practical contexts) is the rational nature of man as created by God. Burke speaks of equity and utility as 'the two foundations of law' and characterizes utility as being, like equity, 'connected in the same manner with, and derived directly from, our rational nature'.[1] On the practical level both the unalterable nature of original justice and the principle of utility will serve as checks on short-sighted or partial utility, which differs from genuine utility by being derived from base interests or passions and not from our rational nature.

With this test of cogency as to whether a particular law or act is in accord with our *rational* nature Burke can avoid many of the problems which arise from the shorter and seemingly simpler question put by the utilitarians: Is it in accord with our nature ? He can continue to grade the parts of our nature and their pleasures in the old, Aristotelian way without encountering many of the problems which await the utilitarians as they try to sort out the various pleasures. No arrangement of pleasures in terms of intensity, &c., is necessary to his hierarchy of pleasures arranged in terms of their contributions to our rationality and welfare. Nor is he committed to any identification of pleasure with the good and of pain with evil. Indeed, he is especially vehement in denying such identifications.

[1] *Works*, VI, 323.

It might be said that just as Burke avoids a democratic chaos of competing pleasures all aspiring for a higher moral grade in terms of their intensity, duration, propinquity, &c., so, too, he avoids the democratic chaos in determining what is politically good for the community. The test of reasonableness makes the counting of noses unnecessary, Burke thinks. It is well known that Burke restricts his sense of 'the people' in the England of his day to about four hundred thousand in number; and there is no reason why a similar restriction cannot be said to hold for his sense of 'community', as these four hundred thousand upper and middle class Englishmen by virtue of their education and station in life should, according to Burke, know best what is just and useful for the whole community. Even if this be debated, there is no reason in Burke's theoretical apparatus why he should have been concerned with making government more responsive to the *wishes* of the many and every reason why he should have been concerned with making it more acceptable to reason: which is in fact the way he declared himself to have behaved in his political undertakings. (Of course, the utilitarians were not always democratic in their conception of the political process; still there is an affinity between their ethics and democratic political thought which is lacking in the case of Burke.) As John MacCunn observed, the sense of 'people' (and of 'community') in Burke is so different from what it is in Bentham and the utilitarians that it is a misnomer to call Burke a utilitarian.[1] Given Burke's organic conception of society, his traditionalism, his doctrine of virtual representation, and his ethical and religious beliefs, the resemblances between Burke and the utilitarians appear ultimately superficial.

[1] *The Political Philosophy of Burke* (London, 1913), 49.

II

BURKE'S ADHERENCE TO THE
NATURAL LAW

So far it is difficult to see in Burke anything going beyond St. Thomas's view of law as 'an ordinance of reason for the common good' (*Summa Theologica*, I–II, qu. 90, art. 4), provided one notes also what Bentham and the utilitarian critics of natural law later ignored, namely that the Thomistic natural law tradition attached considerable importance to considerations of utility and expediency in the making of human laws.[1] This observation brings us to the problem of Burke's relation to this tradition and to the 'discovery' of Burke's adherence to the natural law; and while the discovery of Burke's natural law affiliations involved chiefly the filling in of the gap between Burke's religiosity and his doctrine of expediency, it was a long time before this gap was filled. The attempt to specify what Burke was committed to in his acceptance of natural law has been part of a larger, and in my opinion more dubious, effort to mark more sharply than hitherto the distinctions between classical and Christian theories of natural law, on the one hand, and modern natural law theories, on the other. This effort, inspired by Leo Strauss and continued by Peter Stanlis and Richard H. Cox, has been intent upon emphasizing the differences and down-grading the continuities between the classical and the modern, and it has concentrated importantly upon showing that John Locke, despite his protests to the contrary, was

[1] Ewart Lewis, 'Natural Law and Expediency in Medieval Political Theory', *Ethics*, L (January 1940), 144–63. Lewis noted the importance of the test of expediency for Aquinas and explicitly connected Aquinas and Burke on this point years before the current 'discovery' of Burke's relations with Thomism and the natural law.

an opponent of natural law in the traditional sense and was committed to the hedonism, egoism, and 'utilitarianism' of Thomas Hobbes. To Strauss and his adherents, traditional natural law is objective, with a universal, rational, intelligible order of values and with an emphasis upon society taken as a whole, while modern natural law is subjective, nominalistic, and individualistic, with an emphasis not upon man's reason but upon his will. The opposition between the two conceptions of natural law is also held to be a case of the natural law versus the natural rights doctrines of Hobbes, Locke, and their followers.[1]

The first and most obvious objection to this treatment of the history of ideas is that if we are going to emphasize the discontinuities between classical and modern we will ultimately have to carry this keenness for diversity back into the classical and Christian conceptions of natural law. There are differences worth noting between the classical and the Christian doctrines. The Christian doctrines of Original Sin, Revelation, and Grace must affect and alter significantly the legacy of Aristotle and Cicero (between whom there are also significant differences). It is scarcely adequate to comment as Stanlis does that the 'fusion of classical and Christian thought achieved its artistic supremacy in the *Divine Comedy* of Dante and reached its theological perfection in the *Summa theologica* of St. Thomas Aquinas. St. Thomas's aphorism, "Grace does not abolish Nature but perfects it," is a perfect summary of the harmony of Christianity and Natural Law.'[2] Also, within Christianity, between the time of the Church Fathers and the Reformation, the natural law tradition is an evolving one with significant variations and two distinct levels of expression: the juristic and the philosophical or theological. Within the classical and the Christian traditions there are

---

[1] Leo Strauss, *Natural Right and History* (Chicago, 1953); Richard H. Cox, *Locke on War and Peace* (Oxford, 1960); Leo Strauss, 'Locke's Doctrine of Natural Law', *What is Political Philosophy? and Other Studies* (Glencoe, 1959), 197–220; Peter Stanlis, 'Natural Law and Revolutionary "Natural Rights"', op. cit., 14–28. [2] Stanlis, op. cit., 9–10.

crucial differences concerning the derivation, the content, the knowability, and the applicability of the natural law: Is the natural law divine in origin or is it independently derivable from universal principles of justice and right or is it derivable simply from human nature ? What is its relation to Revelation ? Is it a body of universal and immutable principles or is it more like what Stammler later would call 'natural law with a changing content' ? How is the natural law affected by the Fall of man and his sinfulness ? Can it be known by everyone or chiefly by philosophers, jurists, or the Church ? Can it be applied universally, and if so what is its relation to that 'necessity which knows no law' ? If we are going to ignore the differences among Aristotle, Cicero, Augustine, Aquinas, the canon lawyers, Bracton, &c., on these points, then what could possibly count as a significant difference between Locke and Aquinas ?

When Stanlis writes that 'Like St. Thomas Aquinas and Coke before him, and to a degree Rudolph Stammler in the twentieth century, Burke conceived of a Natural Law with a changing content and dynamic method, guided by the principles of prudence, subject to growth by the recognition of new values emerging from the historical development of civilization',[1] he seems not to notice that this is but one of the classical and Christian conceptions of natural law. A reviewer has found Stanlis guilty of distorting even this one tradition, specifically the Thomistic distinction between natural law and divine law, by his overemphasis upon the theistic sources of natural law. While reason is ultimately a gift from God, it can, according to Aquinas, know the natural law without any direct divine intervention;[2] and it is also worth noting that Burke as an Anglican would presumably not have accepted the Catholic Church as the interpreter of natural law. Another critic has gone so far as to say that Burke's Anglicanism and his

---

[1] Stanlis, op. cit., 112.

[2] J. L. Montrose, Review-Essay, *Natural Law Forum*, VI (1961), 204, 216–17.

alleged failure to share in the 'traditional Christian' view of Revelation as 'enlarging' the content of natural law keeps him from having a Christian natural law philosophy,[1] but this (if we remember that Richard Hooker was an Anglican) seems extreme. The two criticisms taken together illustrate, however, the problem of speaking of *the* Christian, or even the Thomistic, conception of natural law without a reasonably elaborate specification of what is meant.

A second (and equally obvious) objection to this frame of reference concerns its curious antipathy to Locke who in his 'muddled' and 'inconsistent' way is held to be ultimately a Hobbesian, a psychological egoist, and a hedonist. He is also said to have denied in effect the knowability of natural law and of the truths of revealed religion, to have contributed to the advent of both anarchic individualism and democratic collectivism, and to have been in large part responsible for the growth of the revolutionary doctrine of the Rights of Man later expressed during the French Revolution. This reading of Locke has been ably criticized by others,[2] and I shall discuss it but briefly, as my interest in Locke is for present purposes a function of my interest in Burke. I must, however, express my preference for two older theses, one asserting the fundamental agreement between Locke and Aquinas where natural law is concerned, the other affirming that Burke's place in the history of political thought is within the Lockian tradition which he alters but does not destroy. In short my preference is for an interpretation which stresses the continuity between Aquinas (whom Lord Acton called 'the first Whig'), Locke, and Burke; and which is

[1] James F. Davidson, 'Natural Law and International Law in Edmund Burke', *The Review of Politics*, XXI (July 1959), 483–94. This is a criticism of Stanlis's 'Edmund Burke and the Law of Nations', which appeared in the *American Journal of International Law* for 1953.

[2] Charles H. Monson, 'Locke and His Interpreters', *Political Studies*, VI (1958), 120–33; Paul E. Sigmund, Review of Cox's *Locke on War and Peace*, *Natural Law Forum*, VII (1962), 202–8; John W. Yolton, 'Locke on the Law of Nature', *Philosophical Review*, LXVII, (1958), 477–98.

strengthened by the discovery of Burke's commitment to natural law. (Previously scholars had felt that it was Burke not Locke who was odd man out where natural law is concerned.) Some of the reasons for these preferences will emerge in the course of this study; here I shall cite briefly several reasons why Locke should still be included in the natural law tradition.

The suspicion that Locke was 'unsound' on the natural law is admittedly an old one; evidence for it is to be found in the exchange of letters between Locke and James Tyrrell. While the youthful Locke had written eight essays on the laws of nature, the mature Locke refused to allow the publication of these essays which in fact remained unpublished for nearly three centuries;[1] and while he appealed to the law of nature in his mature political work he wrote that it was 'beside his present purpose' (*Second Treatise*, chap. 12) to demonstrate the existence and content of the natural law. This was to say the least unfortunate because of the suspicion that the theory of knowledge in Locke's *Essay on Human Understanding* undercuts the possibility of our knowing the laws of nature. Against this uncertain background Strauss and others have suggested that Locke, 'a cautious man', only appeared to be following the lead of Hooker and hence Aquinas and that covertly he was a Hobbesian and with Hobbes a precursor of utilitarianism and its denial of natural law. This interpretation, obviously, presupposed the accuracy of the Strauss–Oakeshott[2] reading of Hobbes's *Leviathan* as being a sharp departure from traditional natural law doctrine, a reading which is challenged by Howard Warrender's *The Political Philosophy of Hobbes, His Theory of Obligation* (Oxford, 1957). But assuming Hobbes to have made a radical

---

[1] See John Locke, *Essays on the Law of Nature*, edited by W. Von Leyden (Oxford, 1954 and 1958). In his polemics against Locke Stanlis makes no mention of these essays.

[2] Leo Strauss, *The Political Philosophy of Hobbes* (Oxford, 1936); Strauss, *Natural Right and History*, 165–251; Michael Oakeshott, Introduction to Hobbes's *Leviathan* (Oxford, 1946), xxx–lxvi.

departure from the tradition in part by his reductive analysis of moral virtues and responsibilities in terms of psychological egoism, where is the evidence that Locke made a similar reduction ? As for the importance attached by Hobbes and Locke (and Burke also) to self-preservation and the right of self-defence, this can be thought of as being in the spirit of Aquinas's judgement that 'every substance seeks the preservation of its own being, according to its nature; and by reason of this inclination whatever is a means of preserving human life, and of warding off its obstacles, belongs to the natural law' (*Summa Theologica*, I–II, qu. 94, art. 2).

The allegation of hedonism is more difficult to refute; but J. W. Gough's judgement that Locke's was a *modified* hedonism in which pleasure and pain may be the consequences of and the means by which we recognize good and bad actions, but are not the motives of a good man's conduct, seems defensible.[1] It is doubtful that such a modified hedonism need affect logically any possibility of our knowing or obeying the laws of nature. As for the knowability of the laws of nature, Locke's empiricism may pose a problem here; but I fail to see why epistemology need be assumed to wear the trousers in all questions where an author's theory of knowledge and his moral and political convictions are allegedly in conflict. The evidence is that Locke was a rationalist in his conception of natural law and an empiricist in his theory of knowledge. If there be an inconsistency here, why must it be decided at the expense of Locke's belief in the rationality and intelligibility of the natural law ? (Locke's denial of the doctrine of innate ideas, to which Strauss's school attaches great importance, is irrelevant to the question of Locke's position relative to medieval natural law theorists, as none of them held such a doctrine.) Concerning Christianity, Locke considered the natural law to have obligatory power because it is the will of God, and Locke believed he had

[1] *John Locke's Political Philosophy* (Oxford, 1950), 16.

demonstrated the existence of God; his *The Reasonableness of Christianity*, while Unitarian in tendency, affirmed the truth of the Gospels and the Messiahship of Christ.

The notion that Locke was an anarchic individualist is absurd, for Locke's conception of human equality was in terms of moral equality and human potentials and not in terms of political or intellectual equality.[1] Also in error is the picture of Locke as a democratic collectivist, or a 'majority rule' democrat.[2] Locke was no more attracted to the idea of an extended suffrage or to restrictions upon property rights than Burke would later be; and his definition of political power in terms of the 'public good' is good Thomistic doctrine. Where the French doctrine of the Rights of Man is concerned, if one takes this to be a thesis proclaiming absolute, inalienable rights (as Burke would interpret it in his attacks upon it), ultimate authorship for that doctrine cannot be laid upon Locke. In both the state of nature and in civil society men are, according to Locke, limited in their exercise of the executive power of the law of nature, in the state of nature by other men and in civil society by the government. This means that a man who has violated a law of nature may be punished, that is, his right to life, liberty, or property may be limited or taken away altogether. The extent of Locke's influence upon radical thought in France and England in the eighteenth century has sometimes been exaggerated by scholars, and to reconstruct Locke's arguments in the light of the use made of them by subsequent generations of radicals is an unhistorical exercise.[3] Finally, it could perhaps be said that the *spirit* of Locke shows he belonged among the

[1] This reading is in agreement with Martin Seliger, 'Locke's Natural Law and the Foundation of Politics', *Journal of the History of Ideas*, XXIV (July–September 1963), 333–54.

[2] The thesis that Locke was a 'majority rule' democrat is argued by Willmoore Kendall, *John Locke and the Doctrine of Majority-Rule* (Urbana, 1941).

[3] The decline of Locke's influence among the English radicals is argued convincingly by H. V. S. Ogden, 'The State of Nature and the Decline of Lockian Political Theory in England 1760–1800', *American Historical Review*, XLVI (October 1940), 21–44. Ogden, however, includes Burke among the utilitarians

advocates of *Ethica Ordine Geometrico Demonstrata*: Descartes, Hobbes, Spinoza, and Leibniz; and that this serves to set him apart from Burke and the Thomistic tradition. Certainly Locke believed that morality is a demonstrative science, but he did not conceive of the application of moral truths and rules to practical circumstances as being demonstrative. In a passage that reads like pure Burke he wrote: 'Polity and prudence are not capable of demonstration. . . . But whether this course in public or private affairs will succeed well . . . is but probability grounded upon experience or analogical reasoning but no certain knowledge or demonstration.'[1]

The Strauss-inspired frame of reference for handling the differences between classical and modern natural law becomes especially relevant to the present study when it attempts to mark this distinction in terms of Thomistic duties versus Hobbesian (and Lockian) rights. Strauss concedes that the differences between the natural law of the seventeenth and eighteenth centuries and the premodern natural law might be spoken of as a 'shift of emphasis' from natural duties to natural rights. 'But', he writes, 'quantitative changes of this character become intelligible only when they are seen against the background of a qualitative and fundamental change, not to say that such quantitative changes always become possible only by virtue of a qualitative and fundamental change.'[2] Strauss's construction of the 'shift of emphasis' as a quantitative change intelligible only against the background of a qualitative and fundamental change is an attempt to sharpen a difference of degree (as it had previously been seen) into a difference in kind, hence his use of the (in this case)

who abandoned the doctrine of natural rights. For Stanlis's interpretation of Locke in the terms of Locke's radical followers see Stanlis, op. cit., 125–59.

[1] For this point and this quotation from Locke's *Journal* for 26 June 1681, I am indebted to A. P. Brogan, 'John Locke and Utilitarianism', *Ethics*, LXIX (January 1959), 79–93. Brogan is, however, convinced that the mature Locke was a utilitarian.

[2] Leo Strauss, *Natural Right and History*, 182.

peculiarly inappropriate quantitative–qualitative language. In analysing Burke, Strauss's effort to attain a more precise distinction than the evidence actually warrants leads him to fall back upon his by now familiar strategy of suggesting that an author may not really mean what he says: '*The practical character of Burke's thought partly explains why he did not hesitate to use the language of modern natural right whenever that could assist him in persuading his modern audience of the soundness of a policy which he recommended.* He spoke of the state of nature, of the rights of nature or of the rights of man, and of the social compact or of the artificial character of the commonwealth. But he may be said to integrate these notions into a classical or Thomistic framework.'[1] I shall discuss the effects of this orientation upon Burke scholarship shortly, but first the orientation itself should be examined.

The older scholarship which Strauss seeks to set aside had seen the difference between modern and pre-modern as a *qualitative* difference in degree. A difference in degree and not in kind because, as Gierke suggested, the medieval theorists had already grasped 'the thought of the absolute and imperishable value of the individual'. According to medieval doctrine, 'absolute protection against Positive Law was due to those rights which were directly conferred by pure Natural Law without the intermediation of any entitling act. . . . In this sense Medieval Doctrine was already filled with the thought of the inborn and indestructible rights of the Individual.'[2] If this be so, Hobbes (and Locke) cannot, where the doctrine of rights is concerned, be used as a great dividing line because there is not all that great a difference to divide. As Montrose remarks: 'A difference between "natural law" and "natural rights" may be no more than one of language and aspect. Whereas "laws" are concerned with abstract possibilities of appli-

---

[1] Strauss, op. cit., 296. My italics. For Strauss's doctrine of the 'hidden meaning' see his *Persecution and the Art of Writing* and 'On a Forgotten Kind of Writing', *What is Political Philosophy? and Other Studies*, 221–32.

[2] Otto Gierke, *Political Theories of the Middle Ages* (Cambridge, 1951), 81–82.

cation, "rights" are concerned with the application of legal propositions to specific individuals. A law which forbids any person to inflict harm on any other person gives John Doe a right not to be injured.'[1] Montrose remarks, too, that the distinction between natural law as concerned with the common good and natural rights as concerned with the welfare of individuals is inadequate. The classical writers knew that the common good is the good of individuals, while the modern writers are aware that individual claims to rights may require limitation for the general welfare. Man's social nature *is* recognized by Grotius, Pufendorf, Wolff, Locke, and Rousseau—so is it especially noteworthy that it is recognized by Burke too ?

From this brief review of the Straussian frame of reference I pass now to the question of Burke's belief in the natural law. The 'discovery' of Burke's affinities with Thomistic natural law can, I think, survive the highly probable demise of the frame of reference in which it has found expression, provided this discovery is suitably qualified. One of the necessary qualifications has already been suggested, namely that this discovery does not serve to separate Burke sharply from the Lockian tradition. That the discovery must also be recast or reinterpreted in other ways if it is to outlive its Straussian context will soon become evident. First, I shall dispose of some ill-founded initial objections to the thesis that Burke accepted the natural law. One of these objections concerns Burke's alleged hostility to theory of any sort, the other concerns Burke's intellectual biography with emphasis upon its practical and pragmatic dimensions. The two objections are, obviously, different sides of the same coin, and both show the impress of the utilitarian reading of Burke discussed earlier.

Burke is all too well known for his pejorative use of words such as *theory*, *metaphysics*, and *speculation*, and for his bitter indictments, especially at the time of the French

[1] Montrose, op. cit., 214–15.

Revolution, of metaphysicians, calculators, and even philosophers. Where the Aristotelian and Thomistic distinction
between speculative and practical reason is concerned
Burke seems to come down hard on the side of practice; and
if this is so, how can he be associated with the Thomistic
natural law tradition ? Sir Ernest Barker, who seems to
have been the first serious commentator actually to call
Burke a Thomist in his principles,[1] also wrote, on another
occasion, that 'To Burke any speech of natural law and
natural rights is metaphysics, and not politics.'[2] (On the
first occasion, Barker explicitly stated that Burke rejected
natural rights, and he did not discuss Burke in connexion
with the natural law.) If we accept as correct Father
Canavan's somewhat embarrassed admission that 'Burke
had very little direct interest in metaphysics, properly so
called'[3] (although Father Canavan does not define 'metaphysics, properly so called' for us), then we can construct
from Barker *cum* Canavan the following argument: Burke
considered natural law and natural rights as a part of
metaphysics but not of politics, Burke had little interest
in metaphysics, therefore, he had little interest in natural
law and natural rights. If this is accepted, then Burke's
adherence to natural law is, as J. G. A. Pocock has suggested in another connexion, not essential to our understanding of all the parts of Burke's political thought.[4]
Regardless of how we differ on the question of Burke on
natural rights, this is not the conclusion that Strauss,
Stanlis, Canavan, or I would wish to accept. On this
argument it is chiefly Burke's belief in prudence which
Barker emphasizes that remains to link Burke with Thomism; and this is not enough, for it is doubtful whether

---

[1] *Essays on Government* (Oxford, 1945), 222. Barker's Burke is a Thomist 'even
if unconsciously'.

[2] *Traditions of Civility* (Cambridge, 1948), 311.

[3] Francis P. Canavan, *The Political Reason of Edmund Burke* (Durham, 1960),
46.

[4] 'Burke and the Ancient Constitution—A Problem in the History of Ideas',
The Historical Journal, III (1960), 125–43.

prudence *per se* is sufficient to establish a link with any *moral* philosophy.

A fresh start is necessary. Error crept in with Barker's distinction between metaphysics and politics, not that this is not a Burkian distinction; but what is not Burkian is the placing of natural law and natural rights, which are vitally connected with the moral question of the basis of political obligations and rights, solely on the metaphysical side of this distinction. Burke's conviction that the 'principles of true politicks are those of morality enlarged, and I neither now do or ever will admit of any other'[1] necessarily commits him to the belief that the principles of politics are related to the question of natural law and natural rights; and if he believed in natural law (and natural rights, too, as I shall show) then he must have believed that these were germane to politics. A famous passage in Burke which is sometimes mistakenly offered as evidence of Burke's indifference to natural rights shows Burke speaking of these rights as metaphysical but does not show him affirming the moral irrelevance of these rights:

These metaphysic rights entering into common life, like rays of light which pierce into a dense medium, are by the laws of Nature, refracted from their straight line. Indeed, in the gross and complicated mass of human passions and concerns, the primitive rights of men undergo such a variety of refractions and reflections that it becomes absurd to talk of them as if they continued in the simplicity of their original direction. The nature of man is intricate; the objects of society are of the greatest possible complexity: and therefore no simple disposition or direction of power can be suitable either to man's nature or to the quality of his affairs.[2]

The truth of the matter is that it is not always clear what Burke's frequently impassioned denunciations of *theory*, *metaphysics*, and *speculation* amount to. Where Burke's outbursts are concerned an emotive theory of meaning often seems required: his outbursts must be seen as in

[1] Letter to Dr. William Markham, *post* 9 November 1771, *The Correspondence of Edmund Burke*, II, (Chicago, 1960), 282.
[2] *Reflections on the Revolution in France*, *Works*, III, 312.

large part a reflection of attitude and feeling. The attitude which such outbursts reflect is that of the practical man of affairs whose philosophical interests are pretty much limited to moral philosophy and to aesthetics and who is distrustful of metaphysics and of most abstract speculation. The feeling which such outbursts convey is one of contempt for those whom Jacob Burckhardt would in the nineteenth century characterize as 'terrible simplifiers'. Burke firmly believed that Britain had lost her American colonies because the government had dogmatically insisted upon the exercise of Britain's theoretical rights as an imperial power, and he later saw France and Europe as the victims of the same uncritical following or acceptance of oversimplified theories and speculations about what man and society ought to be like. So much then (for the present) for the attitude and feeling conveyed by Burke's denunciations of theory, metaphysics, and speculation. What about the content, if any, of such indictments ?

Let us consider Burke's case against 'metaphysics'. First, there is the problem (with which students of twentieth-century philosophy are also familiar) of attaching a precise sense to the use being made of *metaphysics*. Does Burke mean to convey a distrust of claims to knowledge about some supersensible reality, or does he mean to convey a distrust of statements which purport to describe the essential characteristics of the world and of human nature ? There is in the *Tract on the Popery Laws* a passage which Lord Acton later seized upon as evidence of Burke's insincerity in matters of faith (although it is the only statement of its kind in all of Burke): 'For the Protestant religion, nor (I speak it with reverence, I am sure) the truth of our common Christianity, is not so clear as this proposition,—that all men, at least the majority of men in the society, ought to enjoy the common advantages of it.'[1] (Unfortunately, Burke is not clear as to what he means by 'the truth of our common Christianity', and he nowhere

[1] *Works*, VI, 334.

affords us a clear statement of his theological tenets, apparently believing that it is sufficient to affirm his allegiance to the Church of England.) While it is possible that Burke's statement that the truth of our common Christianity is 'not so clear as' a certain moral truth about man and society may be only a rhetorical way of saying that the truth of our common Christianity is 'no clearer than' the moral truth in question, even a more literal reading of Burke's statement does not support Lord Acton's charge of insincerity. While Burke believed *parts* of the truth of Christianity to be defensible upon rational grounds, he did not accept clearness and distinctness as a criterion of truth. Ordinarily he was content to accept our 'natural feelings' as a reliable guide where questions such as the existence of God or of Divine Providence were concerned. Burke's preference for following our 'natural feelings' rather than our 'Reasonings' on such questions does not imply voluntarism or irrationalism, but rather it points to his deep distrust of our *private* reasonings when these are not checked against the experience and judgement of the species as a whole. Burke's reliance upon natural feelings and his distrust of speculation except in those cases where speculation concurs with such feelings is evident in the next quotation, taken from a notebook kept by Burke and his 'cousin' William Burke in the 1750's.

If belief in the existence of Divine Providence is part of what Burke would include in 'the truth of our common Christianity' (as seems most probable) and if the following quotation is representative of Burke's treatment of some crucial parts of 'the truth of our common Christianity' (it is), then Burke's judgement that this truth is 'not so clear as' another proposition seems not to affect his sincere acceptance of 'the truth of our common Christianity'. (Whether it should from the logical point of view affect his faith is another matter. But from the point of view of internal consistency, Burke would have no difficulty in believing (1) that the truth of our common Christianity is not so clear as another proposition, (2) that the clearness of a proposition is, in any event, no sure sign of its truth, and (3) that the truth of our common Christianity while not so clear as another proposition—or other propositions for that matter—is still clear enough to be intelligible and to pass any reasonable test of clearness where such a test may be relevant.)

> The Arguments against Providence are from our *Reasonings*, observing a certain order in the works of God. There is nothing at all in our natural feelings against it.
> There is a great deal in our natural feelings for it. . . .
> Metaphysical or Physical Speculations neither are, or ought to be, the Grounds of our Duties; because we can arrive at no certainty in them. They have a weight when they concur with our own natural feelings; very little when against them.[1]

Where this leaves 'the truth of our common Christianity' is roughly where Aquinas left it, as a matter of faith and not of reason. This is especially true if one agrees with F. C. Copleston and others that many of the demonstrations in Aquinas including his 'proofs' for the existence of God are not intended as demonstrations or proofs 'in the strict sense'. To be sure, if the above quotation from Burke were all we had to go on, then Burke's distrust of metaphysics in speaking of super-sensible reality might appear anti-Thomistic; however, as Canavan points out, the limitations of the sceptical side of Burke's thought must be borne in mind, and in fact Burke seems to have believed that we can have some knowledge of God through causality (working back toward Him from His effects).[2] There is here, and elsewhere, too, as we shall see, a considerable difference between the qualified scepticism of Burke and the scepticism of David Hume.

Burke's conception of the 'natural feelings' mentioned above and their relations to reason will be discussed in

---

[1] H. V. F. Somerset, *A Notebook of Edmund Burke* (Cambridge, 1957), 71.
[2] Canavan, op. cit., 44.

Part Two. Meanwhile it seems safe to assume that Burke believed that some knowledge of super-sensible reality is possible, even if this is a knowledge based in part upon faith and natural feeling. Indeed, metaphysical speculations about God, Providence, &c. arouse Burke's animosity primarily when they are aimed *against* claims to religious knowledge in the traditional Christian sense. It is first deism and later atheism that arouses Burke's ire as exceeding the powers of human reason, and traditional Christian metaphysics is part of the old order that Burke wishes to protect. Where the rational approach to God is concerned Burke, as so often, occupies a middle position, distrustful of the rational pretences of the deists, on the one hand, and the emotional enthusiasm of the Methodists, on the other.[1] As a defender of tradition and of the Church of England, Burke's position on metaphysical speculation about the deity seems to be that it is after all an aid but one to be handled gingerly and one that must never be allowed to run against the grain of traditional Christian beliefs, natural religious feelings, or those moral obligations placed upon us by God.

The second question of whether Burke thinks we can have knowledge of the essential characteristics of the world and of human nature is quite complicated; we can, however, confidently state that Burke does not doubt that we can and do have *adequate* knowledge of human nature and the principles of morality. Here as in the case of claims to knowledge about super-sensible reality Burke's position represents a kind of middle ground. We can know something, but we cannot know as much as the radicals and rationalists think we can. It is the speculations of radical and rationalist contemporaries that lead Burke into overstatements of his practical and empirical biases. Such excesses should be seen not as condemnations of

---

[1] For an early attack by Burke on deists, see his favourable review of John Leland's *The Advantage and Necessity of the Christian Revelation*, *Annual Register*, 1764. For Burke on the Methodists, see his *Notebook*, 96–97.

metaphysics *qua* metaphysics or theory *qua* theory but of 'bad' metaphysics or of 'bad' theory. Burke in a speech on parliamentary reform makes this clear and at the same time shows his practical criteria for the truth of theories:

I do not vilify theory and speculation: no, because that would be to vilify reason itself. *Neque decipitur ratio, neque decipit unquam.* No,— whenever I speak against theory, I mean always a weak, erroneous, fallacious, unfounded, or imperfect theory; and one of the ways of discovering that it is a false theory is by comparing it with practice. This is the true touchstone of all theories which regard man and the affairs of men,—Does it suit his nature in general ?—does it suit his nature as modified by his habits ?[1]

This is sufficient, I think, to answer the charge that Burke was so opposed to theory as necessarily to oppose Thomistic natural law theory, especially as this theory places emphasis both upon its conformity to man's essential nature and upon its practical dimensions. It does not answer the question, which I doubt can be answered, of the exact nature of the relations and distinctions Burke may have envisaged as holding between metaphysics and morality. Burke's respect for theory and speculation, in their proper sphere, is evident in the following remarks: 'It is the business of the speculative philosopher to mark the proper ends of government. It is the business of *the politician who is the philosopher in action*, to find out proper means towards those ends, and to employ them with effect.'[2]

Burke's intellectual biography when it is written will in all likelihood emphasize his respect for theoretical considerations in the manner indicated above and will show that his practical posture in the world of affairs presupposed a familiarity with and a commitment to a political philosophy with a Christian base. Where the Thomistic reading

[1] *Speech on Reform of Representation of the Commons in Parliament, Works,* VII, 97.
[2] *Thoughts on the Cause of the Present Discontents* (1770), *Works,* I, 530. My italics.

of Burke is concerned it must, however, be frankly acknowledged that there is no evidence either from the works of Burke or from the list of books in Burke's library of any first-hand acquaintance on his part with the writings of Aquinas. The suggestion that the thoughts of Aquinas were 'in the air' would in most cases be quite inappropriate, given the anti-Catholic biases prevalent in eighteenth-century England. Its implausibility is, however, weakened in the case of Burke when two things are recalled: (1) Burke's mother was a Catholic, and he himself married into a Catholic family, (2) Burke's political career was marked by frequent charges of secret Catholic ties and of Jesuitry. Moreover, Burke's lifelong defence of the Catholics suggests more than a sympathy for the oppressed inspired by love for his family. It points to a profound respect for the Church itself, as does his oft-repeated conviction that Christians regardless of their particular affiliations have more in common than they are wont to acknowledge. Still we do not need to rely upon the Atmospheric Hypothesis or upon the charges made by Burke's political enemies in order to connect him with the natural law tradition.

The absence of any direct references to Aquinas in Burke's writings is but an extreme example of a pervasive difficulty in Burke scholarship. As John Morley observed, 'There is no copiousness of literary references in his works, such as overabounded in civil and ecclesiastical publicists of the seventeenth century.'[1] Even so the traces of Burke's erudition are not quite so obscure as Morley suggests. The readings required of undergraduates at Trinity College, Dublin, where Burke was an undergraduate, afford some clues and show that Burke, while he may never have read Aquinas, was nevertheless exposed to a warmed-over scholasticism. Franco Burgersdicii's *Institutionum Logicarum libri duo*, Eustachius's *Ethica, sive summa moralis disciplinae*, Martin Smiglecki's *Logica*, and

[1] *Burke* (London, 1923), 308.

Robert Sanderson's *De juramenti promissori obligatione* and *De obligatione conscientiae* are all in the Aristotelian–Thomistic tradition. The second work by Sanderson, an Anglican bishop, is an explicit restatement of Thomistic natural law doctrine. From the neo-scholastic authors cited above Burke could easily have first derived his belief that there is a divine order of the universe, his conception of a natural law the basic principles of which command universal assent, and his emphasis upon the importance of prudence in selecting appropriate means to the ends selected by moral philosophy. Burke was a distinguished student at Trinity College, and he continued to be a voracious reader both for general and specific purposes. Evidence of general reading is to be found in his quotations from the Bible, Milton, Shakespeare, Horace, Addison, and Virgil. Two examples of intensive reading and research for specific purposes are to be found in his speeches during the Regency crisis precipitated by King George III's mental disorder, speeches which show him thoroughly conversant with contemporary theories concerning mental illnesses, and in his speeches during the impeachment of Warren Hastings, which prove him to be in remarkable command of the history of English jurisprudence. While Burke often does not name the source of many of his quotations and arguments, he sometimes does. Cicero, Hooker, and Aristotle are mentioned, always favourably; and Locke is referred to, sometimes favourably sometimes not. Textual and/or biographical evidence supports the thesis that save for Aquinas Burke had read the most important formulations of natural law doctrines, classical, Christian, and modern; Sanderson and Hooker (and, I think, Locke) make Burke's presumed failure to read Aquinas not too important.[1] From these three writers alone Burke could have got a view of natural law sufficiently

[1] Canavan, op. cit., 197–211; Arthur L. Woehl, 'Burke's Reading', A Doctoral Thesis, Cornell University, 1928; J. W. Stubbs, *The History of the University of Dublin from Its Foundation to the End of the Eighteenth Century* (London, 1889), 199–200.

similar to that of Aquinas for the purposes of the present inquiry.

Besides Burke's Catholic relations and his readings in philosophy there is a third strand in Burke's biography which serves to link him with the natural law tradition, and this is his familiarity with English law. While this strand has been noticed by Stanlis, its significance has generally been slighted; it has even been said to work against the natural law interpretation of Burke. Burke's father was a lawyer, and after leaving Trinity College Burke went to London to prepare for the Bar. He subsequently abandoned this pursuit in favour first of a literary and then of a political career. He acquired at the Middle Temple an abiding awareness of the limitations of lawyers and of legal procedures which would be much in evidence during his later years in his exchanges with the defence at the Hastings impeachment proceedings. But Burke's distrust of lawyers and his dislike of the existing system (or lack thereof) of training for the legal profession pales into insignificance beside his sincere and often moving protestations of reverence for the law itself. Burke's conception of the English Constitution, his way of thinking about the history of English law, and the influence of English property laws upon his political philosophy will be referred to in due course; for the present it is enough to note that Burke has a veneration for law as an expression of the *reason* of a community.

Later I shall try to show also certain significant parallels between Burke's political philosophy and Blackstone's *Commentaries*, which he reviewed for Robert Dodsley's *Annual Register* in 1767 and 1768.[1] By virtue of these two reviews Blackstone becomes, in my judgement, the strongest link in the chain of evidence connecting Burke with

[1] Burke's labours as editor and reviewer for the *Annual Register* are discussed by Thomas W. Copeland, 'Edmund Burke and the Book Reviews in Dodsley's *Annual Register*', *PMLA*, XLV (June 1942), 446–68. Copeland's attribution to Burke of the authorship of unsigned reviews in this journal from 1758 until at least 1773 is now accepted by all Burke scholars.

the natural law tradition. Blackstone serves, too, to bring into question the alleged hostility or indifference of the English legal profession to the natural law. This hostility or indifference must be questioned now, however, if Burke's knowledge of English law is to count for, and not against, the natural law interpretation of his thought. Blackstone's espousal of natural law suggests that there is something seriously wrong with an interpretation which would place continental law but not English law within the natural law tradition. As even Pollock and Holdsworth admit, not much is said in English law about the laws of nature; enough is said, however, to show that the validity of a custom (and, it was sometimes said, of statutes as well) was to be judged in terms of its reasonableness. We know, too, that Roman and canon law did influence English common law. The extent of this influence is still being debated; but Pollock's conclusion that there is a real link between the medieval doctrine of the law of nature and the principles of the common law, a link consisting mainly of the test of reasonableness, seems warranted.[1] If this is correct, then Burke's exposure to English law represents at least an indirect exposure to natural law; and in the case of his careful scrutiny of Blackstone a direct contact with natural law doctrine.

From this brief survey of circumstantial evidence I pass now to an outline of the content of some of Burke's natural law beliefs. While Burke offers us no formal treatise upon natural law—or upon any aspect of political theory for that matter—his references to natural law are frequent and strategic enough to be taken seriously. First, however, I shall indicate some parts of Burke's reflections which superficially appear to run counter to the thesis that Burke accepted the claims to universality that natural law theories all make. 'I was never wild enough to conceive that one

---

[1] Sir Frederick Pollock, *Essays in the Law* (London, 1922), 57. W. S. Holdsworth, *A History of English Law* (London, 1923), II, 602–4.

method would serve for the whole, that the natives of Hindostan and those of Virginia could be ordered in the same manner', Burke wrote in 1777 in his *Letter to the Sheriffs of Bristol*.[1] 'Nothing universal can be rationally affirmed on any moral or any political subject', Burke stated in 1791 in his *Appeal from the New to the Old Whigs* in a passage where he draws a characteristic distinction between mathematical and metaphysical reasoning on the one hand and morality and prudence on the other.[2] A second look shows that the first quotation is consistent with the emphasis placed by Thomistic natural law theory upon the circumstances and variety of the human condition, and Burke's distinction between the caution of prudence and the certainty of metaphysical demonstration is also Thomistic. But what is not Thomistic is the denial that universal judgements can be rationally affirmed in morals and politics. How, too, is this to be squared with Burke's talk in the impeachment of Warren Hastings of 'those eternal laws of justice which are our rule and birthright' and of 'the primeval, indefeasible, unalterable law of Nature and of nations' ?[3] If nothing universal can be rationally affirmed in morals and politics, then Burke's argument that Hastings was bound by the eternal laws of justice (and not simply by English law) to protect the rights of Indians looks queer.

There are two, possibly three, ways of resolving the apparent contradiction between Burke's denial of the possibility of universal, rational judgements about morals and politics and his insistence that the laws of justice and of Nature are eternal and unalterable. These two, possibly three, ways are to be found in his *Reflections on the Revolution in France*: (1) There may be fixed rules and an occasional deviation, (2) Reason may be presumed to include at least implicitly in all general rules especially those concerning morals a number of correctives or exceptions, (3) General moral rules may in extreme cases require

---

[1] *Works*, II, 227.   [2] Ibid., IV, 80–81.   [3] Ibid., IX, 338, 459.

suspension in favour of moral principles. (3) is suggested by Father Canavan (p. 18); (1) and (2) are my discovery, but I am not sure how separate they are in Burke's mind. Burke sets forth (1) in discussing the hereditary principle of succession, but that it admits of wider moral and political application is obvious:

> It is far from impossible to reconcile, if we do not suffer ourselves to be entangled in the mazes of metaphysic sophistry, the use both of a fixed rule and an occasional deviation,—the sacredness of an hereditary principle of succession in our government with a power of change in its application in cases of extreme emergency. Even in that extremity, (if we take the measure of our rights by our exercise of them at the Revolution [of 1688–9],) the change is to be confined to the peccant part only,—to the part which produced the necessary deviation; and even then it is to be effected without a decomposition of the whole civil and political mass, for the purpose of originating a new civil order out of the first elements of society.[1]

Burke offers (2) in discussing qualifications for political and social power, authority, and distinction:

> I do not, my dear Sir, conceive you to be of that sophistical, captious spirit, or of that uncandid dulness, as to require, for every general observation or sentiment, an explicit detail of the correctives and exceptions which reason will presume to be included in all the general propositions which come from reasonable men. You do not imagine that I wish to confine power, authority, and distinction to blood and names and titles. No, Sir, there is no qualification for government but virtue and wisdom, actual or presumptive.[2]

Whether in Burke's own mind there was a clear distinction between (1) and (2) is uncertain, although there is a

---

[1] *Works*, III, 258–9. Here 'rule' and 'principle' are used quasi-synonymously. In Part Two his quasi-synonymous use at times of 'principle' and 'standard' in his *Inquiry* and the confusion that this engenders will be discussed. There is a great deal of looseness in Burke's use of language. Often he seems reluctant to use the same term twice in the same passage if he can find a synonym. Given contemporary philosophy's awareness of the extreme complexity of the problem of synonymity, this rhetorical or poetic dimension in Burke adds considerably to the problem of interpretation.

[2] Ibid., 296–7. What Burke says of 'every general observation or sentiment' and of 'all the general propositions which come from reasonable men' must necessarily hold for 'fixed rules' and 'principles'. Indeed, this seems to be the point Burke is making. In my own formulation of (2) I have, however, spoken of 'general rules' as being perhaps the best single term available for the present discussion.

readily apparent difference between an exception to a rule which may be justified by criteria not contained in the rule itself (or which may not be justified at all) and an exception which is allowed implicitly at least by the rule in question. Burke seems to have conceived of the principle of hereditary succession as falling under both (1) and (2). In cases of extreme emergency where the welfare of the whole society is at stake there may be necessary deviations from fixed rules; Burke's defence of the Glorious Revolution of 1688–9 is couched largely in terms of the doctrine of necessity. On the other hand, Burke would be prepared to argue that implicit in the rule or principle of hereditary succession are obvious exceptions in the case of would-be kings who are idiots, traitors, or otherwise subversive of the Constitution. For the student of morality, however, (1) and (2) are different, and Burke appears committed to an implicit recognition of this difference. (1) and (2) may provide a resolution to the apparent contradiction in Burke, chiefly by permitting us to explicate his denial of universal, rational rules or principles in morals and politics as meaning that nothing universal can be rationally affirmed in these areas unless note be somehow taken of the exceptions to these universal affirmations. Any universal judgement denying that there are such exceptions would partake of irrationality.

The chief difference between (1) and (2), on the one hand, and (3), on the other, stems from the fact that (3) explicitly recognizes that there may be cases where our criteria for judging an action are at odds with one another. Moral conflicts may be said to arise when there are new cases not covered by old rules, when the applicability of established rules is uncertain, and when existing rules lead or seem to lead to incompatible results. Concerning the last of these possibilities various attitudes can be taken. One might argue that if the rules in question are truly moral and fully universal, a real conflict among them is not possible. But one might also face up to such a conflict as being a datum of moral experience and try to live with this unpleasant reality by arranging or grading moral rules or principles in terms such as *primary* and *secondary* or *unconditioned* and *conditioned*. The latter approach is in the scholastic tradition; and, as Canavan points out, it appears implicit in that passage in the *Reflections* where Burke speaks of 'the dreadful exigence in which morality submits to the suspension of its own rules in favor of its own principles'. Burke writes:

The statues of Equity and Mercy might be veiled for a moment. The tenderest minds, confounded with the dreadful exigence in which morality submits to the suspension of its own rules in favor of its own principles, might turn aside whilst fraud and violence were accomplishing the destruction of a pretended nobility, which disgraced, whilst it persecuted, human nature. The persons most abhorrent from blood and treason and arbitrary confiscation might remain silent spectators of this civil war between the vices.[1]

In the above passage Burke is envisaging a hypothetical situation in which, had the French nobility actually been guilty of the charges levelled against it, a moral man might have stood aside and permitted its destruction by its enemies. The moral rules which he would have to suspend in favour of more fundamental moral principles are not spelled out by Burke, but presumably they have to do with extremely serious matters including the right of members of the old régime to life itself. Hence Burke's talk of 'dreadful exigence'. The rationale for standing aside is also not given by Burke in this passage, but most likely he has in mind a notion of the *common good* which would be furthered by the destruction of any *unnatural* aristocracy. There may be hard cases, Burke seems to be saying, where the preservation of society and hence of the species (man being a social animal dependent upon the social order) will depend upon our taking exception to those moral rules which serve adequately in standard cases. But all such exceptions must be justified by some moral principle or

[1] *Works*, III, 410.

principles which rank higher in the scale of values. In cases of civil and international wars the common good may require the suspension of or deviations from the rules of ordinary morality, but the burden of proof always falls upon the exception maker. Circumstances, for example, might allow Hastings to govern the natives of Hindostan somewhat more harshly than he would be allowed to govern those of Virginia, who have a considerable tradition of self-government and English liberty behind them; but no circumstances, not even the circumstance of having to govern a conquered and sometimes rebellious people, allow him to become a tyrant, presumably because tyranny, in Burke's view, perpetuates the exceptions and furthers a permanent disregard for the eternal laws of justice. Any interpretation of Burke's emphasis upon the importance of changing circumstances in moral and political delibera- tion which sees in this emphasis a licence for an immoral kind of expediency or even for choosing to live on the level of secondary moral principles where life on a higher moral level is at all possible is false.

Previously I have spoken of (1), (2), and (3) as ways of overcoming the apparent contradiction between Burke's denial of the possibility of universal, rational judgements in morals and politics and his belief in the eternal laws of justice and of nature. But, if the sense I have given to the passage first cited by Canavan is correct, then (1), (2), and (3) might be conceived of not so much as alternative ways of overcoming this contradiction as successive *steps* in such an overcoming, steps which, in my opinion, seem close to being the steps we ordinarily would take in unravelling the logic of moral justification and decision making.*

* There might come a time in our moral development when, upon discovering certain hard cases where a lie, for instance, might save a life or several lives, we allow for an occasional deviation from the general rule 'Thou shalt not lie'. But if we continue to follow this rule in the vast majority of cases, we may be uneasy from the moral point of view when we occasionally deviate from it. We may do nothing to alleviate this sense of uneasiness, but if we wish to be fully moral then we may reach step (2) or step (3). Step (3) may be reached either through (2) or independently, although usually, I believe, it comes after (2). (2) enables us to

In this discussion of an apparent but unreal contradiction
in Burke some of the content of his natural law doctrine
has been revealed, but more needs to be done. It is essential
for an understanding both of the content of this doctrine
and of its place in the history of ideas to emphasize that
Burke, like Aquinas and Locke, believed the natural law
to be binding because it reflects God's will.

I allow, that, if no Supreme Ruler exists, wise to form, and potent to
enforce, the moral law, there is no sanction to any contract, virtual or
even actual, against the will of prevalent power. . . . I may assume that
the awful Author of our being is the Author of our place in the order of
existence,—and that, having disposed and marshalled us by a divine
tactic, not according to our will, but according to His, He has in and by
that disposition virtually subjected us to act the part which belongs to the
place assigned us. We have obligations to mankind at large, which are not
in consequence of any special voluntary pact. They arise from the
relation of man to man, and the relation of man to God, which relations
are not matters of choice. On the contrary, the force of all the pacts
which we enter into with any particular person or number of persons
amongst mankind depends upon those prior obligations. In some cases
the subordinate relations are voluntary, in others they are necessary,—
but the duties are all compulsive.[1]

As Burke's thought unfolds in the above quotation, it
becomes evident that not only is the moral law binding
because of God's will but that this is true of every species
of moral obligation or duty. It is, however, possible to

preserve both the generality of our moral rules and to justify our occasional
deviations from these rules on the grounds (if they are true) that such deviations
are allowed for, implicitly at least, by the rule or rules in question. (2) is all right
as far as it goes, but it does not cover, as it is now stated, conflicts between moral
rules. There might be a case (obviously there are many such cases) where, for
example, a rule about not lying and a rule about preserving life or lives, at least a
good life or good lives, may present us with mutually exclusive possibilities:
if we tell the truth, A (or A, B, and C) die; if we do not tell the truth, A (or A, B,
and C) will live. In such cases, we may say that the deviations allowed for if only
implicitly by general rules under (2) are, when a more comprehensive analysis is
made, *fully* justifiable only when our rules are arranged in a hierarchy in which
some rules rank higher and allow of exceptions in fewer cases than do some
rules which we have ranked lower. We might rank the preservation of a good life
higher than telling the truth, for example. And at the top of our hierarchy we
may have a rule like 'Do good and avoid evil' which functions as a kind of ultimate
criterion which all other criteria are, so to speak, powerless to resist.

[1] *Appeal from the New to the Old Whigs* (1791), *Works*, IV, 165–6.

picture God's will as conceived by Burke as existing both above and within His creation. In the *Tract on the Popery Laws* Burke speaks of 'a superior law, which it is not in the power of any community, or of the whole race of man, to alter,—I mean the will of Him who gave us our nature, and in giving impressed an invariable law upon it'.[1] Burke's use of the word *invariable* may suggest Cicero more than Aquinas, and significantly Burke refers to Cicero a few sentences later; still, when all the relevant aspects of Burke's thought are taken into account, e.g. his Christian beliefs, his doctrine of prudence, and his emphasis upon adapting to changing circumstances and novel situations, Burke's is a Cicero filtered through the Christian, scholastic tradition.

It is a corollary of Burke's belief that God impressed an 'invariable law' upon our nature that appeals to Nature are not empty rhetoric to Burke. In the case of human nature there are present in addition to the physical laws which hold for all of God's creation moral laws as well. To live in accordance with Nature in the case of man means chiefly to obey the moral law and hence God's will. The necessity involved in such obedience, a necessity which Benthamites have usually professed not to understand since men as a matter of fact often fail to obey this law, is a *moral* necessity or obligation; but it is not an obligation voluntarily entered into. Appeals to this obligation are frequently made by Burke, and it may be of some value to give a long quotation from the *Reflections on the Revolution in France* in order to show how the concept of Nature functions in Burke's thought. In the passage below Burke is, characteristically, pointing out the advantages of the English Constitution:

This policy appears to me to be the result of profound reflection,—or rather the happy effect of following Nature, which is wisdom without reflection, and above it. A spirit of innovation is generally the result of a selfish temper and confined views. People will not look forward to posterity, who never look backward to their ancestors. Besides, the

[1] *Works*, VI, 322.

people of England well know that the idea of inheritance furnishes a sure principle of conservation, and a sure principle of transmission, without at all excluding a principle of improvement. It leaves acquisition free; but it secures what it acquires. Whatever advantages are obtained by a state proceeding on these maxims are locked fast as in a sort of family settlement, grasped as in a kind of mortmain forever. By a constitutional policy working after the pattern of Nature, we receive, we hold, we transmit our government and our privileges, in the same manner in which we enjoy and transmit our property and our lives. The institutions of policy, the goods of fortune, the gifts of Providence, are handed down to us, and from us, in the same course and order. Our political system is placed in a just correspondence and symmetry with the order of the world, and with the mode of existence decreed to a permanent body composed of transitory parts,—wherein, by the disposition of a stupendous wisdom moulding together the great mysterious incorporation of the human race, the whole, at one time, is never old or middle-aged or young, but, in a condition of unchangeable constancy, moves on through the varied tenor of perpetual decay, fall, renovation, and progression. Thus, by preserving the method of Nature in the conduct of the state, in what we improve we are never wholly new, in what we retain we are never wholly obsolete. By adhering in this manner and on those principles to our forefathers, we are guided, not by the superstition of antiquarians, but by the spirit of philosophic analogy. In this choice of inheritance we have given to our frame of polity the image of a relation in blood: binding up the Constitution of our country with our dearest domestic ties; adopting our fundamental laws into the bosom of our family affections; keeping inseparable, and cherishing with the warmth of all their combined and mutually reflected charities, our state, our hearths, our sepulchres, and our altars.[1]

The above passage suggests many problems of which I shall mention briefly only a few. Burke's language concerning 'the happy effect of following Nature, which is wisdom without reflection, and above it' suggests the now suspect thesis of knowledge by inclination. Also, the praise of a constitutional policy 'working after the pattern of Nature' and of 'preserving the method of Nature in the conduct of the State' would not satisfy those who, following Hume and Bentham, despair of giving a precise sense to the meaning of such phrases. It is, however, possible to attach some sense to these phrases if we attend to

[1] *Works*, III, 274–5.

Burke's remark that 'we are guided not by the superstition of antiquarians, but by the spirit of philosophic analogy.'

Actually in this passage Burke has recourse to two analogies, first with the order of the world and second with the nature of the family. According to the first analogy the English political system is placed in 'a just correspondence and symmetry with the order of the world, and with the mode of existence decreed to a permanent body composed of transitory parts'. By the second analogy, the frame of polity is given 'the image of a relation of blood'; the Constitution is bound up with 'our dearest domestic ties'; and as Burke remarked just prior to the above quotation the whole system of English liberties is conceived 'as an entailed inheritance derived to us from our forefathers, and to be transmitted to our posterity'. In the second analogy Burke proceeds from the family, which in his view is natural to man, to the state, which is held to be conventional (conventional not in the sense of being arbitrary but in the sense of being man-made in a way that the family is not).

Both analogies are central to Burke, but it is the second analogy that usually draws the greater comment. Whenever conservatively oriented thinkers such as Burke introduce the family into political and moral discourse, the question arises as to why the analogy of the family is felt to be so appropriate. Why is the family pattern a criterion for the evaluation and shaping of the political pattern ? Resemblances between state and family might explain psychologically why we feel cosy and at home (if we do) under the English Constitution. But what is the moral worth of this analogy ? We have here perhaps a 'wisdom without reflection' in some vague psychological sense, but in the sense of articulated moral judgements why is it held to be reasonable to pattern the state after the family, as if the family were some ultimate moral criterion and not just another social institution ? In short, the familiar argument goes, has not the philosopher in question covertly derived an *ought* from an *is*, and is not he guilty of the 'naturalistic fallacy' ? It might be argued, if we are going to derive an *ought* from an *is*, why is the monogamous English family a more suitable fact for moral canonization than, say, the polygamous or polyandrous families described by anthropologists ? It might be an historical accident that monogamy appears to be triumphing over other forms of family life; regardless of whether it prevails or not, in the total history of the world more people have probably lived in non-monogamous families than in monogamous ones. If statistical frequency *per se* is not going to determine our selection of the *is* suitable for elevation to *ought* status, then what is ?

It is difficult in a study in the history of ideas to suggest how a philosopher might have answered questions or resolved problems which for him did not exist or existed only dimly. While Burke may well have read that now famous passage in the *Treatise* (Book III, i, 1) concerning the impossibility of deriving *ought* propositions from *is* propositions, a passage where in the opinion of some contemporary moral philosophers Hume was the first to expose what is now referred to as the 'naturalistic fallacy', there is no evidence that Burke's thought was in any way affected by this. (Modern Hume scholars are divided as to whether the impossibility Hume had in mind concerns the impossibility of deriving *ought* propositions from *is* propositions after the manner of his philosophical adversaries or whether it is meant by Hume as a denial of *any* derivation of an *ought* proposition from an *is* proposition unless the *is* proposition in question is conjoined with an *ought* proposition; therefore, the question of how Burke's thought should have been affected by Hume's treatment of this point admits of no simple answer.) It is especially unhistorical to claim as Stanlis does (op. cit., 170) that Burke 'always' distinguished between 'descriptive' and 'normative' nature. Burke did not do any such thing because so far as I can tell, he saw no *reason* to. Commentators may, of course, apply this distinction to Burke's works at times, but when, for example, Burke tells us that 'nature' (along with Providence) opposes a parliamentary union with the American colonies (*Works*, I, 373, 376) he clearly does not have in mind a distinction between descriptive and normative nature.

The truth of the matter is that most moderns outside the Catholic faith have forgotten the rules of the language game played by Burke. The vital connexion between fact and value seen by Burke and Thomists is largely obscured now, although H. L. A. Hart has caught glimpses of it in his treatment of 'The Minimum Content of Natural Law' when he speaks of '*natural necessity*'.[1] The notion that the moral law and all species of obligation depend upon the will of God for their existence is even more obscured despite the revival of natural law thinking in some quarters. My purpose is not to defend Burke's belief in natural law but to explain its function in his political thought and to make clear the rules by which he played the natural law game. Of one thing, however, I am certain: Burke nowhere explicitly commits the 'naturalistic fallacy' of deriving an *ought* solely from an *is*, but this may tell us more about Burke's loose, informal manner of reasoning than about his logical acumen. Of greater importance is the fact that Burke neither implicitly nor explicitly committed the 'naturalistic fallacy' in a wholesale manner, if he committed it at all. Some human inclinations and some of man's political institutions and practices met with Burke's moral disapproval; and even God's will was to be obeyed not simply because it was His will but because it was reasonable and good.

Historically the thesis that there is a natural law has been intimately associated with the belief that there are ends or purposes natural to man, and it was no accident that the waning of the teleological perspective was accompanied by a decline in the fortunes of natural law theory.

[1] *The Concept of Law* (Oxford, 1961), 189–95.

It could indeed be argued that natural law theory loses much or all of its relevance when its teleological pre-suppositions are set aside. The dependence of natural law upon the notion of ends natural to man is illustrated in the following remarks by Jacques Maritain: '. . . there is, by virtue of human nature, *an order or a disposition which human reason can discover and according to which the human will must act in order to attune itself to the necessary ends of the human being. The unwritten law, or natural law, is nothing more than that.*'[1] If this is so, then there can be no further question of Burke's belief in natural law.

In the light of this teleological aspect of the natural law Burke's analogies between the state and the order of the world and between the state and the order of the family are more clearly understood. These analogies are intended as illustrations of how the physical world and the human family (which is built in large part upon physical needs) attain their natural ends. Such analogies may function as imperfect guides as to how the state may achieve its 'natural' end. In Burke's view the end of the state (which is a human artifact) is that it serve as a *means* to the development and perfection of human potentials: '. . . He who gave our nature to be perfected by our virtue willed also the necessary means of its perfection: He willed, therefore, the state: He willed its connection with the source and original archetype of all perfection.'[2]

Burke's view that the state is a means to our moral (and intellectual) development and his belief that a law is made for the common good suggests that an act of the state or a law which does not contribute to these ends is not a genuine law. Historically, natural law theorists as opposed to legal positivists have argued that an unjust law is not a law. In his *Tract on the Popery Laws* Burke writes that if a law transgresses seriously against 'common rights and the ends of just government' then it renders void 'its obligatory

---

[1] *The Rights of Man and Natural Law* (London, 1945), 35.
[2] *Reflections on the Revolution in France, Works*, III, 361.

quality on the mind. . . . It cannot be said to have the properties of genuine law.'[1] Even if the people gave not only virtual but actual consent to such a law, it would still be null and void:

They have no right to make a law prejudicial to the whole community, even though the delinquents in making such an act should be themselves the chief sufferers by it; because it would be made against the principle of a superior law, which it is not in the power of any community, or of the whole race of man, to alter,—I mean the will of Him who gave us our nature and in giving impressed an invariable law upon it. It would be hard to point out any error more truly subversive of all the order and beauty, of all the peace and happiness of human society, than the position, that any body of men have a right to make what laws they please,—or that laws can derive any authority from their institution merely, and independent of the quality of the subject-matter. No argument of policy, reason of state, or preservation of the constitution can be pleaded in favor of such a practice.[2]

Burke goes on to say that it was Hobbes who maintained this error and that Cicero had previously argued with indignation and contempt against just such a view: Burke approves Cicero's verdict that such an opinion is unworthy not only of a philosopher but of an illiterate peasant as well.

Critics sometimes suggest that Burke as he grew older repented or qualified his denial that 'laws derive any authority from their institution merely'. This is a complex point to be discussed later, but in the *Tract on the Popery Laws* Burke makes it clear that human authority is to be judged in terms of its justice and its utility. Burke's reverence for English authority stems not from its parochial or national quality but from its reasonableness in terms of natural law criteria. The early Burke at least was not guilty of deriving a moral *ought* from a legal *is* but judged the legal *is* of positive law, often severely, from the perspective of natural law.

[1] *Works*, VI, 319–320.   [2] Ibid., 321–2.

III

BURKE, HUME, SMITH, AND BEATTIE

FURTHER elaborations of Burke's natural law beliefs will
occur in the course of this study, but enough has been said
for now to establish Burke's commitment to the natural
law. The question remains, however, as to the range of
data that this explanatory principle will cover. Will it
provide an understanding of all of Burke's political thought
or only of restricted portions of it ? Shifting the question
to the historical level, does the mention of Aquinas make
further mention of Hume or Adam Smith superfluous ?
Before the natural law reading of Burke was advanced, it
was held, in the words of H. B. Acton, that 'From Hume
to Edmund Burke the transition is smooth and easy'; and
George H. Sabine seems to have been struck more by the
parallels between Burke and Hume than by the resemblances between Burke and any other philosophers.[1] Does
acceptance of the natural law reading of Burke mean that
the transition from Hume to Burke is no longer to be
regarded as 'smooth and easy' ? This seems inevitable if
one holds with Sabine that, provided one grants the premisses of Hume's arguments, these arguments destroy the
natural law. The problem becomes more complicated,
however, when one attends closely to the concluding paragraph of Book III, ii, 1, of Hume's *Treatise of Human
Nature*:

> To avoid giving offence, I must here observe, that when I deny justice
> to be a natural virtue, I make use of the word, natural, only as oppos'd
> to *artificial*. In another sense of the word; as no principle of the human
> mind is more natural than a sense of virtue; so no virtue is more natural
> than justice. Mankind is an inventive species; and where an invention is

---

[1] Acton, 'Prejudice', *Revue Internationale de Philosophie*, VI (1952), 333;
Sabine, 'Convention and Tradition: Hume and Burke', *A History of Political
Theory* (New York, 1950), 597–619.

obvious and absolutely necessary, it may as properly be said to be natural as anything that proceeds immediately from original principles, without the intervention of thought or reflexion. Tho' the rules of justice be *artificial*, they are not *arbitrary*. Nor is the expression improper to call them Laws of Nature; if by natural we understand what is common to any species, or even if we confine it to mean what is inseparable from the species.[1]

To see Hume as the destroyer of natural law the above passage must be slighted, and attention must be shifted to those more famous passages where Hume proclaims that 'Reason is, and ought only to be the slave of the passions, and can never pretend to any other office than to serve and obey them' and 'Where a passion is neither founded on false suppositions, nor chuses means insufficient for the end, the understanding can neither justify nor condemn it. 'Tis not contrary to reason to prefer the destruction of the whole world to the scratching of my finger.'[2] The restriction of reason's role in moral deliberation to this fact-finding capacity is held by Sabine and others to vitiate the rational pretensions of the natural law; and surely the notion of the natural law as something universal, objective, and rational seems jeopardized by Hume's remarks that it is not contrary to reason to prefer the destruction of the whole world to the scratching of my finger, or to choose my total ruin to prevent the least uneasiness of an Indian or person wholly unknown to me, or to prefer for myself a lesser good acknowledged by myself as such to my greater good.

It is interesting to note, however, the refusal of one Catholic historian of ideas to be especially disturbed by Hume's argument: 'Despite his extreme language, Hume is moving here toward a moderate position that recognizes the guiding function of practical reason, the distinctive contribution of the appetitive powers, and the need for the mutual impenetration of reason and the appetitive powers in human conduct.'[3] The conclusion, intended

[1] *Treatise of Human Nature*, L. A. Selby-Bigge ed. (Oxford, 1960).
[2] Ibid., II, iii, 3.
[3] James Collins, *A History of Modern European Philosophy* (Milwaukee, 1956), 449.

somewhat charitably, is that Hume did not misunderstand
the role of reason in ethics any more than he did in the
more speculative realms (where he allegedly 'reduces'
reason to imagination). My sole purpose in referring to
this reading of Hume is to suggest that Hume's emphasis
upon the limits of reason in moral deliberation, his insistence that the passions determine the ends and reason the
means, is not so completely alien to the Catholic natural
law tradition as historians such as Sabine have imagined.*
Revelation and grace would appear superfluous to the
Catholic were it not for those limitations of reason to which
Hume has here called attention. One need not deny significant differences between the Catholic position and
Hume's in this matter in order to insist upon the obvious,
namely that far greater differences exist between them on
the religious level. And it is the derivation of the natural
law from God's plans for man that is conspicuously missing
in Hume. His insistence upon the artificiality of the virtue
of justice in his special sense of *artificial* is, however, no
cause for undue alarm to the natural law tradition. It is
not improper, Hume writes, to call the rules of justice
'Laws of Nature' if by Laws of Nature 'we understand
what is common to any species, or even if we confine it to
mean what is inseparable from the species'. To speak of
the Laws of Nature as *inseparable* from the species shows
that in his ethical theory Hume has not altogether lost
sight of the Aristotelian notion of essential predication.
Inseparable suggests essential to the species in the traditional sense. It is a recognition on Hume's part that man
has certain minimal requirements for his survival, that the

---

* Could we not say, in the spirit of Hume, that the Laws of Nature may be
reason's means to the ends chosen by the passions, *if* the passions choose survival
(personal and of the species) ? Could one not picture Hume himself as saying: it
is a contingent fact that men opt for survival, no contradiction or logical absurdity
is involved if they do not; but if they do, then the observation of the Laws of
Nature becomes a necessary means to the end of survival ? Is this not what his
talk about 'necessary' to, 'common to', and 'inseparable from' the species means ?
And is 'necessary to the species' not a prime criterion in traditional natural law
thinking for deciding what is to count as a law of nature ?

Laws of Nature (which Hume conceives of in terms primarily of property rights) reflect, in Hart's phrase, those natural necessities without which survival is either impossible or exceedingly unpleasant. It could perhaps be argued from Hume's examples (it is not unreasonable to prefer the destruction of the whole world to the scratching of my finger, etc.) that Hume would have to construe the Laws of Nature as being both artificial and *arbitrary*; and this suggestion of arbitrariness is what goes especially against the grain of traditional natural law. Here one must choose between Hume's generalizations and his examples, and his generalizations seem more consistent with those facts of mutual dependence among men to which he has called attention.

I am not trying to make Hume into a defender of the natural law tradition but rather to point out that his opposition to this tradition is not so complete as that of later utilitarians who in part derived from him, following as it were those famous examples of his out to their logical consequences where the natural law is concerned, and insisting, far more than Hume ever did, upon the obscurity and subjectivity of the traditional moral vocabulary of *reasonable, right, just, obligatory*, &c. But Hume's examples can cut two ways, either against the reasonableness claimed for the natural law, or against the calculating egoism that is usually associated with utilitarianism (I may prefer a stranger's advantage to my own, or I may knowingly prefer a lesser to a greater good for myself). The point of this digression into Hume exegesis is to show that, if it is no longer possible to speak of the transition from Hume to Burke as 'smooth and easy', one can still discover significant parallels between them without being liable to the charge of a 'profound ignorance' of Burke's life and thought (a charge made by Stanlis against Sabine).

One way of preserving the significance of the parallels between Burke and Hume is to revise Sabine's reading of

Hume so that note is taken of the residues of natural law thinking which survive in Hume (as in his description of the rules of justice as being natural to, in the sense of being inseparable from, the species). With this fairly important revision in mind, we can then be struck anew by the force of some of the parallels Acton, Sabine, and others have seen between Burke and Hume. We can avoid that air of Thomistic exclusiveness that often permeates the natural law reading of Burke and leads even the judicious Canavan to write: 'His conception of the proper structure of society, his doctrine of prescription, his theory of conservation and reform—these and other aspects of his thought cannot be understood if Burke is taken as merely an empiricist in the British philosophical tradition.'[1] Unfortunately for Canavan these are *the* aspects of Burke's thought which could be understood along 'British empiricist' lines, for Burke's political conservatism is in these aspects substantially the same as that expressed earlier by David Hume.

What considerations then lie behind Canavan's downgrading of the Burke–Hume parallels? Essentially the same ones, I think, as led Strauss and Stanlis earlier to down-grade the parallels between Burke and Locke. The consensus among them seems to be that a moderate or conservative politics is much more natural or organic to a deeply religious world view such as Burke's than to a watered down Anglicanism (Locke) or to a largely sceptical viewpoint (Hume). Dr. Johnson remarked that Hume was a Tory 'by chance'; and Burke agreed, 'Yes, as he was an Epicurean, it must be by chance.' Hume's lack of religious faith probably explains Burke's unkind remark, made while Hume was dying: 'I doubt that keeping company with David Hume, in a strict light, is hardly defensible. But in the present state of society I see all men. 'Tis making myself of too much consequence not to.'[2]

---

[1] Canavan, op. cit., 81.
[2] These remarks are attributed to Burke by James Boswell. Bryant, op. cit., 108, 224–5.

Regardless of whether one holds that Hume was a conservative 'by chance', the fact remains that he was a conservative. It also remains true that what chiefly marks the difference between the political principles of the Tory Hume and the Whig Burke is not the content of these principles, which are in many respects remarkably alike, but the question of the ultimate derivation of these principles. As for Locke and Burke even the question of the ultimate derivation of their political principles seems not to mark a significant difference; both saw the natural law as an expression of God's will. Here the chief difference seems to involve rather a question of *perspective* toward, and of temporal distance from, the Revolution of 1688–9. So while accepting the thesis that Burke's politics cannot be fully understood within the confines of an exclusively 'British' or 'empiricist' or 'Humian' interpretation, I see good reasons to avoid obscuring totally the no longer 'smooth and easy' but still passable transition from Hume to Burke. Given the admittedly controversial and incomplete reading of Hume sketched above, there is no longer any compulsion to accept an exclusive disjunction between Burke and Hume on the one hand and Burke and the natural law on the other.

The differences between Hume and Burke are, of course, significant. Naturally enough we do not find in Hume the traditional conception of natural law as that part of the eternal law accessible to human reason; he speaks of the human invention of the laws of nature whereas Burke would, I think, be inclined to speak of the discovery of these laws. And we do not find in Burke any distinction corresponding to Hume's separation of natural virtues such as courage from artificial virtues such as justice. Like Thomas Reid (with whom he was acquainted) Burke seems not to have been convinced that the issue between those who ascribed ethical judgements to reason and those who like Hume ascribed them to a 'moral sense' was a vital one, and we do not find him discussing this question, although presumably a strict adherence to Thomistic rationalism would have led him to go against Hume here. It is surely correct, insofar as such remarks contain any truth, to characterize Hume (as Burke did) as an Epicurean and to characterize Burke as a Stoic. Where the writing and interpretation of history is concerned Burke and Hume were in a sense rivals; and Lord Acton for one preferred Burke's youthful *Abridgement of English History* to Hume's *History* and regretted that Burke had, according to legend, given up the writing of history upon learning of Hume's intentions to take up this subject.[1] Despite a favourable review of the first two volumes of Hume's *History of England* in the *Annual Register* where he described Hume as a 'very profound thinker' and wrote approvingly of Hume's using 'the idea of the growth' of the Constitution as the principle upon which to build his history,[2] it is known that he considered Hume to be a careless and partisan historian. Here Burke's Whig commitments and Hume's Tory ones did make for differences.

Burke's biographer, James Prior, reports in a tantalizingly brief sentence that Burke once considered writing a refutation of the philosophical 'systems' of both Berkeley and Hume.[3] Prior reports this while relating the story that Burke, who later became Lord Rector of the University of Glasgow, had earlier been an unsuccessful candidate for the Chair of Logic at that institution; and this story seems doubtful. It calls our attention, however, to a fact which both MacCunn and Stanlis have underplayed and that is Burke's Scottish connexions. Dugald Stewart, Adam Ferguson, Thomas Reid, James Beattie, and Adam Smith were friends or acquaintances.[4] These connexions will be mentioned again in a moment, but for the present the

---

[1] *Essays on Church and State* (London, 1952), 455.

[2] *Annual Register*, 1761.

[3] *A Life of Edmund Burke* (London, 1891), 38.

[4] Ibid., 38, 52, 61, 128, 236, 317, 519. Bryant, op. cit., 243–9. Burke was also acquainted with a large number of Scottish literati and historians, including the distinguished historian, William Robertson.

crucial question is: Given the great philosophical and personal differences that separated Burke and Hume, why should anyone persist in being struck by the resemblances between them? What purpose, save that of biographical completeness, is served by the mention of Hume alongside Burke?

Actually two purposes are served by preserving this relationship: (1) It is relevant to Burke's account of the passions and hence of human nature, providing a key especially to Burke's *Inquiry* and thus into the psychological assumptions of Burke's political theorizing. (2) It tells us something about Burke's natural law beliefs that mention of Aquinas does not, at least not explicitly. The Humian contribution to Burke's account of the passions will be evident in Part Two, and readers of Hume will easily detect traces of Hume in Burke's account of prescription (Part Three). At this point, however, some brief notes on prejudice and prescription may prove helpful, especially if the following remarks about Burke and Aquinas are correct.

It is said that Burke did not understand 'the natural moral law as a rigidly deductive system' but had rather 'a subtle and empirical conception of it'.[1] The subtlety of Burke's conception of natural law poses no problems for those who are struck by Burke's affinities with Thomism; the problem here is altogether different, and it is the perennial one of whether unsystematic authors such as Burke, Montaigne, and Lord Acton (to name but a few disparate examples) are not often endowed by partisan readers with a greater degree of subtlety than they in fact possess. But for those who read Burke from the Thomistic point of view the empirical emphasis in Burke does pose a problem. Aquinas may not have conceived of natural law as a rigidly deductive system, but he did conceive of it deductively in a significant sense. A law of nature is self-evident to Aquinas (meaning the predicate is 'contained

---

[1] Canavan, op. cit., 23.

in the notion of its subject'), and it is said to be 'the first rule of reason'. A human law which is not just, according to Aquinas, is no law at all: 'every human law has just so much of the nature of law as it is derived from the law of nature'. This derivation from the natural law may be in two ways: (1) 'as a conclusion from principles', (2) 'by way of a determination of certain common notions'. (1) is the mode of the 'sciences', (2) the mode of the crafts; but both modes of derivation are found in human law. Aquinas gives as an example of (1) the derivation of 'one must not kill' from the principle 'one should do harm to no man', and as an example of (2) the variety of ways in which a man who has violated the laws of nature may be punished. Now it is true that Aquinas concludes this argument (*Summa Theologica*, I–II, qu. 95, art. 2) by emphasizing the great variety of human affairs and the consequent diversity of positive laws. In matters where particular points in the determination of natural law are concerned Aquinas endorses the 'Philosopher's' opinion that '*we ought to pay as much attention to the undemonstrated sayings and opinions of persons who surpass us in experience, age and prudence, as to their demonstrations*'.

If one is going to read Burke as a Thomist, one is going to have to emphasize the concluding part of Qu. 95, art. 2 and minimize the earlier parts of this article where Aquinas speaks of derivations from natural law, especially derivation in the sense of (1) where the model and the example seem to be conceived of as strictly deductive. Aquinas, following Aristotle and anticipating Burke, is well aware of the differences between speculative and practical reason, and in Qu. 94, art. 4 he discusses how in some particular cases the conclusions drawn from the natural law may fail as to 'rectitude' and 'knowledge' in a way that the conclusions drawn by speculative reason cannot. Still, even if one plays down, as Maritain now does, the deductive side of Aquinas and if one can find in the texts some justification for this, one has to admit that the language at least of

derivation, deduction, and determination is explicitly present in Aquinas and not, ordinarily, in Burke, although one
might argue that it is *presupposed* by Burke. I doubt
whether Burke in his philosophical capacity would be
considered especially subtle by most Thomists, excepting
Father Canavan; but they would be struck by his empirical
inclination, by the zeal with which he attended to the
undemonstrated opinions of persons of experience, age,
and prudence. It is true that Aquinas had said that 'What
pertains to moral science is known mostly through experience' (*Ethicorum*, I, 3), but it is also true that Burke's
writings show an estimate of the importance of experience
to moral science which seems to owe something more to
Hume than to Aquinas. This is evident, I think, in his
treatment of prejudice and prescription.

Prejudice and *prescription* are quasi-technical terms in
Burke. In endorsing prejudice Burke does not mean to
include everything that might ordinarily be considered as
such but rather to call attention, as he does in the *Reflections
on the Revolution in France*, to the 'latent wisdom' that
prevails in many but not all of the opinions dismissed by
men of the Enlightenment as mere prejudice. Prejudice
provides men with motives for doing the good which
reason alone cannot provide, and as Burke pointed out in
his *Tract on the Popery Laws* the 'stable prejudices of time'
make for social order and continuity. Russell Kirk thinks
that Burke at times 'approaches very nearly to a theory of
collective human intellect, a knowledge partially instinctive, partially conscious, which each individual inherits
as his birthright and his protection' and warns of the perils
of ignoring 'this enormous bulk of racial knowledge'.[1]
But this goes too far; no theory of 'collective human
intellect' or of 'racial knowledge' is needed for what can
be explained in terms of a learning theory whereby each
individual receives the vast majority of his opinions un-
critically from others, usually without benefit of formal

[1] *The Conservative Mind from Burke to Santayana* (Chicago, 1953), 33.

demonstration even in cases where such demonstration may be possible. In morals such opinions serve as motives to action in a way that 'naked reason' cannot, being deeply interwoven with our affections and interests. This, according to Hume and Burke, is as it should be, for most of those prejudices which have become customary and habitual have significant uses. They help us get through the vast majority of moral decisions successfully, to resist dangerous novelties and untried methods, to preserve, and ultimately to leave, society in pretty much the order in which we found it. On all that has been said thus far Hume and Burke are in substantial agreement; the principal issue between them concerns the question of whether religion is a useful prejudice or a superstition.[1] Both men attend carefully to what Aquinas calls the 'common notions' of mankind (Hume's 'general opinion' and Burke's 'prejudice'), but their motives for such attention might have given Aquinas reason for serious misgivings. Hume's analysis of the limits of reason in ethics has, as I have already remarked, no explicit parallel in Burke, indeed Burke's scholastic presuppositions seem to suggest that Burke could not have accepted such an analysis *in toto*; but on the practical as distinct from the analytic level both men emphasize the weaknesses of reason and the strength of the passions in moral decisions.

Prescription can be considered a major part of the strategy endorsed by Hume and Burke as a means of meeting on the community level the weaknesses of human reason. Prescription is, of course, a much older notion than this might suggest; the establishment of rights by a long exercise of their corresponding powers figures prominently in the history of English law, and Hume and Burke are not innovators where this concept is concerned. There is, however, as Graham Wallas has pointed out, a difference between the principle of prescription when it is followed in the ordinary manner and when it is made

[1] H. B. Acton, op. cit., 332–6.

part of a deliberate, consciously embraced political policy.[1] Accordingly, it is not the concept of prescription but the emphasis upon this concept as crucial to our understanding of political, social, and economic rights and obligations that marks something new in Hume and Burke. The importance attached to prescription by Hume in the *Treatise* and Burke in his *Reflections on the Revolution in France* is not an isolated facet of their political theories but is an integral part of their overall deference to that which is, to the customs and conventions of society. Social conventions such as rules for the acquisition and transmission of property are artificial in the sense of being man-made, but given man's social nature and the mutual dependence of men there is a sense in which they are natural as well. The important thing for understanding both Hume and Burke is their general refusal to equate artificial with arbitrary.

Prescription may have some rather grim consequences, which are accepted by Hume and Burke as part of the price to be paid for social order and stability. The moral as distinct from the legal significance of possession, of present occupancy, may at times be doubted; and it requires no great moral imagination to conceive of situations where injustice may result from the application of the doctrine of prescription. It seems likely, however, that Hume and Burke could not have been altogether blind to the obvious, that they believed the greater danger to be from the other side, that is from the *challenge* to established possessions, and that they sincerely held that the extension or elevation of the legal principle of prescription to provide moral cover or justification of rights to land, liberty, and political power preserved both the social fabric *and* the requirements of justice in the vast majority of cases in a way in which other rules could not.

There is a significant passage in which Burke purports to ground prescription in natural law and at the same time

[1] *Human Nature in Politics* (London, 1948), 182–3.

admits its grimmer aspects. He has been speaking of the 'solid rock of prescription' as the 'soundest, the most general, and the most recognized title between man and man that is known in municipal or in public jurisprudence'. Prescription is, he thinks,

. . . a title in which not arbitrary institutions, but the eternal order of things, gives judgment; a title which is not the creature, but the master, of positive law; a title which, though not fixed in its term, is rooted in its principle in the law of Nature itself, and is indeed the original ground of all known property: for all property in soil will always be traced back to that source, and will rest there. . . . These gentlemen . . . know as well as I that in England we have had always a prescription or limitation, as all nations have, against each other. The crown was excepted, but that exception is destroyed, and we have lately established a sixty years' possession as against the crown. All titles terminate in prescription,—in which . . . the son devours the father, and the last prescription eats up all the former.[1]

Morton Auerbach comments on the metaphor of the son devouring the father that this 'is to say that "prescriptions" of any kind are irrelevant as arguments against a revolution and that the English are quite capable of ignoring them in an actual revolution'.[2] This is, however, a misunderstanding, for according to Burke prescriptions are always relevant against a revolution but they are not always of one kind; against the king's rights there may be the rights of his subjects, or the king's conduct may have cost him his rights; and prescription may sometimes give way to 'necessity'. Prescription is meant to cover a vast majority of cases, but it may be overridden in certain others. The point about prescription is that it justifies not past possession as such but continuous and present possession. The English have established a right of possession against the Crown, that is, Parliament now exercises powers previously exercised by the Crown. The son has devoured the father, and prescription has sanctified so to speak a successful revolution. But this does not mean that prescription, because it allegedly

---

[1] *Letter to Richard Burke on Protestant Ascendency in Ireland* (1793), *Works*, VI, 412.

[2] *The Conservative Illusion* (New York, 1959), 62.

can be employed to justify a successful revolution after a decent interval of time has elapsed, can be ignored when a revolution is being planned or considered. The essential function of prescription is to provide *prima facie*, but not in every case conclusive, reasons not to challenge the established system of legal and moral obligations and rights.

It could be argued that Aquinas arrived at a similar position, although by a different road. Certainly his judgement that an unjust law is no law is no injunction to rebel against a law if it is unjust. It does remove the endorsement provided by the natural moral law, but prudential considerations may enjoin us to continue to obey an unjust law or laws so long as these are not directly contrary to divine revelation. It is also true that Aquinas advises us to attend not merely to the customs of a people but specifically to those customs that form part of the legal system. In short, he tells us to attend to the facts of human experience; but it seems doubtful that he himself attended to them to the extent that Burke ('the philosopher in action') did. Certainly the concept of prescription and, I think, much of the reality of prescription as well is not present in Aquinas as it is in Burke (and Hume). At the minimum there is a difference in emphasis. With Burke and Hume, as with Hobbes and Locke, a large part of the emphasis derives from a preoccupation with the rights of property.[1]

What I have said about the parallels between Hume's political thought and Burke's does not commit me to the historical thesis that Hume is *the* historical source of those ideas of Burke's which resemble Hume's. In the light of Burke's *Inquiry into the Origin of Our Ideas of the Sublime and Beautiful*, which shows Burke's early familiarity with the *Treatise*, such an historical thesis is, however, not so absurd as is sometimes imagined.[2] It may

---

[1] C. B. Macpherson, *The Political Theory of Possessive Individualism, Hobbes to Locke* (Oxford, 1962), *passim*.

[2] Pocock, op. cit., 126.

perhaps be sounder on a strictly historical plane to insist that Burke's awareness of the importance of custom and habit and of man's second (or social) nature comes more from Montesquieu's *Esprit des lois* than from Hume;[1] but it is not silly to suggest that Hume's ideas were 'in the air'. This notion can be brought to earth as it were, not only by an examination of Burke's *Inquiry* but also by reference to works such as Adam Smith's *Theory of Moral Sentiments* which Burke reviewed in the *Annual Register* as an 'excellent work' that avoids the novelty so dangerous to moral speculation. Burke wrote:

We conceive, that here the theory is in all its essential parts just, and founded on truth and nature. The author seeks for the foundation of the just, the fit, the proper, the decent, in our most common and most allowed passions; and making approbation and disapprobation the tests of virtue and vice, and showing that those are founded on sympathy, he raises from this simple truth, one of the most beautiful fabrics of moral theory, that has perhaps ever appeared. The illustrations are numerous and happy, and show the author to be a man of uncommon observation.[2]

Unfortunately Burke's policy in reviewing books, as he assures his readers, is to review only those books which he can recommend to his readers, 'to raise, not to satisfy curiosity', and to give readers some specimen of each writer's work. In the case of Smith's *Theory of Moral Sentiments* most of the review consists of a lengthy quotation from Smith on the importance of sympathy and imagination to morality; and so from this review we have

---

[1] C. P. Courtney's *Montesquieu and Burke* (Oxford, 1963) provides good grounds for such an argument. It is, however, doubtful that Burke's lack of interest in explaining the French Revolution as an 'historical phenomenon' justifies Courtney's conclusion that 'He does not apply Montesquieu's historical method because he no longer believes in it' (149). There is no reason to suppose that Burke ever accepted any historical method that entails the 'historical determinism' which Courtney sees in Montesquieu's judgement that all political states decay and decline. In view of Montesquieu's own declared belief that human action can offset the effects of material causes (*Esprit des lois*, xiv, 5–6) and his emphasis upon the influence of morality and religious convictions upon the course of history it seems doubtful that he was himself a 'determinist' in Courtney's sense or was committed to an historical method which would rule out the legitimacy of a moral indictment of the French Revolution such as Burke's.

[2] *Annual Register*, 1759.

only the assurance that Burke read Smith and attached special significance to Smith's theory of sympathy. (That Burke had himself advanced such a theory in his *Inquiry* will be shown in Part Two.) The passage Burke quotes from the *Theory of Moral Sentiments* concludes with the reflection that the fear of death, which we can imagine all too clearly, is one of the most important principles in human nature and 'the great restraint upon the injustice of mankind, which, while it afflicts and mortifies the individuals, guards and protects the society'. So we can safely judge that Burke saw the social significance of Smith's (and hence Hume's) theory of the passions, of sympathy and the imagination, as well as at least some of the significance of this for political philosophy.

Burke read widely and voraciously, but there is no reason to suppose that he read or thought systematically. For a man of Burke's active and sociable nature ideas that are 'in the air' in the form of books being currently discussed and reviewed have undoubtedly a significance greater than they would ordinarily have for the 'closet philosopher'. So we cannot here ignore evidence in the form of an uncritical book review while in other cases we might safely do so; nor can we assume that Burke was aware of divergences between the contemporary theory of moral sentiments and the books he had read while receiving a classical education as an undergraduate. More systematic thinkers than Burke have assumed that their favourite books are substantially consistent with one another without examining them closely for differences. The history of ideas would scarcely be so interesting were it not for the fact that many thinkers have a strange collection of favourite texts which, when examined critically or from a different perspective, seem to make odd bedfellows indeed.

One of the greatest oddities in the case of Burke concerns his endorsement of both traditional natural law and the *laissez-faire* economics of Adam Smith, apparently without ever considering their differences. We find Burke seemingly unconscious of his part in fusing the natural law principle of hierarchy and subordination with the principles of a self-regulating market.[1] From this point of view perhaps the greatest champion of duty and obligation appears in the paradoxical position of weakening further the traditional system of duties and obligations that was already disappearing from British society by the last half of the eighteenth century. Various defences of Burke are possible. Burke sincerely believed that 'the laws of commerce . . . are the laws of Nature, and consequently the laws of God'.[2] Accordingly, market price would be conceived of as being in some ultimate sense a just price; if only we could know what God knows, the apparent discrepancy, which had seemed so real to medieval natural law theorists, at times between 'just price' and 'market price' might be narrowed or might disappear altogether. 'Circumstances' *had* changed, and the economy of the eighteenth century bore little resemblance to the economy of the thirteenth. It is unfair to suggest that historically speaking Burke helped to kill the idea of a just price, although he probably helped somewhat to bury it. While it is not historically odd to find that Burke did not feel a need to justify the abandonment of the notion of a just price, it is logically odd that while he championed the idea of a free market at home and, where feasible, free trade among nations, he nowhere noted the economic differences between traditional and modern natural law and appeared to believe that the natural law was univocal in this respect. Nowhere does he actually avail himself of an argument which would say explicitly that the natural law is a body of laws the contents of which may change as circumstances change.

Although the story that Adam Smith consulted Burke while writing the *Wealth of Nations* is unverified, Smith's

[1] For a discussion of Burke's resolution of 'traditional and capitalist moralities' see C. B. Macpherson, 'Edmund Burke', *Transactions of the Royal Society of Canada*, LII (June 1959), 19–26.

[2] *Thoughts and Details on Scarcity* (1795), *Works*, V, 157.

high regard for Burke is well established. Burke was, according to Smith, 'the only man, who, without communication, thought on these topics [of political economy] exactly as he did'.[1] Besides accepting much of Smith's theory of moral sentiments and his economic theory of the self-regulating market, Burke's own belief in Providence, in particular his belief that conditions of poverty and scarcity will not be allowed by God to become permanent, is reminiscent of Smith's notion of the 'invisible hand'. It has also been suggested that Smith, like Burke, had a keen historical sense, the evidence for this being found mainly in the historical sections of the *Wealth of Nations* and in Smith's proposal for a work on jurisprudence which would have followed Montesquieu's historical method.[2]

It proves eventually unrewarding to pursue the parallels between a thinker such as Burke and other philosophers beyond a certain point. One envisages a long list of separate studies, *Burke and Aristotle*, *Burke and Cicero*, *Burke and Smith*, which, while they might be separately illuminating, would together create a somewhat misleading impression of the quality and depth of the various aspects of Burke's thought. Hume and Smith, having served our immediate purpose, can now be withdrawn from consideration; for together they have illuminated the presence in Burke's thought of the concepts of prejudice, prescription, and of market valuation in a way that, clearly, mention of Aquinas cannot. They have served, too, to show Burke's familiarity with a theory of moral sentiments which, to say the least, poses problems for the traditional Thomistic view of the role of reason in ethics.

Still we are not quite through with the Scots. Hume *may* be one source of Burke's denunciation of metaphysics and of the pretences of 'naked reason', but there is another

[1] Robert Bisset, *Life of Edmund Burke* (London, 1800), II, 429. Burke was probably responsible for the favourable review of the *Wealth of Nations* in the *Annual Register* for 1776.

[2] William C. Dunn, 'Adam Smith and Edmund Burke: Complementary Contemporaries', *The Southern Economic Journal*, VII (January 1941), 339–40.

side to Burke: 'The two poles of thought, scepticism and certainty, are always present in Burke; he argues first one cause and then the other with equal fervor.'[1] Just as the Scottish philosopher Hume helps illuminate the sceptical side of Burke (although this is not Hume's only contribution), so the Scottish philosophers who were adversaries of Hume help illuminate the certainty that is also a hallmark of Burke's thought. It may be that they serve only to shore up a certainty that was in evidence in Burke from the beginning, but one cannot treat the service of shoring up, in the sense of providing supporting arguments for theses already subscribed to, as entirely negligible.

The attempt to answer Hume's 'scepticism' concerning the range and powers of human reason by distinguishing between reason and *common sense*, with many of the capabilities which Hume had denied to reason being now transferred to the faculty of common sense, was championed by a number of Burke's Scottish friends; and indeed this attempt is usually labelled as the Scottish common sense philosophy. Burke's friend James Beattie stated the tenets of this philosophy in *An Essay on the Nature and Immutability of Truth, in opposition to Sophistry and Scepticism*, which Burke reviewed favourably and quoted from extensively in the *Annual Register*. Burke's selections from this *Essay* are revealing, for they are aimed at Hume: 'If an inhabitant of another planet were to read *The Treatise of Human Nature*, what notions of human nature could he gather from it ?—That man must believe one thing by instinct, and must also believe the contrary by reason . . . That man ought to believe nothing, and yet that man's belief ought to be influenced and determined by certain principles:—That we ought to doubt of everything, yea of our doubts themselves; and therefore the utmost that philosophy can do, is to give a doubtful solution of doubtful doubts.' Not content to deny that this

[1] J. A. Lester, 'An Analysis of the Conservative Thought of Edmund Burke', A Doctoral Thesis, Harvard University, 1942, p. 133.

is the proper conception of either human nature or of the task of philosophy, Beattie argues vehemently that many philosophical sceptics are infidels without taste or sentiment: 'The views and expectations of the infidel and sceptic are so full of horror, that to a man of taste, that is of sensibility and imagination, they are insupportable. On the other hand, what true religion and true philosophy dictate of God, and providence, and man, is so charming, so consonant with all the finer and nobler feelings in human nature, that every man of taste who hears of it, must wish it to be true: and I never yet heard of one person of candour, who wished to find the evidence of the gospel satisfactory, and did not find it so.' Beattie follows a similar line where the 'moral powers' of man are concerned.

I have quoted at length from Burke's quotations from Beattie because they show the kind of 'argument' that Burke used to reinforce his certainty concerning the 'truths' of religion and morality. Burke was willing to sacrifice certainty in our claims to knowledge about the ultimate nature of the physical world and perhaps some of the certainty in claims to 'metaphysical' knowledge; but in religion and morals his position was altogether different. The arguments from the 'horror' of the atheistic view of the prospects awaiting man, from the 'nobility' of the religious and moral feelings, and the *ad hominem* argument that sceptics were lacking in taste or sentiment are as familiar to readers of Burke as to readers of Beattie.

Prior's remark that Burke had intended at one time to refute the 'systems' of Berkeley and Hume seems odd, for after his *Inquiry* Burke did no work that could be called strictly or wholly philosophical in the manner of the *Inquiry*. Possibly Prior's remark comes from a hasty reading of Burke's review of Beattie where *Beattie* ('the author') is said by Burke to have attempted to expose in his *Essay* the 'sceptical systems of Bishop Berkeley and Mr. Hume'. Burke believed that Beattie's efforts had been extremely successful: 'He has gone to the bottom of his subject, and vindicated the rights of the human understanding with such precision and sagacity, with such powers of reason and investigation, as will do him honour, when the systems he exposes will be remembered only in his refutation. . . . If he may sometimes be thought too warm, it may easily be forgiven, when his warmth neither hinders him from doing justice to the merits of his adversaries, where they have real merit, nor leads him to any intemperance of language, unworthy of himself or of his subject. . . . The author establishes the standard of Truth in *Common Sense*, into which all reasoning is ultimately resolved.'[1] One could get from other Scottish philosophers ideas identical to those Burke found in Beattie; Beattie's principal use is that we know Burke read him with some care and honoured him with a review much longer than many found in the *Annual Register*.

I shall now summarize briefly the findings of this historical section: (1) Burke's philosophy seems consonant with and, in some respects, perhaps ultimately derived from Thomism. (2) But there is no concealing that despite significant resemblances there are significant differences as well, in doctrine or in emphasis. This is true in the case of Burke's treatment of prejudice, prescription, and *laissez-faire*. (3) Hume (along with Smith) remains useful in illuminating certain aspects of Burke in a way that Aquinas does not. (4) Where the 'sceptical' side of Hume was thought to affect adversely traditional moral and religious beliefs, Burke could find these beliefs bolstered by his friends, the Scottish common sense philosophers. (5) The natural law reading of Burke does not compel us to isolate Burke from Locke or from the main streams of British intellectual life in the eighteenth century. There

---

[1] *Annual Register*, 1771. Burke's judgement of the comparative merits of Hume and the common-sense philosophers was a common one which persisted throughout the eighteenth and much of the nineteenth centuries. It is not esoteric, therefore, to emphasize the importance of these philosophers for Burke and his age. On the personal level, Burke's defence of Beattie's 'warmth' in argumentation is also revealing.

was enough variety in that life for Burke to find compatible ideas and friends. We need not picture him as a lonely Thomist born in the wrong century. He was not alienated from his age to the extent that many conservatives (from Burckhardt to Russell Kirk) have often been. Being uninclined to systematic philosophizing Burke was, within the limits of a Christian and conservative frame of reference, freer than many men to pick and choose not only his philosophers but different parts of their philosophies as well. He could, for example, follow (or parallel) Hume to a certain point, and then drop him for Beattie or Reid. This may seem rather casual, but it need not be a false picture of Burke at times. (6) The natural law reading of Burke instead of lending itself to a picture of Burke in 'revolt' against the eighteenth century provides us with a more subtle problem. Since many of Burke's adversaries have traditionally been read as natural law theorists, does this mean that we have (at least) two kinds of natural law theory operative in the eighteenth century (as Strauss and his school argue), one derived from Thomism and the other divorced from it; or does it mean that we have different emphases within the same tradition ? Or might it mean that the natural law reading of Burke, while it helps us understand Burke, does not entirely illuminate the issues between Burke and, for example, the *philosophes* ? (7) This part of my study may, in light of the above considerations, be read as a *qualified* assent to the natural law reading of Burke, most of the qualifications having to do with the fact that Burke was a Britisher living in the eighteenth century and, until the French Revolution, enjoying to a considerable extent the advantages (including the intellectual ones) of his situation.[1]

[1] See Mario Einaudi, 'The British Background of Burke's Political Thought', *Political Science Quarterly*, XLIX (December 1934), 576–98, for discussions of Bishop Butler, Francis Hutcheson, Hume, Reid, and Adam Ferguson, although some of Einaudi's parallels seem uncomfortably general.

IV

THE QUESTION OF CONSISTENCY

THE above outline and tentative resolution of several of the problems concerning Burke's place in the history of ideas was conceived, as I remarked earlier, more as a means of illuminating certain internal problems in Burke's thought than as a means of fixing definitively Burke's exact location in the history of thought. However we approach Burke, whether we are concerned with his philosophical or his active side, we are ultimately led from the question of correspondence (historical derivation, influence, parallelism, &c.) to the question of the coherence or consistency of Burke's thought. On the philosophical level, the question is, can a man who has significant ties with Thomism, Locke, Hume, Adam Smith, and the Scottish philosophers be said to have a coherent world view, although not a systematic one? On the level of political activity, can Burke's positions as the heir of Lockian Whiggism and the founder of modern British conservatism be reconciled? And is it possible for him to have been, consistently, a preserver of the rights won by the English Revolution of 1688-9 and a champion of the rights of the American colonists in the War of Independence, only to turn upon the French Revolution and become perhaps its severest critic?

In his lifetime, the last two questions were often answered in the negative, especially after his dramatic break with Charles James Fox and the majority of the Whigs over the question of the French Revolution. Despite the judgement by Morley that Burke may have changed his front but not his position[1] and despite Woodrow Wilson's verdict that Burke's treatment of political topics

[1] *Burke*, 243-5.

showed 'a singular consistency, a very admirable simplicity of standard',[1] these questions are still sometimes answered negatively. By way of answer and anticipation, Burke defended himself vehemently: '*I believe, if he could venture to value himself upon anything, it is on the virtue of consistency that he would value himself the most. Strip him of this and you leave him naked indeed.*' Burke has an explanation of why the charge of inconsistency was so often brought against him; the fault lay not in any change of heart on his part, or in any betrayal in old age of principles embraced ardently in youth, but in the complex nature of the principles he had held to all his life:

He who thinks that the British Constitution ought to consist of the three members, of three very different natures, of which it does actually consist, and thinks it his duty to preserve each of those members in its proper place and with its proper proportion of power, must (as each shall happen to be attacked) vindicate the three several parts on the several principles peculiarly belonging to them. He cannot assert the democratic part on the principles on which monarchy is supported, nor can he support monarchy on the principles of democracy, nor can he maintain aristocracy on the grounds of the one or of the other or of both. *All these he must support on grounds that are totally different, though practically they may be, and happily with us they are, brought into one harmonious body. A man could not be consistent in defending such various, and, at first view, discordant, parts of a mixed Constitution, without that sort of inconsistency with which Mr. Burke stands charged.*

As any one of the great members of this Constitution happens to be endangered, he that is a friend to all of them chooses and presses the topics necessary for the support of the part attacked, with all the strength, the earnestness, the vehemence, with all the power of stating, of argument, and of coloring, which he happens to possess, and which the case demands. He is not to embarrass the minds of his hearers, or to incumber or overlay his speech, by bringing into view at once (as if he were reading an academic lecture) all that may and ought, when a just occasion presents itself, to be said in favor of the other members. At that time they are out of the court; there is no question concerning them. Whilst he opposes his defence on the part where the attack is made, he presumes that for his regard to the

---

[1] *Mere Literature* (Boston, 1924), 141. 'Edmund Burke and the French Revolution', *Century Illustrated Monthly Magazine*, LXII (September 1901), 784–92. On Wilson's view, however, the standard exhibited so consistently by Burke was that of expediency.

just rights of all the rest he has credit in every candid mind. He ought not to apprehend that his raising fences about popular privileges this day will infer that he ought on the next to concur with those who would pull down the throne; because on the next he defends the throne, it ought not to be supposed that he has abandoned the rights of the people.

A man, who, among various objects of his equal regard, is secure of some, and full of anxiety for the fate of others, is apt to go to much greater lengths in his preference of the objects of his immediate solicitude than Mr. Burke has ever done. *A man so circumstanced often seems to undervalue, to vilify, almost to reprobate and disown, those that are out of danger.* This is the voice of Nature and truth, and not of inconsistency and false pretence.[1]

Along the lines suggested by Burke, it might be argued that it was an 'historical accident' that Burke in his old age often seemed to 'undervalue, to vilify, almost to reprobate and disown' the 'democratic' part of the British Constitution. That part was, in his opinion, already secure enough; further gains for it could come only at the expense of the rights of the monarchical and the aristocratic parts. It was an historical accident that the French Revolution from without and a growth of democratic and radical activity from within Britain forced Burke in his last years to turn upon the 'democratic' member of the British Constitution; his argument is in effect that he would have behaved the same way at the beginning of his parliamentary career if these happenings had occurred then. On this kind of analysis, the fact that Burke did not see fit to apply to the French Revolution a principle he had enunciated during the American Revolution ('*General* rebellions and revolts of an whole people never were *encouraged*, now or at any time. They are always *provoked*'[2]) poses no problem of consistency. The defence suggested by Morley, that Burke 'had always said' that nothing universal can be rationally affirmed on any moral or political subject[3] is not at all needed. If Morley had attended to the fact that

---

[1] *Appeal from the New to the Old Whigs, Works*, IV, 92–94. My italics.
[2] *Letter to the Sheriffs of Bristol* (1777), *Works*, II, 217.
[3] Morley, op. cit., 245.

Burke in 1777 was speaking of *general* rebellions and that Burke in the 1790's insisted that the French Revolution was not a general rebellion but the result of agitation and conspiracy by a comparative few, he would not have seen fit to extricate Burke from an alleged inconsistency concerning his refusal to extend sympathy to the French Revolution by involving Burke in a greater contradiction, namely that of asserting general propositions about revolutions on the one hand and denying the truth of any such propositions on the other.

What is necessary concerning Burke's lack of sympathy for the French Revolution is to understand that, on his view, France before the Revolution had had a chance of evolving, in a general way, along British lines. She had had, as he informed his French correspondents, the basis of a mixed constitution with monarchical, aristocratic, and democratic parts; and he could no more approve the destruction of the monarchical and aristocratic parts in France than he could in Britain. It may, of course, be true that Burke did not 'understand' the French Revolution or why it ever occurred; and it may be, as even sympathetic commentators such as Morley concede, that he just did not know enough about the circumstances in France. But he knew enough to realize that France had, for the foreseeable future, lost the chance to perfect her already existing institutions under a mixed constitution, and this was enough in his mind to justify his condemnation of the French Revolution by appeal to principles he had subscribed to throughout his career. This topic, in my opinion, affords slim prospects for those who following Fox have charged Burke with a practice inconsistent with professed principles.

There are in Burke, as he himself would be the first to admit, significant differences in emphasis. In the *Tract on the Popery Laws* he recommends that in certain cases

people do need to be reminded at times of the principles
of original justice:

When people are gone, if not into a denial, at least into a sort of oblivion
of those ideas, *when they know them only as barren speculations, and not as
practical motives for conduct, it will be proper to press, as well as to offer
them to the understanding; and when one is attacked by prejudices which
aim to intrude themselves into the place of law, what is left for us but to
vouch and call to warranty those principles of original justice from whence
alone our title to everything valuable in society is derived* ? Can it be thought
to arise from a superfluous, vain parade of displaying general and uncon-
troverted maxims, that we should revert at this time to the first principles
of law, when we have directly under our consideration a whole body of
statutes, which, I say, are so many contradictions, which their advocates
allow to be so many exceptions from those very principles ? Take them
in the most favorable light, every exception from the original and fixed
rule of equality and justice ought surely to be very well authorized in the
reason of their deviation and very rare in their use. For, if they should
grow to be frequent, in what would they differ from an abrogation of the
rule itself ? By becoming thus frequent, they might even go further, and,
establishing themselves into a principle, convert the rule into the
exception.[1]

If the *Tract on the Popery Laws* in which Burke is com-
plaining of the unjust power which the Protestant Ascendency in Ireland has over the vast majority of the Catholic
population were compared with the works which Burke
wrote at the time of the French Revolution certain differences in emphasis would be readily apparent. The later
Burke, confronted by a revolutionary movement which
appealed constantly to the principles of original justice,
would dismiss such appeals as irrelevant and as 'barren
speculations'. Law instead of being conceived as a bulwark
against prejudice would be treated as either an expression
of prejudice, in which case Burke would offer his approval,
or as an attempt to destroy prejudice, in which case Burke
would offer his wholehearted resistance:

What is Jacobinism ? It is an attempt (hitherto but too successful) to
eradicate prejudice out of the minds of men, for the purpose of putting all
power and authority into the hands of the persons capable of occasionally

[1] *Works*, VI, 326–7. My italics.

enlightening the minds of the people. For this purpose the Jacobins have resolved to destroy the whole frame and fabric of the old societies of the world, and to regenerate them after their fashion. . . . As the grand prejudice, and that which holds all the other prejudices together, the first, last, and middle object of their hostility is religion.[1]

Differences in emphasis, however, do not necessarily involve contradictions; alleged contradictions often have a way of disappearing if we examine particular cases for differences. In the case of Ireland, a Protestant minority was exploiting, especially in the economic sphere, a Catholic majority and was rationalizing this by an appeal to the Protestant prejudices of the English people.[2] Burke was adamant that such prejudices should not be allowed 'to intrude themselves into the place of law' at the expense of the majority of the Irish people who, while Catholic, were loyal subjects of the British Crown. In the case of France, things were, according to Burke, altogether different. There a revolutionary minority sought to destroy the religious beliefs ('the grand prejudice') of the majority, to use law as an instrumentality for the removal of *all* prejudices which ran counter to their efforts to establish a new régime, and to justify these revolutionary (and to Burke unnecessary) moves by appeals to the principles of original justice or natural law. Burke's basic strategy in these circumstances was, as a rule, not to make a frontal attack upon these appeals (by pointing out their incompatibility with natural law properly conceived) but to deny the relevance of such appeals and to emphasize the advantages of the old régime and its compatibility with the prejudices, sentiments, and aspirations of the majority of the people. But the primary reason why such appeals to first principles were irrelevant in the French case but not in the Irish was that, in Burke's opinion, France had

[1] *A Letter to William Smith on the Subject of Catholic Emancipation* (1795), Ibid, VI, 367.

[2] Burke's indictment of the dominant Protestant minority is accepted as correct by a sympathetic modern historian, Thomas H. D. Mahoney, in *Edmund Burke and Ireland* (Cambridge, 1960).

enjoyed before the Revolution by and large a just civil order whereas Ireland under the rule of a harsh and hypocritical Protestant clique had not. In short, Burke distinguishes what he considers bad prejudices (the desire to persecute men of another sect or faith, &c.) from good ones (the religious feelings, respect for civil order and the rights of others, &c.). It is, I think, usually clear as to the kind of prejudice Burke has in mind; hence his treatment of prejudice provides no warrant for charges of inconsistency, provided one attends to the different senses of prejudice and to the context in which Burke is operating.

I have not the space or the desire to examine all the charges of inconsistency against Burke. Such an effort would perhaps take several volumes; and, since in many cases it is difficult to detect even the appearance of the contradiction cited by his critics, I doubt that such an undertaking could be justified. There are, of course, verbal *oddities* in Burke. For example, we find Burke on one occasion proclaiming that 'We must all obey the great law of change. It is the most powerful law of Nature, and the means perhaps of its conservation.'[1] But elsewhere he writes that there is 'a marked distinction between change and reformation' and comes down apparently against change and in favour of reformation: 'The former alters the substance of the objects themselves, and gets rid of all their essential good as well as of all the accidental evil annexed to them. Change is novelty; and whether it is to operate any one of the effects of reformation at all, or whether it may not contradict the very principle upon which reformation is desired, cannot be certainly known beforehand. Reform is not a change in the substance or in the primary modification of the object, but a direct application of a remedy to the grievance complained of.'[2]

How might the two passages be reconciled? I suggest the following interpretation. Change is inevitable and

---

[1] *A Letter to Sir Hercules Langrishe* (1792), *Works*, IV, 301.
[2] *A Letter to a Noble Lord* (1796), Ibid, V, 186.

perhaps necessary to the very survival of Nature, but the results of change may be quite novel and may alter the essential character of whatever is affected by it. Therefore, the change which takes place in Nature is not to be taken literally as a model for changes in society, although it may be a cause in the sense of providing a reason for such changes. In place of a novel innovation which may have consequences far removed from those intended by us, Burke preferred partial reform, which takes care to preserve the essential features of an institution or practice in, speaking very generally, the way that change preserves the *whole* of Nature while altering (sometimes drastically) its details. Change is necessary but sweeping change is not, especially in human affairs where a partial reformation may serve our purposes better.[1]

There are, however, readers (such as Robert M. Hutchins) who would be unconvinced by my argument, derived from Burke's '*Apologia*', that it was largely an historical accident that Burke seemed much less sympathetic to the democratic part of the British Constitution at the end of his political career than at the beginning and that Burke was substantially consistent throughout. Of course, Morley and others are correct in saying that Burke, strictly speaking, never adhered to democratic principles as we moderns would conceive of them. He preferred virtual representation to actual, resisted all efforts to broaden the franchise (except in the case of Ireland where, he held, circumstances were altogether different), and was content, with the exception of a term as member of Parliament from Bristol, to sit in Parliament as a representative of a 'rotten borough'. And given his *laissez-faire* commitments it goes almost without saying that the notion

---

[1] I have been told that Karl Popper has been planning for years to write a book on Burke. There is an obvious similarity between Burke's views on reform and Popper's own emphasis upon 'piecemeal engineering', just as there is an obvious difference between them in the realm of values, especially concerning whether existence (conceived as duration over a long period of time) is of any intrinsic worth.

of the Welfare State was absent, even in embryo, from his thought.

Still there is a sense in which he was sincere in his deference to the democratic part of the British Constitution. From Hobbes onward British political speculation was preoccupied with consent as the basis of political authority, and Burke was no exception. Consent was thought to be formally expressed through the social contract rather than through a democratic suffrage, and sovereignity once granted was indivisible. This was true of Hobbes and Locke, and to a lesser extent of Burke. Burke's contribution to this tradition was that, following Hume to a point but not abandoning completely the contract theory, he saw the need for a continuing consent and for the recognition of obligations, binding upon both the ruler and the ruled, which exist independently of whether one has contracted or promised to respect them. The question is, did Burke ground these obligations in utility, history, or human nature ? Or in all three ? Or in one at an early stage in his development and in another later on ?

My interpretation is that one can find Burke grounding obligations and rights as well in utility, in history, and in human nature: that the Burke of the American Revolution is most apt to ground them in utility (I ask not what our rights are but what is expedient), that the Burke of the French Revolution is most apt to ground them in history (Our duties and our rights are part of an entailed inheritance), but that the essential Burke, the Burke who dealt not only with France and America but Ireland and India as well, grounds our obligations and rights ultimately in human nature and the ends implanted in that nature, as he thought, by God. And I see no inconsistency here: Burke changed his front but not his position. The *appearance* of inconsistency comes only from a failure to recognize that Burke, the philosopher in action, speaks on different levels; in certain contexts where he does not wish to raise theoretical questions concerning first principles he denies the relevance of these questions in general when he should only deny their relevance on a particular occasion. Sometimes he stops short with utility or with history in such a way as to suggest that there is logically no need to go further when what he really means is that in certain situations there is no need to do so.

Because of Burke's contribution to the conservative European reaction against natural law and especially natural rights it has been traditional to picture him as in sympathy with De Maistre's dictum that he knew not man but men and to emphasize Burke's contribution to an historicism that professes to know only historical and (hence) national men; but this is to confuse contribution with content, to mistake what was chiefly a by-product of a man's thinking (which might have passed largely unnoticed if the French Revolution had not given way to Bonapartism and imperialism, or had been restrained in any of several ways which one must suppose represented genuine possibilities at the time) for the main thrust of his thought. Readers who come to Burke expecting to find a keen, almost nineteenth-century, awareness of historical differences among people and the 'uniqueness' of their respective positions will, I think, often be struck instead by his eighteenth-century way of speaking of human nature and his almost provincial evaluation of this nature from the English point of view. Indeed, the real tension in Burke is not between an anticipation of nineteenth-century historicism and an affirmation of eighteenth-century anti-historicism, but between eighteenth-century anti-historicism (in which human nature figures as a kind of ahistorical constant) and an eighteenth-century Englishman's pride in *historical* English institutions and practices as the finest that man has yet devised. During the French Revolution, Burke's consciousness of the value of things English becomes almost overwhelming, but because he sees the Revolution as a *civil war* in Europe the Revolution has also the effect of reminding him of the communion of mankind. While protesting that he, *qua* Englishman, cannot suggest a Constitution for the French, he gives a long list of conditions he would like to see realized in France and remarks: '*When I know all this of France, I shall be as well pleased as every one must be, who has not forgot the general communion of mankind, nor lost his natural sympathy, in local accidental connexions.*'[1]

It is one of the peculiarities of the historiography of the history of ideas that Leo Strauss who has contributed so much to the natural law interpretation of Burke sees Burke's interpretation of his 'conservative' thought as becoming ultimately more hostile to 'classical' natural law theory than the 'radicalism' of the theorists of the French Revolution! Strauss is in fact so disturbed by Burke's veneration for the British Constitution ('whose sole authority' according to Burke 'is that it has existed time out of mind') that he writes: 'What could appear as a return to the primeval equation of the good with the ancestral is, in fact, a preparation for Hegel',[2] by which he means an identification of what ought to be with what is. If this point were taken seriously, the Strauss–Kirk–Stanlis way of rewriting the history of natural law (which is seen as a kind of 'transcendent' standard for measuring what is) might itself require rewriting. The eighteenth-century radicals who appealed to transcendent, eternal laws of justice more frequently than did Burke, would now belong to the classical tradition and Burke would be excluded! I have suggested above some reasons why Burke's grounding of obligations and rights in history is not to be confused with his more *basic* grounding of obligations and rights in human nature and why his way of talking of the British

---

[1] Edmund Burke to Mons. Dupont, October 1789. *Correspondence of the Right Honourable Edmund Burke* (London, 1844), IV, 108. My italics.

[2] *Natural Right and History*, 318. Strauss's distinction between Burke's 'conservatism' (which is considered good classical doctrine) and Burke's 'interpretation of his 'conservatism' (which allegedly leads to 'historicism'), while artificial to a degree, is one way of adjusting oneself to the verbal oddities and overstatements that every student of Burke encounters in the texts. But it is tantamount to the admission of serious internal difficulties in Burke's thought.

Constitution as having its 'sole authority' derived from its long duration is more of a strategic move stemming from a preoccupation with the non-theoretical contexts in which he usually operated than a denial of the natural law as a set of criteria for judging whatever institutions may exist. We are left, however, with the problem of why Strauss does not take seriously the question of whether Burke's alleged 'historicism' does not in effect commit Burke to an anti-natural law position. There are, I think, two reasons why Strauss and his school persist in being struck more by the continuities than by the differences between Burke and classical natural law theorists: (1) Burke is close to the classical theorists in his emphasis upon the rationality and knowability of natural law and in his refusal to reconstruct the natural law in terms of ethical hedonism or psychological egoism. (2) Burke, like the classical theorists, talks more about obligations or duties than about rights. It is the preoccupation with rights instead of duties that strikes Strauss, Kirk, and Stanlis as the nemesis of traditional natural law doctrine.

In view of the above it is surprising how little attention Strauss gives specifically to Burke on natural rights. He mentions, as was noted earlier, that Burke used the language of natural rights and suggests an explanation of this in terms of 'the practical character of Burke's thought'. Later, in criticizing Burke's interpretation of his conservatism he writes that prescription should not be considered the sole authority for a constitution and says that if it were recourse to natural rights would be super-fluous.[1] Russell Kirk states that on Burke's view man's rights 'exist only when man obeys God's law, for right is a child of law. Very different all this is from the "natural rights" of Locke, whose phraseology Burke often adopts. . . .' But why it is very different is not explained, especially as Kirk quotes approvingly (but with no acknowledgement that Locke had said the same thing)

[1] Ibid., 296, 319.

Burke's judgement that one of the first motives to civil society is that *'no man shall be a judge in his own case'*.[1] Elsewhere Kirk remarks that Burke 'says that natural right is a human custom conforming to Divine intent' but he does not tell us where Burke says this. Kirk then writes that Burke did not think of natural right as a suitable weapon for political controversy—'he had too much reverence for its origin'—without explaining why a human custom, even one conforming to the Divine intent, deserves such reverence. Finally, we are told that Burke dislikes defining natural right closely: 'natural right is an Idea comprehended only by the Divine intellect; precisely where it commences and terminates, we are no fit judges'. First, natural right is said to be a human custom; second, Burke allegedly holds it in such reverence that he does not like to refer to it; and third, only God is said to comprehend it. The object, if any, of all this seems to be that Kirk like Strauss does not want to talk about natural rights: 'natural rights do not exist independent of circumstances. . . . Prudence is the test of actual right.'[2] Stanlis represents a distinct improvement over Strauss and especially Kirk when he affirms that Burke did believe in natural rights, properly conceived, and did not wish to reduce natural rights to civil rights (meaning I suppose that they are not to be equated with legal, actual, or customary rights). Stanlis, however, *appears* to confuse the notion of inherent rights with the doctrine of innate ideas: 'Locke's empiricism and denial of innate ideas is indistinguishable from Hobbes's basic principle that all knowledge is derived from sensation of external objects. In this, Locke contradicts both his professed faith in Christian revelation and his declared belief in the innate rights to "life, liberty, and estate" of traditional Natural Law.'[3] Like Kirk, Stanlis is primarily concerned with showing that Burke's view of

---

[1] 'Burke and Natural Rights', *Review of Politics*, XIII (October 1951), 442–6.
[2] *The Conservative Mind from Burke to Santayana*, 44–47.
[3] Stanlis, op. cit., 21.

natural rights is 'absolutely different' from that of his 'Locke-inspired' radical and revolutionary contemporaries, but Burke's actual view of natural rights is not made sufficiently clear for us to decide this question. Strauss, Kirk, and Stanlis are most successful in calling our attention to Burke on natural law and duty, but the correlative relationship between duty and right is strangely ignored by them.

It is possible to treat Burke as Locke is sometimes treated, that is, to distinguish between the early and the mature philosopher, and to suggest that for the mature Burke natural law largely ceases to matter. This is the tack taken by Robert M. Hutchins, a liberal interpreter of the natural law who concedes that the early *Tract on the Popery Laws* is an 'admirable' statement of the doctrine of natural law and of natural rights but insists that Burke by the time of the French Revolution recanted these beliefs. It is a reflection of our lack of accepted criteria for deciding what is to count as a natural law theory that while conservative natural law advocates such as Strauss, Kirk, and Stanlis are preoccupied with duty and uncomfortable in the presence of 'rights' talk, Hutchins in effect finds such a position incompatible with the natural law.

The mature Burke became, according to Hutchins, so preoccupied with duties that he, deliberately or not, insisted that our duties were really our rights:

The 'real rights of man' which Burke lists in the *Reflections* reveal the extent of the change. They are to live by law, to do justice, to possess the fruits of one's industry and the means of making that industry fruitful; to retain the acquisitions of one's parents, to secure the nourishment and improvement of offspring, and to receive instruction in life and consolation in death. The major members of this list are not rights but duties. In this category fall living by law and doing justice. They are like that other 'right' which Burke confers on men, the right to a restraint on their passions. The rights of property were fictions as far as the bulk of the people of France and England were concerned. They had no property and little hope of getting any.[1]

[1] 'The Theory of the State: Edmund Burke', *Review of Politics*, V (April 1943), 146.

According to Burke, the rights of men are their 'advantages', which is a somewhat misleading way of saying that a right confers certain advantages or privileges upon its possessor. Living by law, doing justice, and having restraints placed upon our passions by the law are clearly advantages or means to advantages, according not only to Burke but to Locke as well. The security of property figures high on Burke's list of rights, but after Locke and Hume this is scarcely surprising. Accordingly, it is wrong to say with Hutchins that the 'major members' of Burke's list are not rights at all but duties. What might be a better argument, one which I take Hutchins to be hinting at, is that if rights and duties are taken as correlative, as they are by the majority of legal and political philosophers, and if most people own little or no property, then the rights of property impose duties upon more people than they confer rights upon. This is perhaps why today most natural law theorists have severely qualified property rights and begun to pay special attention to 'human rights'; perhaps, too, it explains the traditional uneasiness of natural law theorists concerning property, property rights being usually construed as a concession to the corruption of man after the Fall and hence being treated by Aquinas as an 'addition' to natural law. Even in the heyday of 'possessive individualism' property rights were significantly restricted in natural law theory by recognition of the right of *eminent domain*. One can, therefore, see that Burke and some of his modern admirers such as Kirk may have been too comfortable, in terms of the natural law, in their emphasis upon property rights, although Burke regarded stability and security of possessions as a necessary condition for the enjoyment of other rights. It remains true, however, that most of Burke's 'real rights' are not strictly speaking duties, although the recognition of these rights does lead to correlative duties.

Both conservative and liberal natural law readers of Burke reveal in their treatment of Burke on natural rights residues of the older, utilitarian reading of Burke. From Burke's criticism of 'imaginary' and 'speculative' rights, from his sarcasm concerning the 'Rights of Man', it is easy to reach C. E. Vaughan's conclusion that 'Right' to Burke was 'a hated principle'. Vaughan distinguishes four senses of right: legal, constitutional, moral, and abstract. Legal and constitutional rights cannot stand against expediency; and moral rights 'are, or are capable of becoming abstract'. Vaughan admits that Burke appears to believe in natural rights such as life, property, and equality before the law, but thinks this was inconsistent with his 'principles'.[1] Vaughan's belief that Burke had an 'instinctive dislike' for using 'the term Right in any connection' is an over-generalization, I think, from the fact that Burke disliked to speak of rights in *some* connexions, a point which I shall try to establish later in this study. As the historiography of Burke scholarship shows, however, it is no simple task to try to determine the limits of Burke's hostility towards rights-language.

The confusion concerning the questions of the content and the consistency of Burke's views on natural rights is illustrated by John MacCunn in his book on Burke, which in several respects remains the best general survey of Burke's thought: 'For to Burke, as to Bentham, all rights, in so far as they are substantial, are not ultimate but derivative.' After 'substantial' MacCunn has, however, a footnote explaining that this qualifying clause is necessary 'because, of course, the abstract and empty "rights of uncovenanted man", which Burke affirms, are obviously original and not derivative'.[2] This footnote marks as it were a great divide separating Burke scholars to this day. There are those who follow the footnote, denying in effect its compatability with MacCunn's prior claim and denying that on Burke's view the natural rights of man, properly conceived, are abstract and empty (for if they were, why

---

[1] Vaughan, op. cit., II, 3, 11, 16, 19.   [2] MacCunn, op. cit., 207.

would Burke bother to affirm them ?).[1] But to this day there are strong advocates of what MacCunn said in his text. John Plamenatz, for example, thinks Burke is saying that 'Though it is specifically human to have rights, to make and to recognize claims, there are no *rights of man*; there are only claims which are valid within a particular social order. This, I think, is at least part of what Burke had in mind when he condemned what he called the doctrine of *abstract rights*.'[2]

The question of whether Burke believed in the natural law having been answered with a qualified yes, the question persists as to the difference this makes for the whole of Burke's thought. The question of rights, of whether on Burke's view some rights at least are not derivative from and wholly dependent upon this or that social order, provides a test case, so to speak, for the questions as to whether Burke's natural law commitment is meaningful, the range of data this interpretation will cover, and the substantial consistency of Burke's thought. These questions of meaningfulness, range, and consistency concern the work, if any, that Burke's deference to natural law does in Burke's political theorizing. Is it the structure upon which Burke's political theory is erected or is it, in some crucial respects, more like 'icing on the cake' ? I consider natural rights an effective area in which to attempt to answer this question, for unlike Strauss I am not willing to settle for two distinct *kinds* of natural law theory (one concerned chiefly with duties, the other with rights) for the simple reason that, in my opinion, this would make for two species of absurdity and the fragmentation of a significant and internally consistent way of thinking about man and values. So far as I can see, an alleged natural law

---

[1] Canavan, op. cit., 114–20. R. R. Fennessy, *Burke, Paine, and the Rights of Man* (The Hague, 1963), 139. Fennessy's work is a detailed study of the exchanges between Burke and Paine at the time of the French Revolution. It is, therefore, significant to contrast his judgement that the mature Burke still believed in natural rights with Hutchins's opinion.

[2] *Man and Society* (London, 1963), I, 341.

which dealt with natural duties but ignored or condemned natural rights would be curiously incomplete and undeserving of the name *natural law*; and while, of course, this reveals something of the model or criteria for natural law which I have in mind, it is not, I think, an arbitrary or even unhistorical position to take.

PART TWO

BURKE ON HUMAN NATURE

I

HUMAN NATURE FROM THE MORAL POINT OF VIEW

ONE of the basic presuppositions of natural law theory has been the belief that it is possible to talk about man and not just men. 'Human nature' does not strike any natural law theorist past or present as being an unmanageable or embarrassingly vague concept. Rather such a theorist regards a discussion of human nature as being logically prior to and necessary for any worth-while account of man's natural duties and rights. The chief reason for this belief is intelligible enough: the marking of the duties and rights of man requires dependable knowledge of the subject who is said to possess these duties and rights. The discussion of what is possessed presupposes some knowledge of the possessor, of his wants and needs. Because of Burke's awareness of the distinctions among men caused by geography, culture, history, and religion and because he spoke so often of these distinctions it is sometimes claimed that Burke denied in effect one of the prime assumptions of natural law theory, namely that regardless of the effects of geographic, cultural, historical, and religious factors human nature remains in some respects both unchanging and knowable. I hope to indicate that, while Burke does not develop a systematic theory of human nature such as one finds in Hume's *Treatise*, it would be false to claim that Burke has no theory of human nature. I think that Burke, despite his emphasis upon the variety of human and historical circumstances, still held in some degree to the belief that one can distinguish essential human characteristics from non-essential ones, that he still regarded the terms of traditional and eighteenth-century discourse about human nature as being appropriate to their subject-matter, and that he did not attach the tremendous importance to history and nationality—to 'local and accidental connections'—that men in the nineteenth century often would.

One of Burke's most frequent charges against his adversaries, whom he often identifies simply as 'Jacobins',[1] was that they were ignorant of human nature, which would be an odd charge for him to make if he did not believe (a) that something at least can be known of human nature and that 'human nature' is not a vacuous or embarrassingly vague concept and (b) that the things that can be known about human nature are important from both the moral and the political viewpoints. The lawgivers of revolutionary France were in his judgement obsessed with metaphysics and geometry and ignorant of 'anything moral or anything politic,—nothing that relates to the concerns, the actions, the passions, and the interests of men. *Hominem non sapiunt.*' By way of contrast Burke found the men who had framed the constitutions of the republics of antiquity profoundly aware of the nature of morality and of politics and disinclined to play the part of the 'airy metaphysician' or geometrician: 'They had to do with men, and they were obliged to study human nature.'[2]

When considered from the point of view of systematic philosophy Burke's own studies of human nature hardly

---

[1] Canavan, op. cit., 106, advises us not to be surprised by Burke's exceedingly general use during the 1790's of the term *Jacobin* to fit practically all of the men and ideas he opposed: 'Burke was not a scholar, but a practising statesman, and neither by profession nor by temperament was he inclined to make distinctions among ideas all of which he regarded as dangerous to society anyhow.' One wonders what Canavan would think of a 'practising statesman' of today who either would not or could not distinguish between the ideas of communists, socialists, and liberals and insisted upon speaking as though all his adversaries were 'communists'.

[2] *Reflections on the Revolution in France, Works*, III, 474, 476.

begin to fulfil the expectations aroused by remarks such as those quoted in the above paragraph. The only exception to this lack of system and comprehensive analysis is in Burke's *A Philosophical Inquiry into the Origin of Our Ideas of the Sublime and Beautiful* (1756, 1757). Even here there is some doubt as to the relevance of this study in aesthetics to Burke's political thought: Strauss, for example, uses it freely, while Canavan tends to doubt its relevance. My belief is that, properly handled, it can be of real value in revealing some of the presuppositions of Burke's political thought; indeed, it is tempting for a person with training in philosophy to rely exclusively upon this work and to ignore altogether the sketchy, fragmentary, and from the analytic point of view often primitive reflections on human nature that Burke makes elsewhere, especially in his later polemical outbursts. Yet at the risk of appearing to partake of or to sympathize unduly with the deficiencies noted above, I find it obligatory to try to give some account of what Burke has to say about human nature outside of his *Inquiry*. This account I have called 'Human Nature from the Moral Point of View', although clearly *moral* must here be taken to include reference to psychological and even sociological factors as it often did in the eighteenth century's—and in Burke's—use of the term. This will be followed by a consideration of the *Inquiry* which provides some philosophical support for Burke's more general reflections, a support which both the reader and I will probably agree is much needed by the time Chapter I is completed.

In view of Burke's alleged contributions to that historical awareness and sensitivity which would characterize much of nineteenth-century thought and in view of his own work and considerable (though largely posthumous) reputation as an historian it is surprising to come across remarks by Burke which show that he had grave doubts about the efficacy of studying human nature from the historical point of view. Speaking very generally, he may be said to have sensed the tension or incompatibility between the historical point of view and traditional natural law thinking on this subject and to have feared that the historical point of view would emphasize distinctions among men to such an extent that it would become increasingly difficult or impossible to speak significantly of the resemblances or characteristics common to all mankind. While he is prepared to concede a great deal to the historical point of view and to admit that the points in common among men and the respects in which human nature is unchanging are perhaps fewer than the natural law tradition had previously assumed, he is not prepared to abandon this tradition in favour of a newly emerging 'historical school' or mode of thought which, somewhat ironically, would claim Burke as one of its creators.

Indeed, Burke's most frequent recourse to history is for the moral or practical examples it might provide for the makers of political and social policy; formally, if not substantively, his pragmatic use of historical examples, often from Roman history, was thoroughly conventional and no different in kind from that of his contemporaries, including his enemies the Jacobins. When, however, Burke turned to the question of whether we might expect something more from history than illustrations or examples for rules of moral and/or practical conduct, he experienced grave doubts. In 1777 he wrote that 'we possess at this time very great advantages towards the knowledge of human Nature. We need no longer go to History to trace it in all its stages and periods. History from its comparative youth, is but a poor instructor. When the Egyptians called the Greeks children in Antiquities, we may well call them children and so we may call all these nations, which were able to trace the progress of Society only within their own Limits. But now the Great Map of Mankind is unrolld at once; and there is no state or Gradation of barbarism, and no mode of refinement which we have not at the same instant under our View.'[1] Burke goes on to list the different specimens of civilization and barbarism in Europe, Asia, and America which could now be studied, so to speak, in the same instant. The recent travels and explorations by Europeans seemed to Burke, as to many of his predecessors and contemporaries, a better guide for accumulating and interpreting data concerning the resemblances and distinctions between men of different cultures than did the still somewhat parochial science of history. Comparatively speaking, history was seen by Burke as a poor instructor concerning the nature of man.

Burke's second reservation concerning the science of history is an anticipation of the by now familiar argument that the number of variables and possible combinations of variables in human affairs makes the prediction of the future course of events on the basis of past happenings exceedingly difficult. History has its primary use, according to Burke, as 'a great improver of the understanding, by showing both men and affairs in a great variety of views. From this source much political wisdom may be learned,—that is, may be learned as habit, not as precept. . . .' By means of this distinction Burke seeks to warn against the view of history 'as a reportory of cases and precedents' as for a lawyer. After all, he reminds us, we can know former times but imperfectly; 'and our guides, the historians, who are to give us their true interpretation, are often prejudiced, often ignorant, often fonder of system than of truth. . . .' Burke goes on to observe that 'There are some fundamental points in which Nature never changes; but they are few and obvious and belong rather to morals than to politics. But so far as regards political matter, the human mind and human affairs are susceptible of infinite modifications and of combinations wholly new and unlooked-for.'

Burke's position here seems somewhat overstated. Against the distinction he makes above (and occasionally in

[1] Edmund Burke to William Robertson, 9 June 1777, *Correspondence of Edmund Burke* (Chicago, 1961), III, 351.

other contexts as well) between morals and politics, one must set his more characteristic judgement that the principles of politics are those of morality enlarged; and to his judgement that the respects in which Nature changes are few and obvious, one must add that these respects while obvious were also in his view crucial. The reason for the present overstatement is not hard to find. Burke is here discussing the knowledge of history possessed by the French princes who because of the Revolution were forced to live in exile. What good, he is asking, did their knowledge of history do for them ? Despite their excellent knowledge of the past, the current course of events has taken them by surprise; and Burke is clearly projecting his own plight on to that of the *émigrés* when he lists the surprises afforded by recent history:

Very few, for instance, could have imagined that property, which has been taken for natural dominion, should, through the whole of a vast kingdom, lose all its importance, and even its influence. This is what history or books of speculation could hardly have taught us. How many could have thought that the most complete and formidable revolution in a great empire should be made by men of letters, not as subordinate instruments and trumpeters of sedition, but as the chief contrivers and managers, and in a short time as the open administrators and sovereign rulers ? Who could have imagined that atheism could produce one of the most violently operative principles of fanaticism ? Who could have imagined, that, in a commonwealth in a manner cradled in war, and in an extensive and dreadful war, military commanders should be of little or no account . . . that administrative bodies, in a state of the utmost confusion, and of but a momentary duration, and composed of men with not one imposing part of character, should be able to govern the country and its armies with an authority which the most settled senates and the most respected monarchs scarcely ever had in the same degree ? This, for one, I confess I did not foresee, though all the rest was present to me very early, and not out of my apprehension even for several years.[1]

The above should not be taken as a denial of the value of those moral or practical examples which Burke himself so frequently found in history. The great differences between Rome and England did not keep Burke from using

[1] *Remarks on the Policy of the Allies* (1793), *Works*, IV, 468–9.

Rome as an example of the dangers that befall a nation when the people are taught to turn to the government for their bread; and obviously Burke's rules and maxims of prudence have an historical foundation. What Burke is arguing against is not the use of history but its misuse: the mechanical translation of precedents into precepts and the mechanical application of these precedents-turned-precepts without a view to all the relevant differences between past and present circumstances. It is not, I take Burke to be saying, the ingredients of a novel situation which are wholly unique and unexpected. The alleged envy and the alleged moral corruption of the Jacobins, for example, are not unprecedented; but what is often unique and unexpected is the way in which such old forces take new forms or appear in new combinations of circumstances. This is what took the French princes and Burke by surprise. Burke is, however, rigid concerning one thing. If 'history and books of speculation' have failed to enable us to foresee (and to resist) moral monstrosities such as the French Revolution, then 'it would be unjustifiable to go back to the records of other times to instruct us to manage what they never enable us to foresee'. In such cases we can, Burke appears to believe, rely better upon 'our own experience'.[1]

According to Hume, 'Mankind are so much the same, in all times and places, that history informs us of nothing new or strange in this particular. Its chief use is only to discover the constant and universal principles of human nature. . . .'[2] Regardless of the question of the extent to which the above passage supports the thesis that Hume believed in the uniformity of human nature, it may still be used as a kind of measuring stick for deciding upon some of the basic features of Burke's views on history and human nature. Did Burke believe that mankind are so much the

[1] Ibid., 470.
[2] *An Inquiry Concerning Human Understanding* (New York, 1957), 93.

same that history affords us with no surprises in that respect? The answer, as we have seen, is a qualified yes. There are some few but essential points in which human nature never changes, but these belong to morals and not to politics. What is the significance of this qualification? It is, I think, to warn us that while from the moral point of view human nature never changes or takes us by surprise, this is not true from the political point of view. Whether history could surprise us with new or strange information concerning mankind would then depend upon whether it was written from the moral or the political point of view. From the moral point of view, Burke clearly believed that 'men are not changed, but remain always what they always were'[1] and that the 'causes of evil' are 'Permanent'. If, however, the causes of evil are permanent, the 'occasional organs by which they act, and the transitory modes in which they appear' are not. Wickedness is very inventive: 'Seldom have two ages the same fashion in their pretexts, and the same modes of mischief. . . . The very same vice assumes a new body. The spirit transmigrates; and, far from losing its principle of life by the change of its appearance, it is renovated in its new organs with the fresh vigor of a juvenile activity.'[2]

From the political point of view, the historical process may present us with 'surprises' of the sort mentioned by Burke in his discussion of the things which he and the French princes had not foreseen. Yet while these surprises may be of considerable significance and may decide the question of survival for nations and individuals they lose some of their significance when seen from the moral point of view. The French Revolution may surprise us but Frenchmen, because they are men, do not. Moreover, when the political process is seen from the moral point of view this moral perspective has a practical dimension. While we may be powerless to predict the details of political

[1] *First Letter on a Regicide Peace, Works*, V, 249.
[2] *Reflections on the Revolution in France, Works*, III, 419.

change, we can know a great deal about the moral context in which they occur, about the spirit and character of men in general and of particular nations as well. Given, for example, the moral training of the Americans in the principles of English liberty and the training of the French in the principles of Rousseau's sensual self-indulgence, one can make general but useful estimates of how differently the revolutions of these two respective peoples will turn out. One can also, by knowing something about the ways in which human nature does not change, understand that certain characteristic features of man's relations with other men will recur or reappear in civil society, so long as civil society endures, regardless of how ambitious our programmes of social and political change may be: 'You would not cure the evil by resolving that there should be no more monarchs, nor ministers of state, nor of the Gospel,—no interpreters of law, no general officers, no public councils. You might change the names: the things in some shape must remain. A certain *quantum* of power must always exist in the community, in some hands, and under some appellation.'[1] It seems clear that when Burke says that the points in which human nature does not change are moral not political he means to include under the moral appellation considerations that we would today probably label as *psychological* or even *sociological*.

When Hume wrote that the chief use of history is 'only to discover the constant and universal principles of human nature' he opened himself to the charge that in his own *History of England* his practice was insufficient in terms of his theory. Of both Hume and Burke it is, I think, safe to say that they discovered in history only those constant and universal principles of human nature that they had discovered elsewhere in their moral and psychological speculations. However, historical examples and comparisons in the hands of both men are not mere decorative pieces or illustrations. They are, generally,

[1] Ibid., 419.

conceived in the spirit of philosophical analogy about
which Burke usually spoke respectfully. Only Hume's
optimism concerning the possibility of a general and
certain science of politics separates the two men significantly: 'So great is the force of laws and of particular
forms of government, and so little dependence have they
on the humors and tempers of men, that consequences
almost as general and certain may sometimes be deduced
from them as any which the mathematical sciences afford
us.'[1] Burke perhaps attached more importance to the
humours and tempers of men and less to the particular
forms of government than did Hume; and he certainly
believed that the mathematical sciences being different in
kind from politics afford no yardstick for measuring the
results of political thinking. Even here, however, the
difference between the two men is narrowed by Hume's
use of the word *sometimes* in the above passage and by the
fact that what Burke claimed to know about the moral
dimensions of human nature in politics sometimes led him
in practice to make deductions which he felt to be as certain
as any deductions can be.

The fact that Hume, unlike Burke, would turn to the
mathematical sciences for inspiration when contemplating
the possibilities of a political science points to the fact that
Burke was content to operate on a different level. Part of
his distrust of mathematics rested upon the suspicion that
it is far easier to be mistaken in mathematics than in more
ordinary pursuits:

That there is such a City of Rome is a Proposition of which we can
doubt less than that the Square of the Hypotenuse is equal to the Square
of the two Sides, even when the latter is demonstrated.

The highest degree of testimony leaves less doubt than Demonstration.
Besides the force of it is more easily and generally comprehended.[2]

These youthful reflections of Burke provide the slim
foundations upon which he would later develop his

[1] *Political Essays* (New York, 1953), 13.
[2] *A Notebook of Edmund Burke*, 74.

distinction between mathematics and metaphysics on the one hand and politics and morals on the other. They explain, too, I think, some of the appeal which the Scottish philosophy of common sense would have for Burke. Burke never deviated from the following position (stated here with a crudity that may be youthful or deliberate or both):

A man is never in greater danger of being wholly wrong than when he advances far in the road of refinement; nor have I ever that diffidence and suspicion of my reasoning as when they seem to be most curious, exact, and conclusive. Great subtleties and refinements of reasoning are like spirits which disorder the brain and are much less useful than ordinary liquors of a grosser nature. . . .[1]

It is important to note, however, that while Hume regarded general opinion as inconclusive and even suspect in the areas of metaphysics and natural philosophy, he deferred to general opinion in morals on the ground that in this area there is no other standard upon which controversy can be decided (see his essay 'Of the Original Contract'). The reliance upon human testimony and general opinion in morals is also a characteristic of Burke's ethical thought where a sign of the 'reasonableness' of either a moral code or of a custom is the degree of assent it receives from the species as a whole. It is important to note, too, that both men, while believing that there are respects in which human nature in general does not change, believed also that society can be arranged or disarranged in ways so that the amount of good or of evil in the world at any given time will be altered. Both believed in effect that good laws help make good men and that bad laws or the absence of authority contribute significantly to an increase of evil in the world.

Burke, however, because of the French Revolution was confronted with a problem different from any that Hume ever encountered. The French Revolution represented, according to Burke, a deliberate challenge to the thesis that human nature does not change. It was, he believed, an

[1] Ibid., 90.

attempt to make over or re-do the moral nature of man, to substitute licence or a specious freedom for that restraint upon the passions which Burke believed is owed by society to the individual. The significance of the quarrel between Burke and Rousseau is sometimes lost sight of in, for example, detailed discussions of their different conceptions of sensibility; to avoid this we must realize Burke believed that the French Revolution was, following Rousseau's example, intent upon defying the general opinion of mankind and of reversing the traditional uses of the predicates *good* and *evil* so that what had been called good was now to be called evil, &c. If one believes that human testimony is an ultimate datum in morality and if one sees a deliberate attempt being made to alter human testimony along the above lines, then perhaps one can understand better Burke's grave concern and even his charges of madness and insanity against his foes. Such charges by Burke point to two things, I believe: (1) Burke's belief that, despite the limits of human reason, one *knows* what good and evil are; at least one knows the duties of one's own situation; (2) Burke's genuine perplexity before the problem of ultimate disagreement in morals. What is one to do with a man like Rousseau who apparently does not know the duties of his situation? (This, I think, is the general significance of Burke's famous tirade against Rousseau's failure to acknowledge or to perform his duties as a parent.)

Whereas Hume might have said that the disagreement between Burke and Rousseau concerning the duties of a parent points to that ultimate arbitrariness in matters of morals which is caused by the passions, Burke is not prepared to accept this analysis. While Hume believed that, strictly speaking, there is no warrant for attributing moral problems to a struggle between 'reason and the passions' because it is the passions alone which decide what ends we are to pursue, Burke continued to speak in the pre-Humian way of such a struggle and even to speak at times of reason as *directing* the passions and of passion as *auxiliary* to the understanding.[1] In general, however, Burke believed in a fundamental accord or harmony between reason and the passions: 'Never was there a jar or discord between genuine sentiment and sound policy. Never, no never, did Nature say one thing and Wisdom say another. Nor are sentiments of elevation in themselves turgid and unnatural. Nature is never more truly herself than in her grandest forms.'[2]

What moves then could Burke make when the harmony between reason and the passions appears to break down ? Like Rousseau, Burke attached a great importance to moral instruction; and like Rousseau, although for different reasons, he often attributed moral shortcomings to a bad or imperfect moral instruction. Or else he could deny that the harmony between reason and the passions has actually broken down: Rousseau, regardless of what he says or does to the contrary, really *knows* what his duties are: he *knows* that a father should not be self-indulgent to the extent of leaving his children in an orphanage. Finally, Burke could say that Rousseau is insane or mad if it is actually the case that he does not know this. At different times Burke makes all three of these moves. The first move is undoubtedly important, and presumably there will be a variety of reasons why moral education is sometimes better in certain circumstances than in others. Eventually,

[1] 'Strong passion under the direction of a feeble reason feeds a low fever, which serves only to destroy the body that entertains it. But vehement passion does not always indicate an infirm judgment. It often accompanies, and actuates, and is even auxiliary to a powerful understanding; and when they both conspire and act harmoniously, their force is great to destroy disorder within and to repel injury from abroad.' *Second Letter on a Regicide Peace, Works*, V, 407.

[2] Ibid. Burke does not anywhere explain what he means by 'genuine sentiment'; but apparently what marks off his conception of genuine sentiment from that of an enemy such as Rousseau (at least as Burke thought of Rousseau's conception) is that Burke does not contrast genuine sentiment with cultivated sentiment, has no *a priori* preference for the sentiment of the peasant as against the sentiment of a man of letters, for example, and indeed believes that 'sentiments of elevation' may in a sense be more genuine and more truly natural than sentiments more common to the bulk of mankind provided that such sentiments of elevation are in accord with the 'natural' ends of moral and intellectual growth.

however, our attention is shifted to the more puzzling question of why men have so often received a seriously defective moral education. Given the fact that there is no discord between Nature and Wisdom and the fact that the principles of morality are intelligible to the reason of the vast majority of men (leaving aside presumably mental defectives and children), the occurrence of moral failure in a significant number of cases should, I think, have worried Burke much more than it did. In any event, while Burke often explained the moral shortcomings of nations or groups as the result of defective moral instruction, he ordinarily would explain the moral shortcomings of particular individuals he criticizes in terms first of lies and then of madness. Madness is, however, an obviously desperate and final move (it is doubtful whether Burke meant that Rousseau was literally insane when he spoke of him as 'the insane Socrates of the National Assembly'); accordingly, lying seems to play the more crucial part in Burke's explanation of moral failure at least on the level of the individual if not on the level of a nation as a whole. Burke seems to believe that despite a defective moral instruction a person is usually capable of grasping the fundamentals of moral conduct, that he is to be held accountable if he does not do so, and that he is lying if he claims either not to know the principles of morality or that they are other than they are. Since, however, lying is itself a moral failure, how is lying to be explained ?

Burke, of course, does not deny that there are moral difficulties, that duties will sometimes 'cross one another', and that it is difficult to decide which duty to subordinate or to supersede. He denies, however, that our duties are ordinarily subject to doubt in this way and thinks it harmful to morality to insist always upon its complexity and to emphasize difficult or 'extreme cases'.

I admit, indeed, that in morals, as in all things else, difficulties will sometimes occur. Duties will sometimes cross one another. Then questions will arise, which of them is to be placed in subordination ?

which of them may be entirely superseded ? These doubts give rise to that part of moral science called *casuistry*, which though necessary to be well studied by those who would become expert in that learning . . . it requires a very solid and discriminating judgment, great modesty and caution, and much sobriety of mind in the handling; else there is a danger that it may totally subvert those offices which it is its object only to methodize and reconcile. Duties, at their extreme bounds, are drawn very fine, so as to become almost evanescent. In that state some shade of doubt will always rest on these questions, when they are pursued with great subtilty. But the very habit of stating these extreme cases is not very laudable or safe; because in general it is not right to turn our duties into doubts.[1]

By the harmony of reason and the passions Burke does not mean that such a harmony actually exists within each individual from the moment of birth. Like all natural law theorists, Burke sees this harmony as consisting of two things: (1) it is an end, or final cause, towards which man moves; (2) it is natural for man to move toward this end. (2) appears to be a statement on the level of efficient causality. Man has a natural inclination to become more reasonable and more moral, to place, as Burke describes it, the chains of morality upon his appetites and will. Put somewhat differently, Burke seems to be saying that man is naturally inclined to restrain his inclinations: 'For man is by nature reasonable; and he is never perfectly in his natural state, but when he is placed where reason may be best cultivated and most predominates. Art is man's nature.'[2] The complex arrangements and rules of civil society while they did not exist in the state of nature are nevertheless quite natural, especially from the teleological perspective of (1). Morality, Burke seems to be saying, flourishes in society, in those situations in which restraint and discipline are important. Whether in such situations the knowledge of one's duties does not become more difficult, Burke does not say; the exploration of this side of the question he leaves to Rousseau. Apparently, he did not consider it to be a serious problem.

[1] *Appeal from the New to the Old Whigs, Works,* IV, 167–8.
[2] Ibid., 176.

We can return now to the question of why lying or deception figures so prominently in Burke's remarks about moral shortcomings or failures. Men such as Rousseau and the 'Jacobins' claim to have spent a lot of time (too much time, according to Burke) in speculation about moral difficulties. And morality, Burke thinks, just is not that difficult. Therefore, they are not telling the truth when they advise men that self-indulgence, independence of other men, disregard for the rights of property, &c., are good. They are lying to themselves or to others, or both. *Why would they lie? Because their own ambitions go beyond their station and its duties.* In the aspiration of lawyers to become statesmen and journalists to become their official philosophers, Burke saw something profoundly immoral; and if critics were to counter that Burke was himself a journalist trained in the law, Burke would probably reply that he knew his place and kept to it. He did not seek the company of the titled aristocracy socially, and on no level did he seek to subvert the natural order of subordination in which he found himself.

The immorality of radicals and revolutionaries in general could be traced, I think Burke would say, to their refusal to consider the question put by Persius in his *Satires*, '*Humana qua parte locatus es in re ?*', which Burke believed to be 'the best rule in morals and in prudence'.[1] In Burke's *Reflections on the Revolution in France* we find him developing at great length the implications of this rule: 'But whilst I revere men in the functions which belong to them and would do as much as one man can do to prevent their exclusion from any, I cannot to flatter them, give the lie to Nature. They are good and useful in the composition; they must be mischievous, if they preponderate so as virtually to become the whole.'[2] This chain of subordination is the social equivalent of those chains which reason

---

[1] Edmund Burke to Richard Shackleton, 25 May, 1779, *The Correspondence of Edmund Burke*, IV, (Chicago, 1963), 79.

[2] *Works*, III, 289.

and morality impose upon the appetites and the will of the individual in his private capacity. Both sets of chains are seen by Burke as necessary for the survival of the community and of the individual.[1] Rousseau's famous judgement that men are born free and yet everywhere are in chains would probably have been analysed by Burke as follows: if men are born free and yet are in chains not of their own devising this is a likely sign that they are slaves to their passions and for this reason have not been able to realize their human potentials; if, however, men are in chains of their own devising this is a sign that they *are* free since such chains or restraints are a necessary condition of freedom:

Men are qualified for civil liberty in exact proportion to their disposition to put moral chains upon their own appetites,—in proportion as their soundness and sobriety of understanding is above their vanity and presumption,—in proportion as they are more disposed to listen to the counsels of the wise and good, in preference to the flattery of knaves. Society cannot exist, unless a controlling power upon will and appetite be placed somewhere; and the less of it there is within, the more there must be without. It is ordained in the eternal constitution of things, that men of intemperate minds cannot be free. Their passions forge their fetters.[2]

Burke's emphasis upon the restraint of the will and the appetites by the reason of both the individual and the community to which he belongs is, of course, not the whole story where his political philosophy is concerned. While Burke believed that man is by nature reasonable, he profoundly distrusted those 'human reasonings' which did not take into account the whole man: 'politics ought to be adjusted, not to human reasonings, but to human nature; of which the reason is but a part and by no means the greatest part'.[3] This would mean, as Burke argued in *Thoughts and Details on Scarcity*, that the needs of animal man must be attended to, that the mind while it seeks to

[1] *Speech on the Army Estimates* (9 February 1790), *Works*, III, 223.
[2] *Letter to a Member of the National Assembly* (1791), *Works*, IV, 51–52.
[3] *Observations on a Late Publication on the Present State of the Nation*, *Works*, I, 398.

govern the appetites of the body must realize that it and
the human body depend for their survival upon the satisfaction of the minimal needs of appetitive nature.[1] Therefore, alongside Burke's emphasis upon the subordination
of the will and the appetites to reason we must place his
emphasis upon the mutual dependence of all the aspects of
man's nature. Consider, for example, the following passages in which the importance of 'inbred sentiments',
'prejudice', and 'instinct' is emphasized and the contributions of these feelings to the well-being of the individual
is stressed:

We are not the converts of Rousseau; we are not the disciples of Voltaire;
Helvetius has made no progress amongst us. Atheists are not our
preachers; madmen are not our lawgivers. We know that we have made
no discoveries, and we think that no discoveries are to be made, in
morality,—nor many in the great principles of government, nor in the
ideas of liberty, which were understood long before we were born
altogether as well as they will be after the grave has heaped its mould
upon our presumption, and the silent tomb shall have imposed its law
on our pert loquacity. In England we have not yet been completely
embowelled of our natural entrails: we still feel within us, and we
cherish and cultivate, those inbred sentiments which are the faithful
guardians, the active monitors of our duty, the true supporters of all
liberal and manly morals.

You see, Sir, that in this enlightened age I am bold enough to confess
that we are generally men of untaught feelings: that, instead of casting
away all our old prejudices, we cherish them to a very considerable
degree; and, to take more shame to ourselves, we cherish them because
they are prejudices; and the longer they have lasted, and the more
generally they have prevailed, the more we cherish them. We are afraid
to put men to live and trade each on his own private stock of reason;
because we suspect that the stock in each man is small, and that the
individuals would do better to avail themselves of the general bank and
capital of nations and of ages. Many of our men of speculation, instead of
exploding general prejudices, employ their sagacity to discover the latent
wisdom which prevails in them. If they find what they seek, (and they
seldom fail,) they think it more wise to continue the prejudice, with the
reason involved, than to cast away the coat of prejudice, and to leave

[1] *Works*, V, 135–6.

nothing but the naked reason; because prejudice, with its reason, has a motive to give action to that reason, and an affection which will give it permanence. Prejudice is of ready application in the emergency; it previously engages the mind in a steady course of wisdom and virtue, and does not leave the man hesitating in the moment of decision, skeptical, puzzled, and unresolved. Prejudice renders a man's virtue his habit, and not a series of unconnected acts. Through just prejudice, his duty becomes a part of his nature.

We know, and, what is better, we feel inwardly, that religion is the basis of civil society, and the source of all good, and of all comfort. In England we are so convinced of this, that there is no rust of superstition, with which the accumulated absurdity of the human mind might have crusted it over in the course of ages, that ninety-nine in a hundred of the people of England would not prefer to impiety.

We know, and it is our pride to know, that man is by his constitution a religious animal; that atheism is against, not only our reason, but our instincts; and that it cannot prevail long.[1]

Passages such as the above must, however, be handled with care, as such utterances are often cited as evidence of Burke's being fundamentally opposed not merely to the exaggerated 'rationalism' of the eighteenth century but to rational analysis as such. The truth seems to be rather that he opposed the 'rationalism' of the eighteenth century not simply in the name of sentiment, prejudice, and instinct but ultimately at least because of the 'latent wisdom' which a subtle and patient mind can allegedly find beneath the coat of sentiment, prejudice, and instinct. These 'natural feelings' of man were seen by Burke as comprising that aspect of human nature in which the agreement and harmony of Nature and Wisdom is most striking. Prejudice has the effect of reinforcing the dictates of reason and virtue, of habituating man to rational and virtuous conduct without his having in every instance to run through a series of moral calculations. While it is, I think, difficult to determine fully why Burke uses the word *prejudice* favourably so

[1] *Reflections on the Revolution in France, Works*, III, 345, 346, 348, 350, 351.

often (but not always) and while it is probably true, as
H. B. Acton suggests, that Burke's genuflections before
prejudice constitute an act of defiance aimed at the Enlightenment, two things may be said by way of a partial
explanation of Burke's use of this term. First, *prejudice*,
while it had become a pejorative term by the eighteenth
century, is derived from the Latin *praejudicium;* to the
ancients, *praejudicium* meant a precedent or a judgement
based on previous decisions and experiences.[1] I think that
Burke's use of *prejudice* sometimes has this archaic sense,
and *prejudice* in this sense seems complementary to Burke's
emphasis upon the value in English law of judgements
based upon legal precedent (see Part Three). Second, while
Burke's judgement that prejudice is a means of habituating
men to virtuous conduct may seem at first paradoxical, this
effect is softened considerably by Burke's judgement that
the 'moral sentiments' of man are so nearly connected or
interwoven with 'early prejudice as to be almost one and
the same thing'.[2] This, of course, leaves the precise nature
of the relationship between the moral sentiments and
prejudice in general unspecified, but the statement that
there is little if any difference between the moral sentiments
and *early* prejudice makes one suspect that Burke's attach-
ment of *prejudice* to the 'moral sentiments' theory of Hume
and Smith is an innovation of less substantive significance
than various commentators (and perhaps Burke himself)
have appeared to believe.

Despite the difficulties that attend Burke's conception of
prejudice it is clear that in cases where Burke himself could

---

[1] For a discussion of the changing senses of prejudice see Gordon W. Allport,
The Nature of Prejudice (Boston, 1954), 6.

[2] 'The moral sentiments, so nearly connected with early prejudice as to be
almost one and the same thing, will assuredly not live long under a discipline
which has for its basis the destruction of all prejudices. . . .' *Appeal from the
New to the Old Whigs, Works*, IV, 205. I assume 'early prejudice' to refer to the
initial prejudices that one acquires quite early in life before ambition, unpleasant
experiences, &c. have produced a distorting effect. But this apparently overlooks
the effects that ambition, unpleasant experiences, &c. may have had upon our
moral instructors and the fact that as a result our 'early' prejudices might well
be as defective from the moral point of view as our later ones.

not see the latent wisdom inherent in a prejudice, as in the case of the feelings of Christians against Jews and of Protestants against Catholics, he refused to recognize such feelings as 'natural'. It is then not feeling or prejudice *per se* that Burke is defending but rather 'natural' feeling (see his *Notebook*) and 'just' prejudice (see the above quotation where Burke writes that it is through 'just' prejudice that man's duty becomes part of his nature); the glaring weakness here, of course, is the absence in Burke of clearly stated criteria for separating natural from unnatural feelings and just prejudices from unjust ones. However, while Burke does at first say that we cherish our prejudices 'because they are prejudices', his final position seems to be that we *should* cherish only wise and 'just prejudice'. We cherish our prejudices as prejudices because, given our belief that the species is wise and the individual is in comparison foolish, we have *prima facie* reason to suppose that the prejudices transmitted to us are wise and just. And in the vast majority of cases this assumption, Burke believes, is borne out by the facts of experience; but some few prejudices are shown to be unwise and unjust: these we should definitely not cherish.

As is true of Burke's defence of prejudice, his defence of superstition and instinct seems to some extent less striking than one might at first suppose. Superstition is to be tolerated, Burke asserts, but as an alternative to impiety and as an imperfect though useful way of acknowledging, especially among unreflective people, certain great truths about religion. When Burke wrote that 'We know, and what is better, we feel inwardly, that religion is the basis of civil society, and the source of all good, and of all comfort' he did not, I think, mean to imply that it is better to feel certain things inwardly than to know them except in a very qualified and pragmatic sense of *better*. It is better to feel these things than *merely* to know them in the same way that it is better to have our virtues worked into our very nature by prejudice than to have to rely upon 'naked reason' whenever a moral decision is called for. Man should not be left 'hesitating in the moment of decision, skeptical, puzzled, and unresolved'; and the religious feelings or religious instincts prevent this from happening in the religious realm just as prejudice does in the moral realm.

We are now in a position to comprehend the dual nature of Burke's critique of radicals and revolutionaries, especially but by no means exclusively those of the French variety. Against Rousseau and his disciples Burke urges that they have substituted inward feeling for reason; against the rationalists of whom Voltaire is probably a representative specimen Burke argues that they have neglected inward feeling and sentiment in favour of a 'naked' and 'private' reason. In both cases, though Burke does not explicitly make this point, the charges amount to an indictment of subjectivism in the sense of an over-reliance upon either personal feeling or personal reflection. Rousseau in emphasizing the importance of feeling, including the religious feelings, has neglected the need for a rational justification of these feelings at least insofar as they are directed towards specific objects or ends. He glories in feeling as such and is a voluptuary; he has moreover neglected those feelings which incline man to respect the customs, including the social distinctions, of society. Thus while he has understood some aspects of man's sentient nature he has failed to grasp the fact that precisely because man is not wholly rational he needs to be habituated to virtue by a process of social discipline and self-restraint; because of these shortcomings Rousseau has ultimately given a distorted picture even of man's sentient nature.

By a strangely similar process rationalists such as Voltaire have, according to Burke, given a distorted picture of man's rational nature. Just as Burke could under close scrutiny be shown to have certain points in common with Rousseau[1] so there are resemblances between Burke and

[1] See Marion Osborn, *Rousseau and Burke, A Study in the Idea of Liberty in Eighteenth Century Political Thought* (New York, 1940). Although Osborn is

the rationalists. The difference is that in both cases Burke believed his adversaries had mistaken a part of the truth about man's nature for the whole truth, and it was their claims to having the whole truth that Burke considered exaggerated to the point of outright error. The error of the rationalist consisted not in his determination to judge custom, habit, and feeling in the light of reason but in his determination to do this in every instance and to accept nothing until it had passed *his* tests of reasonableness. In the case of both the man of feeling and the rationalist Burke feared that a certain arbitrariness would fatally mar their moral conclusions because of man's natural inclination to exaggerate the goodness of his own feelings and the rationality of his own reflections. The man of feeling was willing to admit neither the need for the rational justification of his feelings nor even the wisdom of checking to see whether his feelings were shared by others; and the rationalist while naturally willing to prefer his reason to his feelings and the feelings of others was all too willing to prefer his reason to that of other men who might have reached other results, who might, for example, have seen the 'latent wisdom' in a prejudice that struck the rationalist only as being absurd and indefensible. The rationalist in practice was then as independent and anti-social as the man of feeling; both, significantly, were curiously blind to the value of those chains of social subordination which Burke believed to be essential.

Burke's organic philosophy inclined him to extend the

overly impressed by the fact that both Rousseau and Burke were 'religious', hated 'tyranny', and loved 'liberty', her book is a useful reminder that the two were not opposed in every respect. For instance, despite Burke's denunciation of republicanism, Burke was, in part at least, a republican in Rousseau's special sense of one who believes that a state should be governed by laws.

Of Burke's inveterate habit of exaggerating the differences between himself and adversaries such as Paine (or Rousseau) Thomas W. Copeland has remarked: 'It is one of the characteristics of a public controversy that it must reduce almost every human affair it touches to an extraordinary simplicity. Problems which any of the controversialists might privately admit to be complex and bewildering have to be presented as very elementary choices between Right and Wrong.' *Our Eminent Friend Edmund Burke*, 177.

organic metaphor[1] in which the different parts of the body
are mutually dependent (1) to human nature in which the
different aspects of that nature (mind, body, and feeling)
are mutually dependent, (2) to society in which all the
individual members are mutually dependent and in which
the various social, political, and religious institutions, in
Burke's opinion, stand or fall together. Regardless of how
he might wish to reform some part of an existing institution,
there was no social, political, or religious institution, at least
not in England and probably not in Europe, which Burke
would have wished to see destroyed. King George III
might fall far short of what a monarch should be, but
Burke cherished the monarchy and sought only to reform
the royal household; if the Church of England might,
from the theological point of view, have little *raison d'être*
apart from Rome, then Burke would cherish her from the
national point of view and content himself with her sharing
in parts of the Catholic tradition. He would, moreover,
never tire of insisting upon the mutual dependence of
church and state; his belief in religious toleration was a
qualified one in which religious freedom would be tolerated
just so far as it did not affect the security of the state.
It was for this reason that, when the security of the English
state seemed threatened by the French Revolution and
some of the Dissenting clergy spoke with approval of
happenings in France, Burke ceased to be a friend of the
Dissenters in their struggles to achieve a greater degree of
religious toleration. It was Burke's belief that all institutions stand or fall together which helped incline him not

[1] The exact nature of Burke's organic conception of society (and of the historical process) is difficult to specify. I believe, however, that MacCunn, op. cit.,
50–57, is correct in saying that Burke does have a recognizably organic conception of society and that on a simple point of fact Vaughan has seriously
misled scholars by asserting that there are no organic metaphors in Burke's
writings (Vaughan, op. cit., II, 25–26). See, for example, Burke's Speech of
15 February 1781, *Speeches*, II, 207–9, where Burke says that the King is 'the
head of the body of his people, from whom they derive, by many communica-
tions of canals, and joints, and hands, that life and nourishment which actuate
the whole frame. If the stomach is sick, the head is disordered; it is affected in
like manner by the other disorders of the body. . . .'

to make distinctions among the allegedly subversive philosophies of even such clearly different thinkers as Rousseau and Voltaire. Regardless of how conservative an individual such as Voltaire might be in some respects, his religious radicalism made him in Burke's judgement subversive in effect of even those social and political institutions which he professed to accept. This was a lifelong conviction on Burke's part. As he explained in the Preface to his *A Vindication of Natural Society:* 'The design [of that satire] was to show that, without the exertion of any considerable forces, the same engines which were employed for the destruction of religion, might be employed with equal success for the subversion of government.'[1]

So long as we have communities there will (as we have seen Burke say) always be some quantum of power in the hands of some person or persons regardless of the appellations applied to these persons and their offices; also, there will be inequalities not merely in the possession of civil and ecclesiastical power but in the possession of property as well: 'Believe me, Sir, those who attempt to level never equalize. In all societies consisting of various descriptions of citizens, some description must be uppermost. The levellers, therefore, only change and pervert the natural order of things: They load the edifice of society by setting up in the air what the solidity of the structure requires to be on the ground.'[2] The change and perversion of the natural order of things is a change in the rightful arrangement

---

[1] Preface to *A Vindication of Natural Society, Works,* I, 4–5.

There is strong evidence that Burke had read Rousseau's *Second Discourse* at the time he was writing the *Vindication* and that his ironic praise of natural society is directed against Rousseau. See Richard Sewall, 'Rousseau's Second Discourse in England from 1755 to 1762', *Philological Quarterly,* XVII (1938), 97–114.

For an unsuccessful attempt to show that Burke intended the *Vindication* as a serious reflection of his views and that the subsequent Preface denying this was added only when Burke was about to enter politics, see Murray Rothbard, 'A Note on Burke's Vindication of Natural Society', *Journal of the History of Ideas,* XIX (January 1958), 114–18. For a refutation of this thesis, see J. C. Weston, Jr., 'The Ironic Purpose of Burke's Vindication Vindicated', *Journal of the History of Ideas,* XIX (June 1958), 435–41.

[2] *Reflections on the Revolution in France, Works,* III, 295.

of things; but some things in the natural order cannot be changed at all. Subordination and power will always be with us, whether the passions are subordinate to or dominant over reason; inequality will always exist so long as society consists of various descriptions of citizens (meaning citizens with different social functions).

Why did Rousseau and others persist in overlooking the fact that subordination and hierarchy will in some form always be present in society and in denying that the pre-revolutionary structure of European society corresponded, however roughly, to the natural order of subordination with mind above the body, reason above the passions? Burke found it difficult to believe in the goodwill of anyone who could overlook or deny this. Only deception and flattery, of oneself and/or of others, could explain the refusal of radicals and revolutionaries, to accept the traditional Christian point of view in these matters. One could not seriously attribute the deficiency of the 'Jacobins' to a deficiency in reason, God had endowed men and especially these clever men with sufficient reason to know the duties of their situation; therefore, the traditional Christian explanation of such moral lapses would have to be invoked, namely that of pride and wilfulness. It is not the appetites or the passions but their arousal and inflammation by the will that seems crucial from the point of view of Burke's Christian beliefs. Burke goes so far as to affirm that 'Duty and will are even contradictory terms.' It is wilfulness which ultimately keeps men such as Rousseau from telling or recognizing the truth about their obligations, much the strongest of which 'were never the results of our option'.

Taking it for granted that I do not write to the disciples of the Parisian philosophy, I may assume that the awful Author of our being is the Author of our place in the order of existence,—and that, having disposed and marshalled us by a divine tactic, not according to our will but according to His, He has in and by that disposition virtually subjected us to act the part which belongs to the place assigned us. We have obligations to mankind at large, which are not in consequence of any special voluntary pact. They arise from the relations of man to man, and the relations of man to God, which relations are not matters of choice.[1]

Unfortunately Burke has little to say about the will and what he does say usually occurs in passages that are especially polemical even by Burkian standards. The relationships he may have envisaged as holding between will, reason, appetite, and passion are not spelled out, as he is more intent upon condemning wilful persons than upon analysing the will. One of the characteristics of wilfulness, of the proud assertion of independence or importance by a person or a class of persons, which so engrossed and outraged Burke, is that it may lead to a betrayal of one's interests. This is not simply to say that since God wills us to do our duties and since He may invoke sanctions against us if we fail to do them it follows that it is in our interest that we should do our duties. Rather, it is a way of indicating that a man with an envious will who is jealous of the position and property of other persons may actually bring harm to himself by altering or overthrowing the system which made possible not only the advantages of other persons but some of his own advantages as well. A man with a small estate may feel safe in helping to destroy larger estates only to find that he has helped unleash forces which in time will destroy all accumulations of property and perhaps even society. Accordingly, it is a fundamental tenet of Burke's position that 'The will of the many, and their interest, must very often differ. . . .'[2] 'We even deny', Burke said in the impeachment of Warren Hastings, 'that there exists in all the human race a power to make the government of any state dependent upon individual will.'[3] Whether in the mass or the individual the will must not be allowed to predominate:

A perfect democracy is . . . the most shameless thing in the world. As it is the most shameless, it is also the most fearless. No man apprehends in his person that he can be made subject to punishment. Certainly the

[1] *An Appeal from the New to the Old Whigs, Works*, IV, 165–6.
[2] *Reflections on the Revolution in France, Works*, III, 299.   [3] *Works*, XI, 200.

people at large never ought: for, as all punishments are for example towards the conservation of the people at large, the people at large can never become the subject of punishment by any human hand. It is therefore of infinite importance that they should not be suffered to imagine that their will, any more than that of kings, is the standard of right and wrong.[1]

In view of what Burke felt concerning the mutual dependence of men and the duties which bind them together, the proper subordination of will and appetite to duty and reason, and the respects in which human nature never changes regardless of time and place, one can see that Burke's indictment of Warren Hastings 'in the name of human nature itself, which he has cruelly outraged, injured, and oppressed'[2] is far from empty rhetoric but points rather to the central place which the concept of human nature has in Burke's thought. It is easy to picture Burke as projecting this same judgement from one wilful individual on to a group of wilful individuals identified somewhat vaguely simply as 'Jacobins', and to say that this judgement serves not merely to summarize Burke's case against Hastings in the impeachment proceedings but his case against the Jacobins in his *Reflections on the Revolution in France* and the *Letters on a Regicide Peace*. It is the heart of his case against tyranny regardless of its form.

---

[1] *Works*, III, 355. Burke like many conservatives assumes that the advocates of democracy think that the *will* of the people or of the majority of them should be the standard of right and wrong. This is, of course, a doubtful historical thesis, but one which must for present purposes be left unexplored.

[2] Ibid., X, 145.

II

BURKE'S *A Philosophical Inquiry into the Origin of Our Ideas of the Sublime and Beautiful*

IN his *Appeal from the New to the Old Whigs* Burke warns that 'it is now obvious to the world, that a theory concerning government may become as much a cause of fanaticism as a dogma in religion. There is a boundary to men's passions, when they act from feeling; none when they are under the influence of imagination. Remove a grievance, and, when men act from feeling, you go a great way towards quieting a commotion. But the good or bad conduct of a government, the protection men have enjoyed or the oppression they have suffered under it, are of no sort of moment, when a faction, proceeding upon speculative grounds, is thoroughly heated against its form.'[1] This passage is characteristically Burkian for a number of reasons: it reflects his belief that any sort of speculation can when carried too far lead to fanaticism and factionalism; it shows his trust of the passions under ordinary circumstances when men act from 'natural' feelings; and it shows his distrust of the passions when they are inflamed by the imagination. It is important, therefore, that we turn now to Burke's *A Philosophical Inquiry into the Origin of Our Ideas of the Sublime and Beautiful* to determine in some greater detail Burke's theories concerning the passions, the imagination, and reason.

We are at first glance hampered because Burke's treatise is directed chiefly to problems concerning aesthetic judgements. The work is, however, an attempt to apply fruitfully to aesthetics a more general theory concerning the senses, the imagination, and the judgement. If we attend

[1] *Works*, IV, 192.

9

to this theory and avoid the temptation of assuming that what Burke says of aesthetic judgements will necessarily hold true of his views on political judgements as well, we can add to our knowledge of Burke's views on human nature and at the same time avoid giving the misleading impression that Burke's treatise *completes* Burke's theory of human nature by supplying all the missing premisses needed to make this theory truly comprehensive and fully intelligible. Because the treatise in its present form appeared in 1757, because it shows how early Burke became concerned with some of the great themes of his later work, and because it is his only strictly philosophical labour on the topic of human nature, it is easy to assume that Burke's later work is but an application to the political area of propositions derived from this earlier work. Such an assumption while it might be of some heuristic value in helping us see the fundamental coherence of Burke's views would, however, if taken literally, be historically false.

Burke's *Inquiry* has usually been related to the 'empiricist' tradition and with good reason. His view that the senses are 'the great originals of all our ideas' and his judgement that beauty is, 'for the greater part, some quality in bodies acting mechanically upon the human mind by the intervention of the senses' show the general soundness of those interpretations which link the *Inquiry* to empiricism. I think, however, that the exact nature of the linkage is more difficult to discover than commentators have ordinarily assumed. Throughout the present investigation I have chosen to avoid insofar as possible the larger question of the logical compatibility of natural law theories with empiricism. This is not due to a refusal on my part to admit there is a real problem here but to considerations of a different order. While many advocates of natural law have tended to argue as if natural law and empiricism were incompatible and some empiricists have argued that empiricism destroys once and for all the pretences of natural law doctrines, I am inclined to make certain reservations. First, I am struck by the complexity of natural law theories and of empiricism; and second, by the fact that not all empiricists have disavowed the natural law. Locke certainly did not; and, as I have argued, even Hume's dissent was far from complete. The first reservation may be met by saying that if natural law theory is a version of ethical cognitivism and if empiricism is a denial of cognitivism in the realm of values, then no one can consistently claim to accept both the natural law and empiricism, regardless of which forms of these doctrines one may choose. And this disposes, presumably, of my second reservation as well. If Locke, for example, held to both the natural law and empiricism, then he was a bad philosopher; and my reservation is only an historical one. Historical reservations may, however, sometimes suggest the need for reconsidering or recasting our arguments. While historically natural law theorists and empiricists have spoken as if the natural law stands or falls with ethical cognitivism, it may be that this is chiefly an historical point, and that logically some important features of natural law theory could survive the demise of ethical cognitivism. Or it may be that the empiricist has drawn his distinction between fact and value too sharply, that a modified empiricism will undertake a genuine comparison of claims to knowledge in all realms rather than rest upon the dogma that *is* and *ought* are of two different logical kinds. This paragraph is much too general to be of use, except perhaps to the student of Burke; for present purposes it serves to pave the way for an attempt on my part to show that authors such as Strauss and Canavan have been overconcerned with the problem of the consistency of Burke's 'empiricism' in the *Inquiry* with his overall natural law commitments. I do not claim that there is no problem here either in general or in Burke, only that a convincing case for there being such a problem in Burke at least has not been made. I question even Canavan's cautious conclusion that 'It is doubtful that Burke's epistemology as it appears, in his early writings, was compatible with the metaphysic implied in his moral and political theory.[1] Rather than present a summary of Burke's *Inquiry*, which is available in several editions, and then discuss the problem of consistency noted above, I shall treat the problem of consistency first and then undertake to assess the contributions of the *Inquiry* to our understanding of Burke's views on human nature.

Strauss writes that 'The most important thesis of the *Sublime and Beautiful* is in perfect agreement with British sensualism and in explicit opposition to the classics; Burke denies that there is a connection between beauty, on the one hand, and perfection, proportion, virtue, convenience, order, fitness, and any other such "creatures of the understanding" on the other,'[2] While ordinarily criticism should follow exposition, I hope that I may be indulged in reversing this rule on the present occasion, for what I take to be a good reason. The currently prominent Straussian interpretation of the natural law has assumed a basic inconsistency between traditional natural law doctrine and empiricism (or 'sensualism') without having explored in detail the nature of this inconsistency, and Strauss himself has gone on to assume that while Burke believed in traditional natural law doctrine the early *Inquiry* belongs to the empiricist or sensualist tradition as against the natural law tradition. Since the *Inquiry* is the only systematic philosophizing Burke ever did, I think it would be well, as a way of indicating why the *Inquiry* should be gone into carefully, to begin by questioning the assumption that what the *Inquiry* and what the natural law tradition have to say about human nature are so at odds. I find four mistakes in the above quotation from Strauss which I shall give now as a kind of opening wedge in my argument that a new look at the *Inquiry* is in fact needed: (1) Burke's 'perfect agreement' with British 'sensualists' such as Hume is not all that perfect; for example, Hume in considering beauty

---

[1] Op. cit., 45.   [2] *Natural Right and History*, 312.

had not as a matter of fact ignored fitness. (2) Burke does not deny that there is *any* connexion between beauty and perfection, proportion, virtue, &c. but instead argues for a more restricted thesis, namely that, strictly speaking, perfection, proportion, and virtue should not be spoken of as beautiful. (See Sections X and XI of Part III, 'How Far the Idea of Beauty May Be Applied to the Qualities of the Mind', 'How Far the Idea of Beauty May be Applied to Virtue'.) (3) It is, therefore, doubtful that what Burke has to say about the distinction between beauty on the one hand and perfection, proportion, virtue, &c. on the other is the most important thesis of the *Inquiry*. From the point of view of political theory, the distinction between the ideas of the sublime and the beautiful and their respective passions seems more fundamental. (4) Strauss appears to believe that the meaning of the phrase 'creatures of the understanding' is self-evident when there is, in my opinion, no clear interpretation which can be said to hold necessarily of this ambiguous phrase. 'Creatures of the understanding' was, of course, used by Locke in support of what might best be called a qualified nominalism concerning the 'general and universal' (*Essay*, III, 3, 11), but it is not very helpful even as a key to Locke. In neither Locke nor Burke does it necessarily imply that ideas such as proportion are *merely* fictions created by the mind. Burke appears intent primarily upon showing that proportion unlike beauty operates more upon the understanding than upon the senses, that a judgement about proportion will owe more to our understanding than will a judgement about beauty.[1] Burke did not believe that a judgement concerning beauty is *wholly* determined (rather he said that it is 'for the greater part') by the qualities of the body acting mechanically

---

[1] This is Canavan's position also, although he does not note the ambiguity of the phrase 'creatures of the understanding'. Canavan, op. cit., 37–39. But might it not be that the logic of 'creatures of the understanding' is more like the logic of 'creatures of pleasure' or 'creatures of habit' than like the logic of 'fictions of mind' or 'contrivances of reason' in that it marks an important characteristic of the creatures in question rather than the *total* dependence of these creatures upon something else—be it pleasure, habit, or the understanding?

upon the human mind, nor did he believe that a judgement concerning proportion is determined *wholly* by man's understanding. Burke simply wishes to deny that a judgement about proportion is a judgement about beauty: he attempts to do this genetically by showing that beauty appeals *more* to the senses and proportion *more* to the understanding. There is then no reason to suppose that Burke encounters any grave epistemological difficulties when he urges his readers to look at the order or proportion in the universe for inspiration in our political constructions. The understanding of this order requires more rational activity than, say, a judgement concerning the beauty of a rose, but such an understanding is well within man's power.

Still an emphasis upon the limits of man's reason is characteristic of Burke; and commentators have tended to believe that this is more evident in the *Inquiry* than elsewhere. Even the scope of the *Inquiry* itself is supposedly affected by Burke's belief that when we go beyond 'the immediate sensible qualities of things' we are soon out of our depth.[1] Yet Burke's *Inquiry does* represent an attempt to go beyond the sensible qualities of things and to offer causal explanations of their effects upon our aesthetic responses:

When I say, I intend to inquire into the efficient cause of sublimity and beauty, I would not be understood to say, that I can come to the ultimate cause. I do not pretend that I shall ever be able to explain why certain affections of the body produce a distinct emotion of mind, and no other; or why the body is at all affected by the mind, or the mind by the body. A little thought will show this to be impossible. But I conceive, if we can discover what affections of the mind produce certain emotions of the body; and what distinct feelings and qualities of body shall produce certain determinate passions in the mind, and no others, I fancy a great deal will be done; something not unuseful towards a distinct knowledge of our passions, so far at least as we have them at present under our consideration. This is all, I believe we can do. If we could advance a

[1] *A Philosophical Inquiry into the Origin of Our Ideas of the Sublime and Beautiful, Works*, I, 209.

step farther, difficulties would still remain, as we should be still equally distant from the first cause. [!] When Newton first discovered the property of attraction, and settled its laws, he found it served very well to explain several of the most remarkable phenomena in nature; but yet, with reference to the general system of things, he could consider attraction but as an effect, whose cause at that time he did not attempt to trace.[1]

It is clear from the above that Burke did not restrict his investigations to the question of 'How' but on the contrary concerned himself with the question of 'Why'.[2] He dealt, as he said, with the efficient causes of our ideas of the sublime and the beautiful; hence his mention of Newton is significant. What then is the real force of his reservations ? His reference to Newton's difficulty in explaining attraction 'with reference to the general system of things' is illuminating. What Burke is doing is pointing to the *incompleteness* of his own causal explanations. The causes of the causes of our ideas of the sublime and the beautiful are not considered. More importantly, the phenomena he does discuss remain unexplained in two important respects: (1) While he can explain the causes of these ideas, he cannot explain why these causes have just the effects they do and no other. They just *do*. In short, Burke seems to be restating the problem of induction and noting his inability to determine the 'necessary connexion' between cause and effect. (2) Burke is admitting that his causal explanations do not solve the mind–body problem; his intuition appears to be that this problem is not soluble, at least not within the framework of causal explanations and inductive procedures (and he generally confesses to a personal incapacity before such abstract problems within *any* framework). Whether

---

[1] *Works*, I, 208.

[2] Strauss writes that Burke believed 'Our knowledge of bodily and mental phenomena is limited to the manner of their operation, to their How; it can never reach their Why.' Op. cit., 312. He offers no explanation of or support for this claim, but it still crops up in the literature on Burke and should, I think, be mentioned here as an example of how Burke's protestations concerning the limited scope of his *Inquiry* and his inability to come to the *ultimate* cause of the phenomena under consideration are turned by some commentators into more drastic and quite different theses concerning the limits of man's rational powers.

Burke is more concerned with calling attention to the incompleteness of his particular inquiry or to the incompleteness in principle of any such investigation is uncertain, although he clearly intends to do both. What is important, however, is his assertion that an inquiry such as his is 'not unuseful toward a distinct knowledge of our passions'.

Burke considered the question of 'Why' on two different levels, the mechanical and the teleological. Roughly speaking, the former provides an historical link with Locke and Hume while the latter points forward in the direction, for example, of Kant's *Critique of Judgement* and of his *Idea of a Universal History from a Cosmopolitan Point of View*. Burke shows no explicit awareness of the differences between the questions 'What causes that ?' and 'What is that for ?' Yet there is a striking difference between his attitudes before these questions. On the level of efficient causality Burke is modesty itself, stressing his personal inability to unravel the 'great chain of causes' that leads ultimately to God[1] and emphasizing the fact that for anyone it is 'extremely hard' (though not impossible) 'to disentangle our idea of the [divine] cause from the effect by which we are led to know it'.[2] But Burke's modesty is much less complete when he asks the teleological question and discusses God's plans for man. Like Kant, he rather easily explains the ambition of man and its attendant difficulties as Providence's way of keeping men from remaining fixed forever on one low level of development: 'To prevent this, God has planted in man a sense of ambition, and a satisfaction arising from the contemplation of his excelling his fellows in something deemed valuable amongst them. It is this passion that drives men to all the ways we see in use of signalizing themselves, and that tends to make whatever excites in a man the idea of this distinction so very pleasant.'[3] Occasionally, as when Burke cannot explain why Providence has made some animals more attractive than others to man, he admits to bafflement: 'But it is

---

[1] *Works*, I, 209.   [2] Ibid., 142.   [3] Ibid., 124.

probable that Providence did not make even this distinction, but with a view to some great end; though we cannot perceive distinctly what it is, as his wisdom is not our wisdom, nor our ways his ways.'[1] Ordinarily, however, Burke is not baffled even by such details; and while he is never actually immodest he does indicate that in studying the human mind we find strong traces of God's wisdom in making something so intricate and so well suited for the execution of His plans. In such an inquiry, 'we may be inquisitive without impertinence, and elevated without pride; we may be admitted, if I may dare to say so, into the counsels of the Almighty by a consideration of his works'.[2]

Concerning the passions, Burke writes that 'a consideration of the rationale of our passions seems to me very necessary for all who would affect them upon solid and sure principles. It is not enough to know them in general; to affect them after a delicate manner, or to judge properly of any work designed to affect them we should know the exact boundaries of their several jurisdictions; we should pursue them through all their variety of operations; and pierce into the inmost, and what might appear inaccessible parts of our nature. . . .'[3] Concerning taste ('that faculty or those faculties, which are affected with, or which form a judgment of, the works of imagination and the elegant arts') Burke believes 'it is probable that the standard both of reason and taste is the same in all human creatures'. The point of his investigations is 'to find whether there are any principles, on which the imagination is affected, so common to all, so grounded and certain, as to supply the means of reasoning satisfactorily about them'.[4] His conclusion is positive: he believes that he has discovered the principles on which the imagination is affected, that 'so far . . . as taste belongs to the imagination, its principle is the same in all men',[5] and that he has the key as to how

---

[1] Ibid., 115.   [2] Ibid., 126–127.   [3] Ibid., 127.   [4] Ibid., 79, 82.
[5] Ibid., 92.

works of the imagination affect the passions. Accordingly, I do not think that either the scope, the ambitions, or the claims of Burke's *Inquiry* are significantly curtailed by his awareness of the limits of human reason.

There is no question but that Burke's interest in aesthetics does in part reflect 'a constant interest in the irrational response to art and life' and that he refuses to attribute the causes of our feelings, the pleasures that arise from imitation, or the delight we experience before scenes of real or fictitious distress to the activities or conclusions of our reasoning faculty.[1] As an account of what Burke has in mind when he speaks of an aesthetic *experience* this is helpful. It is, however, crucial to an understanding of Burke's views on the relation of reason to aesthetics to make a distinction between an aesthetic experience and an aesthetic judgement, between the experience of sublimity or of beauty and the judgement that this or that object in nature or in art is sublime or beautiful. While Burke does not discuss this distinction as such, it may account for his addition of an Introduction 'On Taste' to the *Inquiry; roughly speaking*, we may say that this addition concerns aesthetic judgement while the rest of the *Inquiry* concerns aesthetic experience. Without recourse to some such elementary distinction it is all too easy, I think, to distort the relationship of reason and aesthetics in Burke by overlooking the part that reason or the understanding plays in the *judging* of a work of art, to stop with Burke's appreciation of the irrational in art (and life) or to say that he was 'a champion of Taste as a *subjective* imperative'.[2]

Burke believed the imagination to have a great power over the passions: this is a constant theme throughout his works. In the *Inquiry* he remarks that 'When men have suffered their imaginations to be long affected with any

---

[1] J. T. Boulton's Introduction to Burke's *A Philosophical Enquiry into the Origin of Our Ideas of the Sublime and Beautiful*, xi.

[2] Wilson O. Clough, 'Reason and Genius—An Eighteenth Century Dilemma', *Philological Quarterly*, XXIII (January 1944), 45.

idea, it so wholly engrosses them as to shut out by degrees almost every other, and to break down every partition of the mind which would confine it. Any idea is sufficient for the purpose, as is evident from the infinite variety of causes which give rise to madness. . . .'[1] Burke also affirms that 'the influence of reason in producing our passions is nothing near so extensive as it is commonly believed'.[2] Yet these certainly are not denials that reason *can* affect the passions, and the manner in which Burke speaks of men having 'suffered their imaginations to be long affected with any idea' at least suggests that men need not in all cases allow their imaginations to be so affected. Indeed, the imagination while it produces works of art and affects greatly the passions of man is restricted first by the senses and finally (this is where aesthetic *judgements* enter) by the understanding itself. The senses provide the materials upon which the imagination must work, and the understanding provides the evaluation of the works of the imagination. The dependence of the imagination upon the senses and its powers of representing the images received from the senses and of arranging these images in new ways is explained by Burke in the following passage:

Besides the ideas, with their annexed pains and pleasures, which are presented by the sense; the mind of man possesses a sort of creative power of its own; either in representing at pleasure the images of things in the order and manner in which they were received by the senses, or in combining those images in a new manner, and according to a different order. This power is called imagination; and to this belongs whatever is called wit, fancy, invention, and the like. But it must be observed, that this power of the imagination is incapable of producing anything absolutely new; it can only vary the disposition of those ideas which it has received from the senses. Now the imagination is the most extensive province of pleasure and pain, as it is the region of our fears and our hopes, and of all our passions that are connected with them; and whatever is calculated to affect the imagination with these commanding ideas, by force of any original natural impression, must have the same power pretty equally over all men. For since the imagination is only the

[1] *Works*, I, 112.   [2] Ibid., 118.

representation of the senses, it can only be pleased or displeased with the
images, from the same principle on which the sense is pleased or displeased with the realities; and consequently there must be just as close
an agreement in the imaginations as in the senses of men. A little
attention will convince us that this must of necessity be the case.[1]

Commentators have frequently, and correctly, remarked
that Burke rejects *ethical* hedonism; but this is not to say
that Burke's ethical theory is indifferent to considerations
involving pain and pleasure. It could not be indifferent to
such considerations without being cut off completely from
Burke's theory of human nature in which the pleasure–pain
principle plays an important part. In the *Inquiry* Burke
rejects Locke's argument that the removal or lessening
of a pain is both considered and operates as a pleasure.[2]
Perhaps following Cicero's *De Finibus*, he argues that the
human mind is often in a state neither of pleasure nor pain
but of indifference. Yet having made this qualification
Burke accepts a kind of *psychological* hedonism in that he
uses the pleasure–pain principle to explain why our senses,
our imagination, and our passions are affected in certain
ways. *The pleasure–pain principle is his key to the dynamics
of human psychology in general and of aesthetic experience
in particular*. His use of the principle of the association of
ideas seems not to have that degree of importance usually
attached to it by commentators. However necessary it may
be to Burke's explanation of how words can affect the
passions without their being accompanied in all cases by
appropriate images or by any images at all, the principle
of the association of ideas is used by Burke primarily as a
means of strengthening the claims he makes for the
pleasure–pain principle:

It is no small bar in the way of our inquiry into the cause of our passions,
that the occasions of many of them are given, and that their governing
motions are communicated at a time when we have not capacity to
reflect on them; at a time of which all sort of memory is worn out of our
minds. For besides such things as affect us in various manners, according

---

[1] *Works*, I, 86–87.   [2] Ibid., 102–6.

to their natural powers, there are associations made at that early season, which we find it very hard afterwards to distinguish from natural effects. Not to mention the unaccountable antipathies which we find in many persons, we all find it impossible to remember when a steep became more terrible than a plain; or fire or water more terrible than a clod of earth; though all these are very probably either conclusions from experience, or arising from the premonitions of others; and some of them impressed, in all likelihood, pretty late. But as it must be allowed that many things affect us after a certain manner, not by any natural powers they have for that purpose, but by association; so it would be absurd, on the other hand, to say that all things affect us by association only; since some things must have been originally and naturally agreeable or disagreeable, from which the others derive their associated powers; and it would be, I fancy, to little purpose to look for the cause of our passions in association, until we fail of it in the natural properties of things.[1]

The starting point of Burke's case for there being fixed principles of taste is the assumption that 'as the conformation of their organs are nearly or altogether the same in all men, so the manner of perceiving external objects is in all men the same or with little difference. We are satisfied that what appears to be light to one eye, appears light to another. . . .' If we believed that the senses present different images of things to different men, this scepticism would make every sort of reasoning, including scepticism itself, vain and frivolous. The second step in Burke's argument is that 'as there will be little doubt that bodies present similar images to the whole species, it must necessarily be allowed, that the pleasures and the pains which every object excites in one man, it must raise in all mankind, whilst it operates naturally, simply, and by its proper powers only; for if we deny this, we must imagine that the same cause, operating in the same manner, and on subjects of the same kind, will produce different effects; which would be highly absurd.' Burke asks the reader to consider the sense of taste (from which the *faculty* of taste has taken its name) as a case in point. All men are agreed to call vinegar sour and honey sweet, nor does agreement cease

[1] Ibid., 209–10.

there: 'They all concur in calling sweetness pleasant, and sourness and bitterness unpleasant.' Custom, Burke admits, might make for deviations from this rule: a man might come to prefer the taste of tobacco to that of sugar, &c.; 'but this makes no confusion in tastes, whilst he is sensible that the tobacco . . . [is] not sweet, and whilst he knows that habit alone has reconciled his palate to these alien pleasures'. When it is said that taste cannot be disputed this, according to Burke, 'can only mean, that no one can strictly answer what pleasure or pain some particular man may find from the taste of some particular thing'. We *can* dispute concerning 'the things which are naturally pleasing or disagreeable to the sense. But when we talk of any peculiar or acquired relish, then we must know the habits, the prejudices, or the distempers of this particular man, and we must draw our conclusions from those.' Burke's contention is that 'There is in all men a sufficient remembrance of the original natural causes of pleasure, to enable them to bring all things offered to their senses to that standard, and to regulate their feelings and opinions by it.'[1]

The significance of Burke's claim that the imagination is 'only the representation of the senses' is that what he has said about the senses and the uniformity of their reactions of pleasure or pain when exposed in the appropriate ways to various natural objects can now be applied, *mutatis mutandis*, to the imagination. The imagination, according to Burke, can have no pleasure which does not arise either from the properties of the 'natural object' or from perceiving the resemblance which an imitation of a natural object has to the original. The imagination has as its chief occupation the tracing of resemblances, while the business of judgement lies in finding differences: 'The painter, the shoemaker, the anatomist, and the Turkish emperor' share a common satisfaction when they see a good imitation of a natural object and when they see an agreeable figure; and they feel in common 'the sympathy

[1] *Works*, I, 82–86.

proceeding from a striking and affecting incident. So far as taste is natural, it is nearly common to all.'[1]

The principles of taste, insofar as taste belongs to the imagination, are the same in all men. The causes (the why) and the manner (the how) of their being affected are the same. There is only a difference in degree, which arises either from a greater 'natural sensibility' or from a closer and longer 'attention' to the object. While there is no common measure for settling many disputes relative to the senses and the imagination, 'we find that the principles are the same in all, and that there is no disagreement until we come to examine into the preeminence or differences of things, *which brings us within the province of the judgment.*'[2] What Burke has done thus far, I think, is to perform a *thought experiment* of reducing taste to its barest components and of taking 'taste' in perhaps its simplest sense as one of the senses and offering an analysis of 'the taste of . . .' (honey, vinegar, tobacco) which he then applies to a more complicated case which might best be characterized as 'the taste for . . .' (art, an agreeable figure, a tragedy). Burke's point is that in both the sense of taste and the taste of the imagination the principles (the causes) and the manner of their operation are the same; in the second case this is due to the dependence of the imagination upon the senses—it *must* be pleased by what pleases the senses and displeased by what does not.

If everything Burke has said thus far were true, it would establish only that the principles (the causes) of 'taste of' and 'taste for' were uniform in all men, *not* his original contention that it is 'probable that the standard both of reason and taste is the same in all human creatures'. When Burke made this remark at the beginning of his treatment of taste he showed some confusion between 'standard' and 'principle' and did not appear to notice that 'principles' is ambiguous and can be used (as he himself seems to use it) as referring either to standards (or criteria) or to causes.

---

[1] Ibid., 92.   [2] Ibid., 93. My italics.

This confusion is, I think, evident in the very first lines of Burke's 'On Taste':

> On a superficial view we may seem to differ very widely from each other in our reasonings, and no less in our pleasures But, notwithstanding this difference, which I think to be rather apparent than real, it is probable that the standard both of reason and taste is the same in all human creatures. For if there were not some principles of judgment as well as of sentiment common to all mankind, no hold could possibly be taken either on their reason or their passions, sufficient to maintain the ordinary correspondence of life. It appears, indeed, to be generally acknowledged, that with regard to truth and falsehood there is something fixed. We find people in their disputes continually appealing to certain tests and standards, which are allowed on all sides, and are supposed to be established in our common nature. But there is not the same obvious concurrence in any uniform or settled principles which relate to taste.[1]

While Burke has said that 'it is probable that the standard both of reason and taste is the same in all human creatures' and while it is clear from the rest of the above quotation that the standard of reason in matters of truth and falsity is, according to Burke, already agreed upon, by his own admission we still lack a common measure, test, or standard for settling our differences in the realm of aesthetics. Even in the simplest cases of 'taste of' and 'taste for' the alleged discovery by Burke of the principles (in the sense of the causes) of taste and the alleged uniformity of our feelings of pleasure and pain when we eat honey or taste vinegar or see a bust by Houdon do not imply that we have an agreed upon standard or set of criteria for resolving disputes in such cases as we have, according to Burke, for settling disputes in some other realms. We cannot, Burke appears to believe, hope to state what these standards are until we bring our philosophical analysis to bear upon the much neglected discipline of aesthetics and begin exploring the ways in which the judgement actually becomes involved with and reacts to our feelings of pleasure or pain and our initial, pre-critical aesthetic experiences. Thus while it is

[1] *Works*, I, 79.

probable that the standard of taste is the same in all men as, according to Burke, the standard of truth and falsity is, what this standard is can only be discovered by our considering *all* the various elements that enter into the appreciation of a work of art. This is why what Burke has to say about what we should call 'good taste' and 'bad taste' and what Burke himself calls 'refined judgment' and 'wrong taste' is crucial to an account of Burke's aesthetic theory.

In the plastic arts Burke often seems willing to let the passions and the imagination carry the day with the judgement playing a role chiefly of assenting to their responses of pleasure or displeasure. A likeness of the Grand Canyon, provided, of course, that it is a likeness, is ordinarily acceptable to our judgement if our passions and imagination respond to it favourably. But, according to Burke, it is the verbal arts which can arouse the passions and influence our behaviour to a much greater extent. It is rhetoric and poetry that must be judged not solely in terms of the likenesses with reality or the rearrangements of the familiar they provide or of the pleasure and pain we feel at the prospects they offer, &c. They must insofar as they affect our passions and our behaviour be judged by rational standards; and in cases where the rhetoric and poetry in question concern themselves with moral issues the judgement can apply the (Burke thinks) universally acknowledged standards of right and wrong, good and bad, in judging these works of art. The function of the judgement in some cases is then, as I interpret Burke, not simply to answer the question, 'Do I enjoy X?' but to consider the question, 'Should I enjoy X?' The enjoyment of X I call an aesthetic experience; the consciousness of the enjoyment of X conjoined with the exploration of the question of whether I should enjoy X I call the aesthetic judgement. In some cases the question of should I like X is not concerned with the fidelity of a copy to some original, its technical merits, &c. but is rather a moral question which can be answered by the application of already agreed upon moral standards. In brief I read Burke as saying that in the areas of truth and falsity and of morality we have universally accepted standards for settling disputes, that probably universally acceptable standards in the area of taste could be elicited from our experience and would in fact already have been agreed upon if agreement in aesthetics was as vital to our existence as it is in other areas, and that in cases where this is appropriate our aesthetic responses may be evaluated and even shaped in part by the standards already agreed upon in other areas of human experience. In the context of the present undertaking, it is the moral element in our judgement of certain works of art that merits closer attention, especially as commentators in the past have neglected this aspect of Burke's aesthetics and indeed his concern with aesthetic *judgement* in general.

Many works of the imagination, Burke writes, are not confined to representations of sensible objects or even to efforts upon the passions, 'but extend themselves to the manners, the characters, the actions, and designs of men, their relations, their virtues and vices. . . .' It was this aspect of the imagination that would greatly concern Burke in his later years in his polemics against the 'diseased' and 'unnatural' imagination of Rousseau and the radicals. Yet properly handled the imagination in its moral capacity is of great value, Burke maintained. Throughout his writings he emphasized that most learning is by emulation rather than by formal demonstration, and in the *Inquiry* he shows himself keenly aware of the moral significance of imitation. When the imagination enters the realm of morals and manners it comes within

the province of the judgment, which is improved by attention, and by the habit of reasoning. All these make a very considerable part of what are considered as the objects of taste; and Horace sends us to the schools of philosophy and the world for our instruction in them. Whatever certainty is to be acquired in morality and the science of life; just the same degree of certainty have we in what relates to them in works of imitation. Indeed it is for the most part in our skill in manners, and in the observance of time and place, and of decency in general, which is only to be learned in those schools to which Horace recommends us, that what is called taste, by way of distinction, consists; and which is in reality no other than a more refined judgment. On the whole, it appears to me, that what is called taste, in its most general acceptance, is not a simple idea, but is partly made up of the primary pleasures of sense, of the secondary pleasures of the imagination, and of the conclusions of the reasoning faculty, concerning the human passions, manners and actions.[1]

Burke has often been criticized for drawing too sharp a distinction between beauty and proportion and utility; and it has not been noticed how in passages such as the above he refuses to separate aesthetics wholly from morality but seems intent rather upon construing good taste as in some cases a morally good taste. 'Whatever certainty is to be acquired in morality and the science of life; just the same degree of certainty have we in what relates to them in works of imitation': is not the certainty Burke speaks of in the latter case *derivative* from our certainty in morality and the science of life ? There are, I think, at least two senses of 'good taste'. The first and perhaps currently more prevalent sense is the one in which a person who refuses to wear loud ties or to drive purple Cadillacs is said to have good taste; the moral significance, if any, of this is not readily apparent. But there is another sense of good taste where a consideration of others (manners), a proper regard for time and place, &c. does at times seem a virtue from the moral point of view. Why does Burke seem to concentrate upon this second sense of good taste to the neglect of the former ? There is, I think, something counter-intuitive from the outset in Burke's insistence that the standards of taste are probably the same in all men. He tries to overcome this by remarking that if we had the 'same interesting motives' to fix standards in taste as in matters of reason we should do so: 'I make no doubt but that the logic of taste, if I may be allowed the expression,

[1] *Works*, I, 94–95.

might very possibly be as well digested, and we might come to discuss matters of this nature with as much certainty, as those which seem more immediately within the province of mere reason.'[1] Still there is, I think, room for considerable doubt. Notice, however, what would happen if we approached this assertion from *within* Burke's philosophy keeping in mind several of Burke's more basic assumptions. If we held with Burke that in some cases the standards by which we judge a work of art are in part at least moral standards or are influenced by the standards of morality and if we firmly believed that certain moral standards are as universally applicable as the standards of reason itself because they are themselves in some sense (unfortunately unspecified by Burke) reasonable, then his case for the probable universality of standards in art appreciation ceases to be wildly implausible. In *some* cases at least these universal standards will simply be the standards of morality applied to an aesthetic context. The fact that men often do not seem to agree on the standards concerning the propriety of (morally) good taste in, for example, the treatment of sexual subject-matter in the various arts would not, I think, pose serious problems for Burke's position. Burke's argument is not that in fact men do agree on such standards but that if certain confusions and obscurities could be removed from the field of aesthetics, if critical reason attended to aesthetics as it has in the past attended to other disciplines, men *could* agree as to what such standards are. In the present case they could upon reflection see, I presume Burke would say, that the obscene or the shocking is as easily detected as such in art as it is in life and ought to be judged as severely in art as in life (and perhaps even more severely because its 'corrupting' influence might be greater and might affect more people, if the obscene work of art becomes popular, as it might).

There is a passage in the *Inquiry* where Burke remarks 'But art can never give the rules that make an art.' This is

[1] *Works*, I, 80.

usually, and rightly, interpreted as a plea for our attending more closely to the need for an improved aesthetics, but it might also be in part an indirect way of denying the complete autonomy of art from moral considerations:

But art can never give the rules that make an art. This is, I believe, the reason why artists in general, and poets, principally, have been confined in so narrow a circle: they have been rather imitators of one another than of nature; and this with so faithful an uniformity, and to so remote an antiquity, that it is hard to say who gave the first model. Critics follow them, and therefore can do little as guides. I can judge but poorly of anything, whilst I measure it by no other standard than itself. The true standard of the arts is in every man's power; and an easy observation of the most common, sometimes of the meanest things in nature, will give the truest lights. . . .[1]

This passage when considered by itself seems to be little more than a suggestion that artists and poets stop imitating one another and begin to imitate nature. But when viewed in the light of Burke's overall philosophy how is his suggestion that artists and poets imitate nature to be interpreted? Perhaps the nature in question should be conceived of not solely as an aesthetic norm but as a moral norm as well. We have seen that when Burke advises his readers to 'follow nature' in political, social, and religious matters the nature in question is, to a considerable extent, to be construed as a moral norm. I suggest that when Burke advises artists and especially poets to follow nature this advice has moral as well as aesthetic dimensions. But what about his advice to observe 'the meanest things in nature'? Obviously, he does not mean by 'meanest' the depraved, the crippled or the freak, but rather the lowliest, the most humble, and the most obscure. Even this is to some degree moral advice because in Burke's philosophy all of Nature (properly understood) is held to partake of and to exhibit the goodness of its Creator.

[1] Ibid., 128. It is interesting to note that the true standards of the arts are in every man's power. So, too, are the true standards of morality, according to Burke.

Like Hume, Burke is fully aware of the factors that make for variety in our judgements of taste,[1] although he is more optimistic than Hume concerning the possibilities of our fixing the standards of taste. The factors Burke calls attention to as making for variety in taste are the ones Hume had mentioned: differences in sensibility and judgement. Like Hume, he bemoans the dangers to aesthetic judgement of prejudice and hasty opinion. I submit, however, that one reason why Burke is not in the final analysis so impressed as Hume by the great variety in our aesthetic tastes is that he believes that in some very important cases aesthetic judgement is in part an expression of moral judgement and as such is subject to continued improvement. As moral judgement is universal and rational, then, Burke believes, there is some hope for aesthetic judgement.

Burke at one point goes into some detail as to what goes wrong and why in cases of bad, mistaken, or 'wrong' taste, and this passage is important enough to quote at some length:

The cause of a wrong taste is a defect in judgment. And this may arise from a natural weakness of understanding (in whatever the strength of that faculty may consist), or, which is much more commonly the case, it may arise from a want of a proper and well-directed exercise, which alone can make it strong and ready. Besides, that ignorance, inattention, prejudice, rashness, levity, obstinacy, in short, all those passions, and all those vices, which pervert the judgment in other matters, prejudice it no less in this its more refined and elegant province. These causes produce different opinions upon everything which is an object of the understanding, without inducing us to suppose that there are no settled principles of reason. And indeed, on the whole, one may observe, that there is rather less difference upon matters of taste among mankind, than upon most of those which depend upon the naked reason; and that men are far better agreed on the excellence of a description in Virgil, than on the truth or falsehood of a theory of Aristotle.

A rectitude of judgment in the arts, which may be called a good taste, does in a great measure depend upon sensibility; because if the mind

[1] J. T. Boulton disagrees, although he believes that Burke and Hume are in accord on 'fundamentals'. He thinks that Hume 'emphasizes the factors making for variety', Burke 'those making for uniformity of taste among all men'. Op. cit., xxix–xxx.

has no bent to the pleasures of the imagination, it will never apply itself sufficiently to works of that species to acquire a competent knowledge in them. But though a degree of sensibility is requisite to form a good judgment, yet a good judgment does not necessarily arise from a quick sensibility of pleasure. . . .[1]

The above passage shows that while Burke uses the pleasure–pain principle to explain why the senses and the imagination are affected in certain ways, his use of this principle becomes limited in the case of aesthetic *judgement*. A degree of sensibility to the pleasures of the imagination is a necessary but not a sufficient condition for a good judgement in aesthetics: 'But though a degree of sensibility is requisite to form a good judgment, yet a good judgment does not necessarily arise from a quick sensibility of pleasure. . . .' Reason forms a final and indispensable element in our judging a work of art. Reason in aesthetics, as in other areas, may be kept from arriving at the truth by inexperience, ignorance, inattention, prejudice, rashness, levity, obstinacy: 'in short all those passions, and all those vices, which pervert the judgment in other matters'. But this does not lead us to suppose that 'there are no settled principles of reason'.

Accordingly, I can see no reason to suppose that in the final analysis Burke viewed taste as 'a *subjective* imperative'. Indeed, Burke's entire treatment of taste points in the opposite direction, whether he is considering the taste of the senses, the imagination's taste for. . ., or that taste in which the senses, the imagination, and the judgement are joined. Indeed, where the *Inquiry* is frankly advisory rather than descriptive it urges that the standards of taste should be agreed upon by all men; this *could* be done not only because the principles of the senses and the imagination are the same in every man but also because the true (rational) standards of the arts are in every man's 'power' (within every man's capacity). Burke writes:

Before I leave this subject, I cannot help taking notice of an opinion which many persons entertain, as if the taste were a separate faculty of

[1] *Works* I, 96.

the mind, and distinct from the judgment and imagination; a species of instinct, by which we are struck naturally, and at the first glance, without any previous reasoning, with the excellence or the defects of a composition. So far as the imagination and the passions are concerned, I believe it true, that the reason is little consulted; but where disposition, where decorum, where congruity are concerned, in short wherever the best taste differs from the worst, I am convinced that the understanding operates and nothing else; and its operation is in reality far from being always sudden, or, when it is sudden, it is often far from being right.[1]

In brief, I believe Burke is trying to mark a distinction between what I have called 'taste of' and 'taste for' on the one hand and a truly aesthetic taste on the other by reference to the role that judgement and rational discrimination play in the latter. In the case of 'taste of' there is properly speaking no aesthetic element; in the case of 'taste for' (which is really a compound of the senses and the imagination) there could occur something that might be called an aesthetic experience; one could derive pleasure, I suppose, from attending the performance of a tragedy written by a dear friend, in part because one is predisposed in favour of tragedy (has a 'taste for' tragedy) as a dramatic form and in part because the production of this particular tragedy represents a personal triumph for our friend who may have laboured under the most adverse conditions to write it and have it produced. But a truly aesthetic judgement would, while taking account of such a pleasure, tend to discount it. And should the tragedy in question violate certain rules, for example, that we consider essential to tragedy properly conceived, then we are, if I read Burke correctly, under a kind of obligation, once we have arrived at such a judgement, to refrain from having an aesthetic experience when this tragedy is performed. An aesthetic experience in its *finest* sense would occur only when the senses, the imagination, and the judgement concur.

Another way of putting the above is that on Burke's view there are two levels of aesthetic experience, the cognitive and the non-cognitive. The cognitive level is reached

[1] *Works* I, 98.

when we go beyond the pleasures or pains of the senses and of the imagination and seek to evaluate the natural or artificial objects which have given rise to these reactions. It is on this level that aesthetic *judgement* enters; and, as we have seen, the understanding's role in this judgement shows that it is permissible to speak of Burke as a rationalist in aesthetics in much the same way as it is permissible to speak of him as a rationalist in politics. In both cases, however, this description must be qualified by an emphasis upon Burke's awareness of the limits of reason and of the importance of large areas of activity or experience which, while not in the vast majority of cases irrational, cannot be described as the deliberate product of man's conscious reason. In politics such areas belong to custom, habit, and prejudice which, although they usually exhibit a 'latent wisdom', do not exhibit conscious choice and rational planning. In aesthetics such areas belong to our non-cognitive or pre-cognitive experience of beauty and sublimity. Beauty, for instance, may appeal to our senses and our imagination and may arouse our passions independently of our judgement that this or that object is beautiful. Beauty, 'since it is no creature of our reason, since it strikes us without any reference to use, and even where no use at all can be discerned, since the order and method of nature is generally very different from our measures and proportions, we must conclude that beauty is, for the greater part, some quality in bodies acting mechanically upon the human mind by the intervention of the senses'.[1] This is important; but its importance is qualified by its obvious incompleteness, just as in the parallel case of what Burke says about the ways in which custom, habit, and prejudice determine our social and political behaviour the importance Burke attaches to these things is qualified by his acknowledgement that they and the behaviour they cause are subject to rational review, provided this review is properly carried out. In aesthetics this rational review is carried out

[1] Ibid., 191.

by the faculty of taste in which the influence of the passions is discounted and the analytic powers of man are in control. Aesthetic judgement like political judgement is, despite the sensuous materials with which it must deal, in the final analysis rational.[1]

While Burke's *Inquiry* appears largely consistent with his political philosophy, what does it contribute toward a clarification of his views on human nature as these views relate more to political philosophy than to aesthetic theory ? The answer lies, I believe, primarily in his treatment of the passions which I shall now discuss. First, however, Burke's treatment of the effect of words upon the passions should be noted. Eloquence and poetry can, according to Burke, affect the passions more than any other arts and often more than nature itself can. The reasons for this are threefold: (1) 'We take an extraordinary part in the passions of others, and . . . we are easily affected and brought into sympathy by any tokens which are shown of them; and there are no tokens which can express all the circumstances of most passions as fully as words. . . .' (2) There are many things of a very affecting nature which might seldom occur 'in the reality', meaning within our own experience (such as war, death, and famine); and there are many ideas which 'have never been at all presented to the senses of any men but by words' (God, angels, devils, heaven, and hell). Words representing such things and such ideas make a profound impression and have a great influence upon the passions. (3) By words 'we have it in our power to make such

---

[1] Canavan, op. cit., 40–41, argues that 'Burke's distinction between the principles by which the sublime and beautiful affect the passions and those by which order and proportion operate on the understanding is of considerable importance, because it shows that his aesthetic theory cannot be used to interpret his moral and political theory. . . . The theoretical principles elaborated in *The Sublime and Beautiful*, because they are the principles of taste and not of reason, cannot therefore furnish one with a guide to Burke's moral and political theory.' Canavan makes too much of the first distinction, I believe; and in his distinction between the principles of taste and those of reason, he has not noticed the crucial difference between 'principles' of taste and 'standards' of taste. In neither case has he attended to the part Burke assigns the understanding in his definition of taste.

combinations as we cannot possibly do otherwise' (Burke's examples: 'the angel of the Lord' and Milton's 'universe of death'). Burke's main point in discussing the power of words especially of what we might call emotive words is that 'We yield to sympathy what we refuse to description.' By 'the contagion of our passions, we catch a fire already kindled in another, which probably might never have been struck by the object described'.[1]

From the above the importance of sympathy and the 'extraordinary part' it enables us to take in the passions of others is evident; sympathy provides an important link between Burke's aesthetics and his political philosophy in that it is one of the mainsprings of human reactions regardless of whether they be in art or in politics. From the point of view of the history of ideas Burke's treatment of sympathy shows the influence of Hume's *Treatise*; taken together with his treatment of those passions which concern self-preservation it places Burke's *Inquiry* within the mainstream of empiricist psychology. So, too, does his use of the pleasure–pain principle to classify the passions into those which relate to self-preservation and those which relate to society.

Most of the ideas which can make a powerful impression on the mind, either of pleasure or pain or some modification of these, may, according to Burke, 'be reduced very nearly to these two heads, *self-preservation*, and *society*; to the ends of one or the other of which all our passions are calculated to answer'. The passions which concern self-preservation turn chiefly on pain or danger; and they are more powerful than those passions which relate to society:

Whatever is fitted to excite the ideas of pain and danger, that is to say, whatever is in any sort terrible, or is conversant about terrible objects, or operates in a manner analogous to terror, is a source of the *sublime*; that is, it is productive of the strongest emotion which the mind is capable of feeling. I say the strongest emotion, because I am satisfied that the ideas of pain are much more powerful than those which enter on the part of pleasure.[2]

[1] *Works*, I, 258–61.   [2] Ibid., 110.

Of the passions which belong to society there are those concerning the society of the sexes 'which answers the purpose of propagation' and those concerning 'that more general society, which we have with men and with other animals, and which we may in some sort be said to have even with the inanimate world'. The passions relating to generation have their origin in gratifications and pleasures 'of a lively character, rapturous and violent, and confessedly the highest pleasure of sense'. The passions relating to general society have their origin in pleasures also, but these pleasures are not so lively or violent:

Good company, lively conversations, and the endearments of friendship fill the mind with great pleasure; a temporary solitude, on the other hand, is itself agreeable. This may perhaps prove that we are creatures designed for contemplation as well as action; since solitude as well as society has its pleasures . . . [but] an entire life of solitude contradicts the purposes of our being, since death itself is scarcely an idea of more terror.[1]

The idea of beauty finds its origin in those passions which relate to society, in love, affection, sympathy, and tenderness.

The passions which Burke conceives of as social passions are, he admits, especially complicated and 'branch out into a variety of forms, agreeably to that variety of ends they are to serve in the great chain of society. The three principal links in this chain are *sympathy*, *imitation*, and *ambition*.' By the first of these passions we enter into the concerns of others and are prevented from being indifferent spectators of things that other men do or suffer: 'this passion may either partake of the nature of those which regard self-preservation, and turning upon pain may be a source of the sublime; or it may turn upon ideas of pleasure and society. . . .'[2] In general, however, sympathy, like imitation and ambition, is distinguished more by pleasure than by pain:

Whenever we are formed by nature to any active purpose, the passion which animates us to it is attended with delight, or a pleasure of some

[1] *Works*, I, 116.   [2] Ibid., 117.

kind, let the subject-matter be what it will; and as our Creator has designed that we should be united by the bond of sympathy, he has strengthened that bond by a proportionable delight; and there most where our sympathy is most wanted,—in the distresses of others. If this passion was simply painful, we would shun with the greatest care all persons and places that could excite such a passion; as some, who are so far gone in indolence as not to endure any strong impression, actually do. But the case is widely different with the greater part of mankind; there is no spectacle we so eagerly pursue, as that of some uncommon and grievous calamity; so that whether the misfortune is before our eyes, or whether they are turned back to it in history, it always touches with delight. This is not an unmixed delight, but blended with no small uneasiness. The delight we have in such things hinders us from shunning scenes of misery; and the pain we feel prompts us to relieve ourselves in relieving those who suffer; and all this antecedent to any reasoning, by an instinct that works us to its own purposes without our concurrence.[1]

Burke's characterization of the social passions of imitation and ambition also emphasizes the pleasures that attend both imitation and that ambition which leads us to cease imitating other men and to try to surpass them. 'It is by imitation far more than by precept that we learn [almost] everything; and what we learn thus, we acquire not only more effectually, but more pleasantly. This forms our manners, our opinions, our lives. It is one of the strongest links of society; it is a species of mutual compliance, which all men yield to each other, without constraint to themselves, and which is extremely flattering to all.'[2] The passion of ambition has its pleasant aspects: for example, to think of excelling other men and of the distinction that excellence may bring is exceedingly pleasant.

In the cases of sympathy, imitation, and ambition Burke emphasizes the naturalness of these passions and the fact that their operation is antecedent to and largely independent of the operations of our 'reasoning faculty'. The same point is made concerning the passions that belong to self-preservation. The great power of the sublime, a power much greater, according to Burke, than any possessed by beauty, derives in large part from the fact that 'it anticipates

[1] Ibid., 119.   [2] Ibid., 122.

our reasonings, and hurries us on by an irresistible force':

The passion caused by the great and sublime in *nature*, when those causes operate most powerfully, is astonishment: and astonishment is that state of the soul in which all its motions are suspended, with some degree of horror. In this case the mind is so entirely filled with its object, that it cannot entertain any other, nor by consequence reason on that object which employs it. Hence arises the great power of the sublime, that, far from being produced by them, it anticipates our reasonings, and hurries us on by an irresistible force. Astonishment, as I have said, is the effect of the sublime in its highest degree; the inferior effects are admiration, reverence, and respect.[1]

Burke's account of the origins of the sublime and the beautiful, his sharp distinction between the sublime and the beautiful, and especially his characterization of beautiful objects (as small, smooth, and delicate) has struck many readers of the *Inquiry* from the eighteenth century to the present as an unconvincing *tour de force*. But these aspects of the *Inquiry* if they fail ultimately in the realm of aesthetics serve to instruct the student of Burke's political philosophy in a number of ways. Chiefly, it must be admitted, this is done through an addition of details to our knowledge of his views on the passions. Even if Burke had not written the *Inquiry* much of what we have given above is stated in or can be inferred from the political writings. One partial exception to this occurs, however, in Burke's treatment of those passions that attend the sublime and are concerned with self-preservation. In none of his other works is there so great an emphasis upon self-preservation or so sharp a contrast between the passions of self-preservation and those of society.

To draw the whole of what has been said into a few distinct points:—The passions which belong to self-preservation turn on pain and danger; they are simply painful when their causes immediately affect us; they are delightful when we have an idea of pain and danger, without being actually in such circumstances; this delight I have not called pleasure, because it turns on pain, and because it is different enough from any idea of positive

[1] *Works*, I, 130

pleasure. Whatever excites this delight, I call sublime. The passions belonging to self-preservation are the strongest of all the passions.[1]

Besides those things which either directly suggest the idea of danger or those which produce a similar effect from a mechanical cause, Burke affirms that he knows of 'nothing sublime, which is not some modification of power'. At first, it might seem that the idea of power could equally belong to pain or to pleasure, but in reality this is not so. If we remember that the idea of pain in its highest degree is much stronger than the highest degree of pleasure and that this is true through 'all the subordinate gradations', then we can see that 'where the chances for equal degrees of suffering or enjoyment are in any sort equal, the idea of suffering must always be prevalent'. Pleasure often 'follows the will', and no great efforts of power are necessary for its enjoyment: 'But pain is always inflicted by a power in some way superior, because we never submit to pain willingly.' Power is generally accompanied by terror at the pain it might inflict.[2]

Burke does not discuss *political* power in the *Inquiry*, but I find Burke's general discussion of power illuminating from the political point of view. It helps to explain why Burke seldom sees the power of government as being an indifferent instrument capable of good or bad use but often tends to see rather its terrible aspects: its actual or potential dangers to human life, liberty, and property. Government can arouse the strongest passions in a man not when it promises to better society but when it threatens his life. Thus the strength of government, like the strength of the horse Burke discusses in the *Inquiry*, may come under two descriptions: it can be socially useful and can occasion feelings of pleasure, but it can be a creature of destruction capable of giving more pain than it could ever give pleasure. The energies of government must, therefore, be held in check and used with restraint; and the users of such energies must respect and even fear their power.

[1] Ibid., 125.   [2] Ibid., 138–139.

The distinction between the passions associated with the sublime and those associated with beauty is also applied by Burke to the virtues:

Those virtues which cause admiration, and are of the sublimer kind, produce terror rather than love; such as fortitude, justice, wisdom, and the like. Never was any man amiable by force of these qualities. Those which engage our hearts, which impress us with a sense of loveliness, are the softer virtues; easiness of temper, compassion, kindness, and liberality; though certainly those latter are of less immediate and momentous concern to society, and of less dignity. But it is for that reason that they are so amiable. The great virtues turn principally on dangers, punishments, and troubles, and are exercised, rather in preventing the worst mischiefs, than in dispensing favors; and are therefore not lovely, though highly venerable. The subordinate turn on reliefs, gratifications, and indulgences; and are therefore more lovely, though inferior in dignity. Those persons who creep into the hearts of most people, who are chosen as the companions of their softer hours, and their reliefs from care and anxiety, are never persons of shining qualities or strong virtues. It is rather the soft green of the soul on which we rest our eyes, that are fatigued with beholding more glaring objects.[1]

The above remarks are made in Section X of Part III of the *Inquiry*. In Section XI Burke states that from Section X we may 'easily see how far the application of beauty to virtue may be made with propriety' and then proceeds to warn against affixing the name of beauty to virtue, proportion, congruity, and perfection as a 'loose and inaccurate manner of speaking' that 'misled us both in the theory of taste and of morals; and induced us to remove the science of our duties from their proper basis (our reason, our relations, and our necessities). . . .'[2] Burke does not explain how this manner of speaking has led to such results; and, in any event, the fact remains that he has himself found it illuminating to arrange virtues in terms of beauty and sublimity.

This arrangement is of considerable relevance to Burke's politics. It helps to explain why in his political practices and theoretical exercises he chose to exalt wisdom and justice over reliefs, gratifications, and indulgences. Political wisdom and justice involve, Burke thought, matters of life

[1] *Works*, I, 188–9.　　　[2] Ibid., 190.

and death and are therefore of ultimate concern in a way that easiness of temper, compassion, kindness, and liberality are not. It is well known that Burke's conception of justice bears practically no relation to those considerations of compassion, kindness, and liberality which, while they do not account for the content of what we now call 'social justice' (as the critics of social justice often allege), at least help to explain the feelings that 'social justice' often arouses in us. One reason why Burke's conception of justice is so restricted is his conviction, evinced in his *Inquiry*, that one can make a sharp separation of virtues in terms of their reference to the passions of society and to those of self-preservation, that the passions of society are less intense than the passions concerned with self-preservation, and that the loss of the pleasures associated with the social passions is of less importance than the experience of the pains, dangers, or fears that the prospect of the loss of life itself involves. The power of government, while it can, usually by indirect means, gratify some of the social passions, cannot and should not be expected to gratify them all. Political wisdom and justice require a restriction of the direct use of such powers insofar as possible to a preservation of life and of those conditions in which life can flourish: a maintenance of law and order, equality before the law, and those (unequal) arrangements of property sanctioned by time and custom. The power of government is the potential cause of so much pain and even death that to use it freely as an instrument of benevolence and compassion is to invite people to misconstrue its fundamental nature and to neglect the dangers that constantly attend it even in the best regulated of societies.

The chief difference between Burke's aesthetics and his political philosophy is that while it is correct to say that Burke preferred 'on grounds of intensity the sublime to the beautiful' in art,[1] he greatly feared and respected, on grounds of intensity, the sublime in society and politics.

[1] Boulton, op. cit., xi.

PART THREE

BURKE ON NATURAL RIGHTS

AN INTRODUCTION

IF we grant the comparatively new interpretation of Burke as a champion of natural law—and the purpose of Part One of this study was to show as clearly as possible why it appears to be for the most part a valid interpretation—then we are left with two important problems on our hands. The first problem is this: a champion of the natural law is one who insists upon judging positive law, social habit, and custom from the perspective of natural law, while Burke at times gives the impression that he is alarmingly lax or indifferent especially in cases where it is English law, habit, and custom that are to be judged. A natural law theorist would not praise prejudice at the expense of reason, but Burke appears occasionally to do this. In Part Two I have tried to show that Burke really preferred the natural law to prejudice and would in the final analysis accept only what he called *just* prejudice, i.e., a prejudice which is in accord with the natural law. Burke for all his deference to prejudice and his criticisms of what he calls 'private reason' is ultimately willing to pass judgement on prejudice in terms of the criteria of the natural law as he understands it. I have also tried in Part Two to suggest that Burke's treatise on aesthetics does not neglect the role of reason in the formation of our aesthetic judgements and that nothing he says there about the senses, the imagination, or the passions rules out the possibility of man's being able to discover the principles of natural law by the use of reason. I submit that Burke in discussing prejudice, positive law, habit, and custom is not suggesting an alternative or an antithesis to natural law or reason. Rather he is proposing that an advocate of natural law look at prejudice, positive law, habit, and custom with initial sympathy as a means of eliciting from them their 'latent wisdom'. If, however, one cannot find any wisdom in these things even after a careful, sympathetic analysis and if one decides that they run counter to the natural law, one must pronounce them morally bad and in cases where the situation is sufficiently serious and circumstances permit one should resist such prejudices, laws, habits, and customs regardless of how firmly entrenched they may be.

In Part Three I shall consider in some detail the second major problem confronting the natural law interpretation of Burke, namely that of his position on natural rights (see the concluding pages of Part One). I shall undertake to answer these questions: Did Burke believe in natural rights? Did he believe in historic rights?* If he believed in both, which did he regard as more essential and in the event of a clash between natural and historic rights which would he defend? If he believed in natural rights, why did he disapprove of speculation about such rights? Why did he criticize the 'Rights of Man'? Problems which I shall refer to but shall *not* discuss in their own right after I have finished these introductory remarks involve the, in my opinion, somewhat tired question of Burke on the social contract and the still largely unexplored question of Burke on the right of revolution. The reasons for this neglect are threefold: (1) I cannot in one essay discuss

---

* By 'historic rights' I mean any rights or privileges which one has *exercised* over a long (but unspecified) period of time. My use of historic rights corresponds in this respect with Ernest Barker's in that passage where he remarks that Burke 'championed the American colonists because he believed that they were standing for historic rights. . . . He equally championed the monarchy, the nobility, and the Church of France because he believed that they had historic rights. . . .' (*Essays on Government*, 212.) But, for reasons that I shall try to make clear, I cannot accept Barker's interpretation of historic rights as excluding and being opposed to natural rights in Burke's thought.

everything that bears on the question of Burke on natural rights, (2) what Burke has to say about the social contract is often obscure and especially unsystematic and as a result the exact status of the right of revolution, whether it is legal or moral or both, is quite complicated, and (3) the questions of whether a political philosopher believes there was a social contract and whether, as a result, he believes there is a legal right of revolution are logically separate from the larger and logically prior question of whether man has any rights that belong to him *qua* man. (I shall have more to say about (3) shortly.)

While there is no clear-cut division of opinion among commentators on the questions of Burke on natural rights, the social contract, and the right of revolution, certain general lines of division may be noted. An old and still influential interpretation of Burke holds that he did not really believe in natural rights or that at least the *mature* Burke did not, that his essential commitment was to historic rights and especially to the historic rights of Englishmen, that the social contract played either a vague part in Burke's thought or no part at all, and that in Burke's eyes the right of revolution is largely or wholly irrelevant from both the moral and the legal point of view.[1] Another line of interpretation holds that while Burke did believe in natural rights, his chief concern was in upholding the historic rights of Englishmen, that while he 'expanded' considerably the language of the social contract he remained loyal to the basic insight of contract theory, namely that government is somehow accountable to its subjects for its conduct and that ultimately it depends for its survival upon their consent, and that while opposed in general to revolutions he still held, as a Whig and an heir to the Revolution

[1] See Ernest Barker, *Essays on Government*, 211–12, 218–21; Alfred Cobban, op. cit., 44–45, 49–53; W. A. Dunning, *A History of Political Theories from Rousseau to Spencer* (New York, 1920), 182–3; F. J. C. Hearnshaw, *The Social and Political Ideas of Some Representative Thinkers of the Revolutionary Era* (London, 1931), 92–93; J. G. A. Pocock, op. cit.; Arthur K. Rogers, 'Burke's Social Philosophy', *American Journal of Sociology*, XVIII (July 1912), 52, 68; C. E. Vaughan, op. cit., 53–54 (but see 16–19).

of 1688–9, to the belief that a revolution is sometimes justifiable.[1]

I wish here to indicate briefly the general lines that my interpretation of Burke on natural rights will follow, and in so doing I will in passing say some things which I believe hold true of Burke on the social contract and the right of revolution but which I shall *not* attempt to *establish* as true in the present study and which I consider helpful but not essential to an understanding of what I shall say later in Part Three. As I indicated in Part One, a significant part of what it means to have a theory of natural law is that such a theory allows at least implicitly for both natural duties and natural rights. If a person has a theory of natural duties but not of natural rights (as Burke is sometimes alleged to have) or if a person has a theory of natural rights but not of natural duties (as Hobbes, Locke, and the French Revolutionists are sometimes alleged to have), then that person, in my opinion, does not have a natural law theory regardless of what he or anyone else may say; this may seem a harsh and unduly restrictive opinion unless attention is given to my qualification 'at least implicitly'. What is meant by the notion of a natural law theory's implicit allowance for natural rights or natural duties can perhaps be seen in the following examples. (1) Aquinas can be said to allow implicitly for natural rights. Although in his discussion of natural law he speaks of duty and not of right, his overall picture of man as a creature uniquely favoured by God and possessed both as a species and as an individual of great moral worth (even if this worth is often ignored or undeveloped by man) indicates that there are elements in Aquinas's philosophy from which a conception of natural rights can be derived (as Maritain, for example, does). (2) Hobbes speaks of natural rights but not of natural duties. His psychological egoism seems to

---

[1] Elements of this composite picture are to be found in MacCunn, op. cit., 191–213, Charles Parkin, *The Moral Basis of Burke's Political Thought* (Cambridge, 1956), 10–11, 20, 22–26, and to a lesser extent in R. R. Fennessy, op. cit., 73–75, 91, 111.

some commentators to make it (logically) impossible for a Hobbesian to speak of natural duties, even the natural duty of the subject to obey the sovereign. But if one takes seriously what Hobbes says about '*in foro interno*', then it may be possible after all to say that to the extent that conscience is at all operative in Hobbes's philosophy, then to that extent it makes sense for a Hobbesian to speak of natural duties as well as natural rights and that indeed the preservation or continuance of a subject's loyalty to his sovereign in some cases seems to require something like the notion of a natural duty. While I am satisfied with the above reading of Aquinas, I am much less satisfied with the above reading of Hobbes largely on the rather standard ground of not being able to see how a truly moral (as distinct from a merely prudential) theory of duties (or of rights) is compatible with psychological egoism. But my point is that whenever one has ground for suspecting that a given theory not only fails to make even an implicit allowance either for natural duties or for natural rights but appears to be incompatible with one of these, then one has reason to doubt whether the theory in question is a natural law theory after all. In the case of Burke, if it could be shown that he not only failed to hold a theory of natural rights but that what he says about natural duties is under close analysis logically incompatible with a belief in natural rights, then this would show that he was not a natural law theorist.

The importance of the questions I shall consider is now evident. If in crucial cases Burke opted for historic rights as against natural rights, then all his remarks about the eternal laws of justice, &c. are not sufficient to establish conclusively his belief in the natural law. On the other hand, the significance of the much-discussed question of Burke on the social contract and its relevance to the natural law (and natural rights) reading of Burke are much less evident. For obviously one can hold to a theory of natural rights without believing that there ever was either a

pre-civil or a pre-social state of nature or that either
society or civil society owes its existence to a social contract.
Yet in the terms of the political dialogue of Burke's age,
advocates of natural rights still sometimes employed the
state of nature and the social contract as means of explaining (heuristically and sometimes historically as well) how
man could in civil society still be said to possess and to be
entitled to exercise some at least of his 'natural' rights.
There is, of course, an ambiguity about the words 'nature'
and 'natural' as found in 'rights of nature' or 'natural
rights'. They may refer to rights actually possessed and
exercised at a given time when man lived in either a pre-
social or a pre-civil condition or both or to rights which it
is, from the moral point of view, illuminating to imagine
they would have possessed and exercised had there ever
been such a state of nature; but such words as 'nature' and
'natural' may also refer to rights possessed by man *qua*
man (as distinct from man *qua* Englishman) and as such
they need not be related logically to any historic condition
or conditions, i.e., there is no logical reason why man
should have *exercised* these rights at *any* time, for the point
is that he has *possessed* them at all times simply by virtue
of being a man. That he may have exercised them most
fully either in the state of nature or for that matter in the
England of Burke's day is irrelevant. Yet given the uses
made of the state of nature and the social contract, especially in the period from Locke to the time of the French
Revolution, it is significant that Burke, while he appears to
sense the logical irrelevance of the state of nature to the
questions of duty and right, still speaks of the social
contract affirmatively and still believes that it is of some
relevance to the consideration of both duty and right (and
not merely duty as is sometimes alleged). It is occasionally
suggested that Burke's conception of duty and right follows
logically from his conception of human nature conjoined
with the principles of justice and utility and that Burke's
treatment of the themes of mutual dependence and of

natural subordination makes mention of the social contract logically superfluous where the grounding of rights and duties is concerned. This is probably true, but it ignores the relevance of Burke's judgement that the politician (and, I presume, the political philosopher) should follow a pattern of reasoning different from that of the metaphysician and of the geometrician who proceed by a process of abstraction, of abstracting out, in the case of a geometrical example, circumstances such as the colour of a square. The politician, Burke says, must take account of *all* the circumstances. In the present case, this would mean that besides man's social inclinations one must take account of the social contract, or in modern language, the social contract serves to reinforce what from the strictly logical point of view can be discovered independently of it.*

Burke sometimes referred to questions concerning the definition and demarcation of natural rights with contempt as metaphysical questions. Yet, as I have suggested earlier, he does not always make the distinction between metaphysics and mathematics on the one hand and morals and politics on the other as sharply as some commentators have supposed (he even says that in politics we perform operations that might be spoken of as moral computations or subtractions). The suggestion that to Burke consideration of natural rights belong to metaphysics, that consideration of historic rights belongs to morals and politics,

---

* That famous passage in which Burke writes that 'Society is, indeed a contract' but one which cannot be dissolved at pleasure and is 'but a clause in the great primeval contract of eternal society' (*Reflections on the Revolution in France, Works*, III, 359) has been much criticized by a long line of scholars from Vaughan to Sabine who find it confused, vague, or metaphorical, and in any case a distortion of contract theory. Certainly it does neglect the idea of express consent and does frown upon the idea that the social contract may easily be dissolved, but as a somewhat poetic expression of the doctrine of *tacit* consent and of a tacit contract which it is *rational* for each succeeding generation to reaffirm it seems fairly intelligible. I think that the social contract is largely but not wholly a *tacit* contract in Burke's opinion, much as it was in that of Lord Rockingham. 'I wish to find a consent, and acquiescence in the *governed*, and I choose therefore to have recourse to what I think an original *tacit compact*. . . .' Lord Rockingham quoted by G. H. Guttridge, *English Whiggism and the American Revolution* (Berkeley, 1942), 74.

and that, therefore, natural rights are from the moral and political point of view irrelevant seems to me mistaken. Burke's major point, and certainly he is novel here in his emphasis at least, is rather that we cannot from the moral and political point of view speak of natural rights without speaking also of historic rights. Historic rights are part of the circumstances that we cannot afford to lose sight of without oversimplifying our picture both of these rights and of the men who possess them.

It is neither the ignoring of historic rights nor the contrasting of these rights with natural rights to the dis-advantage of natural rights that marks Burke's version of the natural law. *We can in discussing rights and duties no more ignore or dismiss historic rights than we can in the discussion of knowledge ignore prejudice which may and usually does exhibit a 'latent wisdom' of its own. And for the same kind of reason: historic rights, if examined with any sympathy and insight, may turn out to be expressions of natural rights, in many cases quite adequate expressions.* Burke's dislike of definitions in the moral and political realms, while it is one of the most irksome features of his thought, has its rationale. It reflects his fear of pre-mature, oversimplified definitions which have the effect of making our distinctions too sharp. Although Burke's age is largely pre-sociological in its interests, the following example is not un-Burkian: Burke is keenly aware of distinctions between social classes in manners, in economic functions, and in political competence. Yet he does not offer defini-tions of the various classes (whether he would even have called them classes seems immaterial). One reason for not doing this may be his fear of the partial and pre-mature definition which in emphasizing obvious differences in manners, functions, and competence ignores significant similarities among classes such as a common nationality and common economic and political interests. In the case of natural and historic rights Burke's reluctance to define these rights, especially natural rights, is traceable in part to his reluctance to contribute to a situation in which the comparing and contrasting of such rights might sharpen in our minds their distinctions and minimize their resemblances. Burke is often described as a mystical thinker; yet his celebrated sense of mystery and his emphasis upon the unity of classes in a nation, of nations in mankind, and of mankind in a special relationship with God, are in some small part at least a reflection of his fear that the definitions offered by reason are often so incomplete and so divisive in morals and politics that it would often be better were they never attempted: 'Metaphysics cannot live without definition; but Prudence is cautious how she defines.'[1] Rather than do the hard and sometimes, he thinks, harmful job of analysis and definition Burke sometimes does no work at all.

Burke's contribution to the natural law tradition is that he brings into focus the questions, 'Might not historic rights be in some important cases natural rights as well ?' and, 'Is it not wise, therefore, to look for resemblances as well as differences, to search out cases where the two coincide instead of always approaching civil institutions and practices with a general suspicion that might in fact be as mistaken as the general scepticism of those rationalists who are determined to doubt everything until it passes *their* tests of reasonableness ?' Still, however valuable these questions might be to the natural law, the problem must remain of what to do about hard cases where *after* a Burkian analysis has been made historic rights still appear nil or unsatisfactory from the perspective of natural law. After all, as critics have complained, the historic rights of Englishmen in the eighteenth century are a small and unrepresentative class of historic rights for the men of that age, and however they stand out in terms of the eighteenth century they now scarcely seem an adequate approximation to the natural rights of man. So what difference does Burke's doctrine of historic rights

---

[1] *An Appeal from the New to the Old Whigs, Works,* IV, 81.

make in the final analysis ? If it means that in no case at all may a man turn his back upon his (perhaps meagre) historic rights and make what Locke called an 'appeal to heaven' in the name of natural rights, that a revolution is *never* to be justified in terms of natural rights, then Burke's deference to natural rights and natural law would be strangely ineffective and inconsequential. More specifically, his relation to the Whig heritage would appear odd : he would be willing to profit from the Settlement brought about by the Revolution of 1688–9 while being opposed in principle to there ever being any revolution at all. But if it turns out that Burke does in some cases recognize the right of revolution as being at least a *moral* right regardless of whether it is legally permissible, then what becomes of Burke's doctrine of historic rights ?

Stated summarily, here is Burke's dilemma : if he believes in historic rights but not natural rights he is no natural law theorist. If he believes in natural rights but not the right of revolution he is an ineffectual natural law theorist. If he believes in both natural and historic rights but concedes that natural rights are more fundamental and more rationally defensible, and if he concedes that in *some* cases the realization of *some* natural rights can and should be achieved by a revolutionary turning of one's back upon woefully inadequate or non-existent historic rights, then what is the philosophical significance, if any, of his doctrine of historic rights ?

HISTORIC RIGHTS AND NATURAL RIGHTS

THERE are two versions of the thesis that Burke or at least the mature Burke did not believe in natural rights. The first version is that this is true without qualification; and the second version is that this is true *in effect*, that while Burke sometimes showed a measure of respect for some 'natural rights' his more basic sympathy for historic rights and his deference to the principle of utility were, in the final analysis, incompatible with the natural rights philosophy and that if Burke had been more logical he would have recognized this more clearly than he did. The first version seems to me to proceed without taking account of the total evidence; the second version because it does attempt to do justice to the complexity of Burke's unsystematic and scattered remarks on rights seems more subtle, and I shall consider it at greater length in this chapter. While both versions of this thesis eventually turn out to be, in my opinion, mistaken, both deserve consideration as they call attention to vital aspects of Burke's reflections on rights. Both versions of the thesis that Burke did not believe in natural rights rest chiefly upon three considerations: (1) Burke's reluctance to discuss and to define those rights which belong to man *qua* man, (2) Burke's belief that the discussion and definition of such rights might contribute to social disorder and in some cases to the destruction of society, and (3) Burke's willingness and even eagerness to discuss those historic rights which belong to man *qua* citizen of a particular political community.

Burke's reluctance to discuss and to define those rights which belong to man *qua* man is perhaps most evident in his *Reflections on the Revolution in France*, but it would be erroneous to regard this reluctance as being simply a reaction against the French Revolution and its proclamation of the Rights of Man. Indeed, Burke's reluctance to discuss the rights of man can be seen as part of an overall reluctance to discuss rights of any sort, whether of the individual or of that division (geographic or social) of society to which he belongs. This overall reluctance was especially pronounced during the time of England's difficulty with her American colonies. Burke's reluctance to discuss the question of the respective rights of the home government and those of the colonies may have been, as political historians usually regard it, an unconvincing piece of political fence-straddling—after all, Burke's own party had been responsible for the Declaratory Act which asserted the right of the British government to make laws and statutes 'of sufficient force and validity to bind the colonies in all cases whatsoever'.[1] The desire of Burke and his friends to placate the colonies was hamstrung by a desire to acknowledge the 'rights' of both the home government and the colonial governments at a time when most people were becoming convinced that the 'rights' of both parties to the dispute could not *all* be acknowledged, that there was in short a real conflict between the rights claimed by the two sides. Burke's proposed solution to this problem said in effect 'Let us stop talking about rights and talk about expediency (in the sense of what can we do for the common good of both parties)'. What distinguished Burke from lesser politicians was that even when fences had to be straddled he sought to justify this action in terms of principle. If Burke was unwilling to discuss the rights of the home government and of the colonies, this was, he assured his listeners, due to an overall reluctance to discuss the question of rights (and not due to any difficulty that

---

[1] A quotation from the Declaratory Act in Samuel Eliot Morison and Henry Steele Commager, *The Growth of the American Republic* (New York, 1956), I, 153.

the Rockingham Whigs had got themselves into). In his *Speech on American Taxation*, 19 April, 1774, Burke argued:

Again, and again, revert to your old principles,—seek peace and ensue it,—leave America, if she has taxable matter in her, to tax herself. *I am not here going into the distinctions of rights, nor attempting to mark their boundaries. I do not enter into these metaphysical distinctions; I hate the very sound of them. Leave the Americans as they anciently stood, and these distinctions, born of our unhappy contest, will die along with it.* They and we, and their and our ancestors, have been happy under that system. Let the memory of all actions in contradiction to that good old mode, on both sides, be extinguished forever. Be content to bind America by laws of trade: you have always done it. Let this be your reason for binding their trade. Do not burden them by taxes: you were not used to do so from the beginning. Let this be your reason for not taxing. These are the arguments of states and kingdoms. Leave the rest to the schools; for there only they may be discussed with safety. But if, intemperately, unwisely, fatally, you sophisticate and poison the very source of government, by urging subtle deductions, and consequences odious to those you govern, from the unlimited and illimitable nature of supreme sovereignty, you will teach them by these means to call that sovereignty itself in question. When you drive him hard, the boar will surely turn upon the hunters. If that sovereignty and their freedom cannot be reconciled, which will they take? They will cast your sovereignty in your face. Nobody will be argued into slavery. . . .

I look, I say, on the imperial rights of Great Britain, and the privileges which the colonies ought to enjoy under these rights, to be just the most reconcilable things in the world.[1]

With the above passage in mind we can construct the following argument which Burke consistently applied to controversies about rights, whether of the American colonies, of Ireland, of India, or of man *qua* man. First, attempts to define rights, to mark their boundaries, are 'metaphysical', meaning here in part that it is a deductive exercise which can be safely done only in an academic atmosphere. In the practice of politics such deductions may 'poison the very source of government', i.e., may alienate the governed from the government upon which they depend for that peace and stability without which

[1] *Works*, II, 72–75. My italics.

'happiness' is impossible. Second, when conflicts over rights do erupt in politics, a logical analysis of the claims involved may only harden the divisions among the opposed parties. The more rights are analysed, the more 'subtle deductions' are drawn, the more important the question of rights becomes. In principle you may reach an impasse that in practice could be avoided. (This is especially likely in view of man's general weaknesses in the speculative realm, Burke thinks.) How to avoid such an impasse ? By attending to past practices. Leave the Americans (also the English, the Irish, the people of India, and the French) 'as they anciently stood'. The criteria provided by 'ancient' systems will not, of course, be the same in all cases; indeed, Burke's overall thesis is that allowance must be made for differing historical circumstances and that attending to historic rights is the best way of doing this. Third, it is the duty of the statesman to reconcile opposing parties, to seek peace while preserving unity. To do this, he must divert attention from those questions that agitate and divide men and he must emphasize unifying factors. If men are divided over questions of rights, the statesman should persuade them to look away from present controversies: (a) to a 'happier' past when such issues did not excite them, and (b) to the miserable future that awaits them if they continue to ignore the consequences of their present differences. (Sometimes this puts the statesman in an embarrassing position: certainly Burke could not have honestly believed by 1774 that the 'rights' of the home government and the 'privileges' of the colonies were 'just the most reconcilable things in the world'—his careful locution of 'privileges which the colonists ought to enjoy under these rights' reflects the strain of the controversy, and he himself often speaks simply of the 'rights' of the colonists. But such an embarrassment is apparently worth the price in Burke's opinion. The statesman is obliged to act *as if* controversies over rights were 'just the most reconcilable things in the world' in the hope that his example and his influence will persuade the disputants that their controversies can be resolved peacefully.)

Besides showing a tendency to exaggerate the credulity of disputants who might often be presumed to know that their differences just are not the most reconcilable things in the world, Burke's argument places a considerable burden upon both the (relatively) happy past and the unhappy future which the disputants are invited to inspect. If things were so good 'as they anciently stood', why the present discontent and divisions ? Burke's answer is often in terms of a conspiracy on the part of a few either in power or in quest of power. Sometimes the conspirators are clever (as with the Jacobins in France); sometimes they are stupid and short-sighted (as with the Protestant Ascendency in Ireland); usually they are primarily avaricious (as with the English adventurers in India); but conspiracy of some sort seems essential to Burke's system as an explanation of how we have got from past order to present chaos.* Without the conspiracy hypothesis the historical systems, arrangements, and practices endorsed by Burke might themselves come under question and might eventually lose their relevance as criteria for evaluating and resolving present difficulties; at any rate, it is difficult to see exactly how the *source* of our present difficulties might provide criteria for their solution. As for the future Burke seems to assume that he knows (and that the disputants can learn) the consequences of their continuing to disagree and that moreover these consequences will be bad for *all* the parties concerned. Perhaps this follows from Burke's conception of society as being in some respects like an organism, but it certainly does not follow, as Burke appears to believe, that all or most parts of society will be hurt equally.

* The behaviour of the British government toward the American colonies is not explained by Burke as a conspiracy but as a combination of ambition and stupidity. North and others have not, Burke thinks, conspired illegally. The powers of taxation are rightly theirs, but on Burke's analysis there is a sense in which they have conspired against the historical privileges of the colonies to tax themselves as well as against the dictates of prudence which warn men not to seek to exercise every right they possess regardless of circumstance.

Moreover, Burke's general position, one which he urges constantly against reformers and radicals, is that there is often a considerable gap in politics between intention and expectation on the one hand and the results or consequences that flow from our actions on the other. Certainly this argument might reasonably be applied against Burke's own thesis that serious disputes if allowed to continue unimpeded will lead to civil war or revolution within a country or empire and that this civil war or revolution will be a disaster for the country or empire in question. Even if this be true, even if the opposing party or faction does not simply capitulate before the force of argument and/or numbers, can the probable course of civil war or revolution be gauged as accurately as Burke seems to assume ? If a right is as Burke says an advantage (meaning, I think, that a right confers an advantage) and a claim to a right is a claim to an advantage or advantages, might not a struggle over rights result from the belief that it is to one's advantage to struggle and even to fight if necessary for one's rights ? Is this not a perfectly rational belief in some cases ? Does it not sometimes turn out to be a correct estimate of the situation ? Either the American colonists or the home government stood to benefit in the event that their respective side won either the dispute between the two parties or the armed conflict that broke out when the dispute could not be resolved peacefully: if the colonists won they would gain a greater degree of independence or, as it turned out, total independence from the home government; if the home government won, the imperial structure might have been tightened considerably and revenues increased. Burke seems almost indifferent to this kind of approach; in his eyes disputes and especially actual conflicts over rights appear often as the result of inflamed passions (often deliberately inflamed by a few who believe that they stand to gain or to increase their power by such tactics) and not as the result of a rational assessment of what one's rights are or a rational calculation of the probability of securing these rights by a struggle. While this Hobbes-like fear of civil war and revolution is typical of Burke, it is not, however, the whole of Burke; while it reflects Burke's usual emphasis, it is not a comprehensive picture of Burke on rights. When others of Burke's arguments are considered at least some of that initial appearance of oddness in Burke's views which I have tried to point out in this paragraph will be qualified considerably.

Because of the frequent charges of insincerity made against Burke's political reflections it is especially helpful when we can find in his pre-political writings foreshadowings of principles or methods of approach which he would follow afterwards. In his *Notebook* there is a piece called 'A Plan for Arguing' which has usually been ignored but which is quite important because it presents in outline form the questions that Burke *always* considered to be the right questions to ask about 'right' and 'rights'. Burke begins by dividing arguments into three kinds: those used to convince us of some 'natural truth', those used to convince us of 'some Matter of fact', and those used 'to persuade us to do something'. Arguments of the first kind are to be taken from 'the Investigation of its Properties and the Analogy they bear to each other'; Burke says nothing more concerning this kind of argument. The 'credibility' of matters of fact is decided, Burke says, in six ways: (1) by its 'Probability with Regard to General Experience', (2) by 'its Agreement with the particular circumstances of time, place, manners, Customs etc.', (3) by the 'Credit of the Relator' (his 'impartiality', his 'consistency' with himself, and his 'consistency' with others), (4) on his being a 'Competent Judge of the Matter of fact', (5) on his having sufficient means of being informed, and (6) on his being credulous or incredulous. Burke's main interest in his 'Plan for Arguing' lies, however, with those arguments that persuade us to do something. Such arguments are taken from (1) 'Justice', (2) 'Interest', or (3) 'Affection'. Burke has very little to say about Arguments taken from Interest or Affection and much of what he does say about Arguments from Interest reappears in what he says later about 'Convenience'. Arguments from Interest are, he says, 'very extensive' as they consist in a wide variety of Relations and Circumstances; he considers them briefly in terms of a division between 'present advantages' and 'Consequences'. Arguments from 'Affection' he divides into those drawn from 'the passions, or from Authority'. He does little or nothing to justify or even to explain these divisions, and for present purposes we may safely ignore them.

It is only in Burke's treatment of Arguments drawn from Justice that the relevance of this brief outline to our present inquiry becomes apparent. Here, Burke tells us, four considerations are to be taken into account: (1) Does it 'suit' the 'Law of God'? (2) Does it suit 'the general Notion of Virtue'? (3) Does it suit the 'Laws of the land'? and (4) Does it suit the 'Law of Opinion'? While this fragment bears no date (the editor of the *Notebook* places it between 1750 when Burke arrived in England to study law and 1756) it shows in its consideration of the 'Laws of the land' and elsewhere probable traces of Burke's legal studies. (Of even greater overall significance perhaps is Burke's inclusion of the 'Law of Opinion' as being relevant to Arguments from Justice. Of course, it might be argued that Burke is more concerned in this context with the pragmatic than with the logical or the epistemic dimensions of argument; however, Burke's mention of both the 'Law of Opinion' and 'the general Notion of Virtue' points in the direction of his later concern with general opinion as a kind of ultimate datum in morality, a topic discussed in Part Two above.) Burke invites us to pass over whatever regards 'Speculation' and to consider those things which belong to 'Civil Life' where the 'Deliberative' approach holds sway. What questions, he asks, would it be appropriate to take into account when considering 'whether certain things are fit to be done or forborne upon the

Principles of Justice on the one hand—and of Convenience on the other ?' He gives the following answer:

On the head of Justice it is fit to ask—
Whether, the thing is capable of Right, viz Propriety.
Who has the right ? how it is capable of right ?
Whence has he it ?
What are its Limits ?
How long has it subsisted ?
What infringements have been made ?
What opinions have been formed on it ?
Are they weighty, numerous, popular ?
Is there any admittance of an Adversary ?
What is the name of the thing and the Right, and whence is that name
    derived ?
What is it like—or unlike ?
  In its substance
  In its reason
  In its use
Now as to Convenience—
  Is the thing necessary ?
    Whence does the Necessity arise ?
    How have we done before ?
    Are there no other Expedients ?
Is it necessary at this time ?
  In this manner ?
  In this Extent ?
Is it expedient, near, remote, certain, or contingent ?
  does it unsettle nothing else ?
  does it introduce any Evil or Good ?
  does it agree with other parts of a System ?
  Will it offend or please ?
  Will it fall in with, or contradict, opinion ?
  the Consequence, if we omit it, simply, or drop, after having begun it ?
  Is the thing difficult or easy—time,
                    Manner,
                    our strength,
                    opposite,
  How may the Difficulty be overcome ?—by Perseverance ?
                              calling help ? what help ?
                              taking new method ?
                              persuing the former ?
What is against us—is it so much as thought ?
What balances ?

What have others done in our Circumstances ?
What opinions have been about it ? . . .[1]

Burke's discussion of Justice and Convenience in the
above obviously foreshadows his treatment in the *Tract on
the Popery Laws* of the principles of equity and utility as
'the two foundations of law' (see Part One of this study).
It is important here to note that Burke's treatment of
Justice and Convenience occurs only as these principles
relate to 'Civil Life': this is an anticipation of Burke's later
insistence that the question of rights be discussed only
with reference to civil society where these rights will be
exercised. Of the questions Burke asks concerning the
source, justification, limits, and duration of a 'right' it
is obvious that these questions might conceivably be
answered differently from the four perspectives afforded
by the 'Law of God', 'the general Notion of Virtue', 'the
Laws of the land', and 'the Law of Opinion'. Burke
himself does not make this point, nor in his listing of these
four criteria (if that is what they are) is there any statement
that Burke has arranged them in terms of their importance.
It seems reasonable, however, to suppose that this is what
he has done; whether consciously or not, he has ordered
these criteria in this brief fragment in a way which is
consistent with his more mature position. Certainly the
Law of God is primary, and the general Notion of Virtue, if
it be taken as the notion general to mankind, ranks higher
with Burke than the Laws of the land. The relative position
of the Laws of the land and the Law of Opinion is harder
to determine; if, however, the Law of Opinion is taken as
the opinion of a particular people at a particular time, then
given the vagaries and instability of public opinion at any
moment Burke clearly prefers the Laws of the land as the
expression of the more durable and reasonable aspects of
the Law of Opinion over a long period of time, a time
during which the Law of the land has also had the opportunity to move closer to the general Notion of Virtue of

[1] *A Notebook of Edmund Burke*, 47–48.

the species and even to the Law of God. Still this fragment reflects a tough-minded appetite for facts as being valuable to a decision in questions of right. Burke besides insisting that it is Civil Life that he is speaking of considers it important to know not only who has the right in question and whence it comes from but how long he has had it and what opinions exist concerning it. The question of how long, of the duration of the right in question, presumably refers back not to the (timeless) Law of God but to the general Notion of Virtue, the Laws of the land, and the Law of Opinion. It is either a legal or a historico-sociological question or both, meaning it is a question about the Law of the land with reference to the provisions it has made concerning a particular right and the length of time such a right has been acknowledged and/or it is a question about the general opinion of mankind or the opinion of a particular people concerning a certain right and the length of time mankind or a certain group of men has held this opinion. This in turn is followed by a series of questions which Burke candidly places under the heading of Convenience to mark them off from those questions which concern Justice.

While it is obviously unwise to claim too much for a youthful fragment, Burke's 'A Plan for Arguing' does present in capsule form those questions which he would later insist (but never again in so systematic a way) are the right questions to ask about a right. It was the opinion of the mature Burke that his adversaries had ignored *in toto* or in large part just these questions and had ignored all or most of his multiple criteria (the Law of God, the general Notion of Virtue, the Laws of the land, and the Law of Opinion) in their evaluations of arguments from Justice. Obviously a separate study would be required to evaluate with any precision the correctness of Burke's indictment of his adversaries on this point, and I can only repeat the strategy announced in Part One, namely that I shall proceed insofar as possible *as if* what Burke says about his contemporary world were true, in order to determine whether a coherent, consistent construction can be placed upon what Burke is doing as a philosopher. My impression, however, is that while Burke is in general unfair in claiming that his adversaries ignore or misinterpret the Law of God, that they are either out-and-out atheists or atheists in effect, he has rightly pointed out their neglect of the general notions of mankind, the laws of the land, and the opinion of the land. Two different interpretations of the natural law seem at issue here. On the one hand, there are those who approach both general opinion and positive law critically, presupposing that much of it will be shown to be absurd when examined rationally and that the duration of an opinion or a law is largely or wholly irrelevant to the question of its value; on the other hand, there are those who like Burke are severely critical of this external perspective, who insist upon some initial sympathy at least for general opinion and positive law on the grounds that these represent the experience and learning of the species or a sizeable part thereof and that the 'latent wisdom' of the ages is apt to be superior to the most acute reasonings of the most superior individuals of our day. Burke obviously belongs to the second group not only in general (see Part Two) but also, one might say especially, where the question of rights is concerned.

Years before the French Revolution Burke went so far as to indicate that the very question of whether man has any rights by nature is an improper question, although probably what he had in mind was his more characteristic conviction that the *discussion* of this question in the heat of a political controversy is improper. In his *Letter to the Sheriffs of Bristol* Burke complains about 'those people' (Burke as usual does not name his adversaries) who have 'split and anatomized the doctrine of free government, as if it were an abstract question concerning metaphysical liberty and necessity, and not a matter of moral prudence and natural feelings'. Of course, Burke himself is to some

degree willing to treat the doctrine of free government as
if it were in part at least an abstract question, but what
he is objecting to, in this characteristic overstatement
of his position, is the treatment of the doctrine of free
government as if it were either largely or wholly divorced
from considerations of a more practical nature. His
position seems to be that there comes a point where the
theoretical consideration of a question apart from the
practical context in which it occurs becomes harmful,
even to theory. His adversaries, he claims, have 'cor-
rupted philosophy' in their asking (or in their manner of
asking) 'whether man has any rights by Nature'; such
people are 'endeavoring to tear up, along with practical
liberty, all the foundations of human society, all equity
and justice, religion and order. Civil freedom . . . is a
blessing and a benefit, not an abstract speculation.'[1] In
advance of the French Revolution Burke has stated his
grievances against an approach to politics that would treat
questions concerning rights and civil freedom as if these
questions had no dimensions which mark them off from
questions such as those concerning metaphysical liberty
and necessity. Against this approach Burke urges a reliance
upon moral prudence and natural feeling. Much of his
argument against the rationalistic approach to religion
(Part Two) applies, *mutatis mutandis*, against what he takes
to be the rationalistic approach to politics; and in both
cases there is an emphasis upon the harmful moral and
political consequences of these approaches. In both
cases, Burke's adversaries are held to be guilty of an
over-reliance upon the powers of analytic reason in the
individual.

In the *Reflections on the Revolution in France* Burke
defends his reluctance to discuss those rights which belong
to man by nature by pointing out the incompleteness of any
discussion of rights which neglects the circumstances, the
relations, and the effects of the enjoyment of the right in

[1] *Works*, II, 228–9.

question: 'But I cannot stand forward, and give praise or blame to anything which relates to human actions and human concerns on a simple view of the object, as it stands stripped of every relation, in all the nakedness and solitude of metaphysical abstraction. Circumstances (which with some gentlemen pass for nothing) give in reality to every political principle its distinguishing color and discriminating effect. The circumstances are what render every civil and political scheme beneficial or noxious to mankind.' This is especially true of the newly won liberty of the French. The spirit of liberty in action is a strong principle at work; 'The wild gas, the fixed air, is plainly broke loose: but we ought to suspend our judgment until the first effervescence is a little subsided, till the liquor is cleared, and until we see something deeper than the agitation of a troubled frothy surface. I must be tolerably sure, before I venture publicly to congratulate men upon a blessing, that they have really received one.' In the case of liberty Burke professes to love 'a manly, moral regulated liberty' but 'abstractedly speaking, government, as well as liberty is good. . . .' Should I, therefore, Burke asks, have congratulated France ten years ago in her enjoyment of a government, without inquiring into the nature of that government? Should I now congratulate that nation upon its freedom without further inquiry? 'Is it because liberty in the abstract may be classed amongst the blessings of mankind, that I am seriously to felicitate a madman who has escaped from the protecting restraint and wholesome darkness of his cell on his restoration to the enjoyment of light and liberty? Am I to congratulate a highwayman and murderer who has broke prison upon the recovery of his natural rights?'[1] The effect of liberty upon men, Burke warns, is that they may do what they please; and liberty when men act in bodies is power: we ought, therefore, to see what it will please men to do with their newly won liberty before we risk congratulations. The discussion of

[1] *Works*, III, 240–1.

the merits of liberty in the abstract may lead us to impru-
dent and pre-mature enthusiasms in particular situations,
and a decision based chiefly upon the merits of liberty
in the abstract may lead us to neglect those circumstances,
relations, and effects which ought to count heavily in
decisions on the practical level.

Burke indeed affirms that 'The pretended rights of these
theorists [such as Dr. Price] are all extremes; and in
proportion as they are metaphysically true, they are morally
and politically false. The rights of men are in a sort of
middle, incapable of definition, but not impossible to be
discerned.' It is characteristic of Burke that he would use
extreme language in attacking extremism; it is especially
difficult to see how claims to rights could be morally and
politically false *in proportion* as they are metaphysically
true. Burke's main point seems to be simply that those
propositions which seem most indisputable or self-evident
when examined abstractly may sometimes lead to the most
absurd or harmful consequences in the actual context
of moral and political decision-making. Burke does not
present us with a logical argument here; at times he seems
to be opposed to any application of metaphysical or abstract
principles in the practice of morals and of politics but more
typically (and more defensibly) he seems to be opposed
simply to the *misapplication* of the conclusions of abstract
reasoning in moral and political decision making. His
judgement that the rights of men are in a sort of middle
reflects his basic assumption that in morals and politics
prudence usually dictates that we accept a medium rather
than an extreme; equally characteristic is his denial that
the rights of men can be defined. He clearly does not mean
by this that they cannot be known or 'discerned'; rather his
point seems to be the practical one that they cannot be
spelled out in advance in detail, that the variety of situations
in which men find themselves are too great for a prior
enumeration of all the rights they might reasonably claim
in each of these situations.

'The rights of men in government are their advantages,' Burke continues, 'and these are often in balances between differences of good,—in compromises sometimes between good and evil, and sometimes between evil and evil. Political reason is a computing principle: adding, subtracting, multiplying and dividing, morally, and not metaphysically or mathematically, true moral denominations.... Men have no right to what is not reasonable and to what is not for their benefit. . . .'[1] This is more tantalizing than precise, but I attach particular importance to the phrase 'in government' as telling us about the context which Burke has in mind. Rights if recognized imply advantages or privileges for their possessor; and in the context of civil society and of governmental decisions about rights within civil society the test of reasonableness (including the crucial question of whether men will benefit from the recognition of these rights) is, according to Burke, different from the tests of reasonableness that would ordinarily be sufficient in the more abstract contexts of metaphysics and mathematics. There is a kind of computing that goes on in decisions affecting men in civil society but it deals with 'moral denominations' and not, Burke repeatedly stresses, with numbers as such. In the civil and political context one does not count for one, as the utilitarians would have it, at least not until we know more about the one that is being counted.

In both the *Reflections* and the *Appeal from the New to the Old Whigs* Burke frequently attacks the 'pretended rights of man'. The force of Burke's 'pretended' seems directed more against the claim that men have certain rights regardless of the contexts in which men find themselves than against the actual rights in question. The pretended rights that were anathema to Burke were those which were said to hold with equal validity in two contexts that were quite separate and distinct, namely that of the state of nature and of civil society. Burke singled out for

[1] *Works*, III, 313.

criticism the thesis contained in the French Declaration of
the Rights of Man 'That all men are by nature free, are
equal in respect of rights, and continue so in society.'[1]
Burke seems to read this as implying that men continue so
in all respects in civil society; on this (perhaps dubious)
reading, the thesis in question ignores what is to Burke a
fundamental truth: that in different contexts men have
different rights and that the same right may take on different
dimensions in different contexts. A man may be said to be
free both in the state of nature and in civil society and yet
what it means to be free will differ significantly for these
two contexts.

With his sensitivity to circumstances, to what Popper
and others now call 'situational logic', would Burke admit
that there might be some situations *in* civil society where
the Rights of Man and those rights claimed for Englishmen by Dr. Price (that of choosing their own governors,
cashiering them for misconduct, and of framing a government for themselves)[2] might safely be enjoyed by the
people ? Could Burke be interpreted as saying simply that
as a matter of fact, owing to certain features of their
historical circumstances, the structure of their legal and
political system, &c., the Englishmen (and also the Frenchmen) of his day just happen not to be in situations where
they can properly claim such rights as those championed
by Dr. Price ? Or could he be read as arguing from what he
takes to be a more or less standard case or model of civil
society which admittedly does not cover *every* variety of
civil society ? Would he concede that the Rights of Man
might actually be compatible with the existence of some
kinds of civil society ? Burke appears to take a much
stronger position which denies in effect that men can enjoy
these rights in *any* civil society and which asserts that in
situations where men do enjoy these rights you will find

[1] Quoted by Burke in Speech on Quebec Government Bill (6 May 1791),
Speeches, IV, 5–6.
[2] *Reflections*, *Works*, III, 251.

not civil society but a state of nature. In short, Burke is saying that a large part of what it *means* to live in civil society and to be a people is that the people do not have these rights: 'The pretended *rights of man*, which have made this havoc [the French Revolution and its aftermath], cannot be the rights of the people. For to be a people, and to have these rights are things incompatible. The one supposes the presence, the other the absence, of a state of civil society.'[1]

From an allegedly faulty construction of what it means to live in civil society or to be a people, havoc in morals and politics has resulted. When Burke speaks of Europe as being in a state of 'civil war' part of what he has in mind is that in those countries in which there are factions that are dedicated to the principles of the French Revolution and the Rights of Man there occurs not merely a challenge to this or that ruler or policy but a challenge to the very foundations of civil society itself. Ordinarily a Whig following Locke might make a distinction between society and its government and thus be prepared to show at least an initial sympathy for a people seeking to change its government. Such indeed was the first reaction to the French Revolution on the part of Charles James Fox and a majority of the Whigs. Burke on the abstract level is no enemy to such a distinction, and he himself uses it, for example, in his treatment of the Irish problem; but he is an enemy to the application of this distinction both to the French situation and to England's internal affairs by Englishmen sympathetic to the French Revolution. The rights now being claimed on behalf of various peoples against their government are incompatible not only with classic 'old' Whig doctrine but are incompatible with the very notion of there being a people at all. To put Burke's argument in a somewhat more modern form: civil rights are being claimed which if acknowledged would have the effect of marking the end of civil society.

[1] *An Appeal from the New to the Old Whigs, Works,* IV, 188.

Political historians usually find it difficult to take Burke's argument seriously, largely because of his faulty conception of the causes and the goals of the French Revolution and kindred movements. Historians of ideas have usually shied away from assessing Burke's argument, partly for reasons not unlike those of the political historians and partly for reasons having to do with the imprecise and sweeping manner in which Burke makes his case against the Rights of Man. One could say, using Burkian language, that Burke's own case is stated so abstractly and with such a disregard for the circumstances that one does not see how the Rights of Man and especially the political rights of choosing and cashiering one's governors or even of changing the government will produce in all or most circumstances the dissolution of civil society that Burke says they must. However, Burke's assessment of the import of the Rights of Man, even if it is incorrect, helps render intelligible both his own reluctance to discuss natural rights and his belief that such discussions were disruptive of all forms of civil society. Where a calmer philosopher might have said, 'Yes, there are natural rights, but they are not always what you think they are. We agree here and here, but we disagree on these points', Burke in the heat of controversy indulges in sweeping polemics against the motives and positions of his adversaries. He is led to this extreme in part by his conviction that the alleged rights of men are often but rationalizations or 'pretexts' behind which 'pride, ambition, avarice, revenge, lust, sedition, hypocricy, ungoverned zeal, and all the train of disorderly appetites' hide: 'These vices are the causes of those storms [and miseries that affect the world]. Religion, morals, laws, prerogatives, privileges, rights of men, are the *pretexts*. The pretexts are always found in some specious appearance of a real good.'[1]

There is in Burke a deep fear of the anarchic consequences that the Rights of Man allegedly imply which

---

[1] *Reflections, Works*, III, 418.

is closely akin to what Bentham would also feel. Burke in speaking of the effects which the doctrine of the Rights of Man had upon the French West Indian colonies asserts that prior to the appearance of this doctrine the colonies in question were 'most happy and flourishing' (a standard ploy of Burke's):

As soon as this system arrived among them, Pandora's box, replete with every mortal evil, seemed to fly open, hell itself to yawn, and every demon of mischief to overspread the face of the earth. Blacks rose against whites, whites against blacks, and each against one another in murderous hostility; subordination was destroyed, the bonds of society torn asunder, the every man seemed to thirst for the blood of his neighbour.[1]

On the occasion of a debate over the proposed repeal of the Test and Corporation Acts in 1790 Burke proclaimed (in justification for his about-face concerning religious toleration for the Dissenters):

Abstract principles . . . he disliked, and never could bear; he detested them when a boy, and he liked them no better now he had silver hairs. Abstract principles were what his clumsy apprehension could not grasp; he must have a principle embodied in some manner or other, and the conduct held upon it ascertained, before he could pretend to judge of its propriety and advantage in practice. But, of all abstract principles abstract principles of natural right—which the dissenters rested on, as their strong hold—were the most idle, because the most useless and the most dangerous to resort to. They superseded society, and broke asunder all those bonds which had formed the happiness of mankind for ages. He would venture to say, that if they were to go back abstractedly to original rights, there would be an end of all society. Abstract principles of natural right had been long since given up for the advantage of having, what was much better, society, which substituted wisdom and justice, in the room of original right. It annihilated all those natural rights, and drew to its mass all the component parts of which those rights were made up. It took in all the virtue of the virtuous, and the wisdom of the wise. It gave life, security, and action to every faculty of the soul and secured the possession of every comfort which those proud and boasting natural rights impotently held out, but could not ascertain. . . .[2]

The above quotation in which Burke speaks of natural rights as the most idle, the most useless, and the most

[1] *Speeches*, IV, 8.   [2] *Speeches*, III, 475–6.

dangerous of abstract principles is alarming for a number of reasons. First, when Burke is speaking in this manner of the incompatibility of various rights and society he ordinarily speaks of the Rights of Man and hence appears to be referring specifically to the French Declaration of the Rights of Man. Here, however, he speaks of natural rights in the same way in which he usually refers to the Rights of Man, thus indicating that, at least on this occasion, he makes no distinction between them. Moreover, he appears not to have in mind any distinctions among the various natural rights but to be making an all-inclusive condemnation of them. Second, this passage jeopardizes not only the thesis that Burke believed in natural rights but also, if I am correct in my assessment of what it means to hold a natural law theory, the thesis that Burke believed in the natural law. Third, the above passage creates the impression that Burke considers natural rights to have failed in securing the ends sought by man who has found these ends secured by society instead. Society has annihilated 'all those natural rights' and has drawn 'to its mass all the component parts of which these rights were made up'. The second part of this claim seems unusually tangled, but the total effect of this two-part description of what society has done is to suggest that those ends which man had sought to realize by claiming certain rights to be 'natural' can now be realized by society *independently* of all such claims. Society gives life, security, and 'action' (freedom of action, or realization of the potential for growth ?) to every faculty of the soul. 'Natural rights' or 'original rights' seem to have lost all relevance to man circumstanced as he is in civil society, except the wholly negative relevance of reminding him that to claim these rights is to alienate oneself in effect from the advantages and securities offered by civil society. (I speak of civil society where Burke speaks of society but clearly means civil society. The same imprecision is to be found in Locke. Since Locke expressly and Burke tacitly admit there may be a loose social arrangement in the state of nature that might be spoken of as constituting a 'society', the word 'civil' seems a helpful addition to mark those occasions when they clearly are speaking of a more complex social arrangement than is to be found in a state of nature and one marked by the presence of a government.)

My position, however, is that Burke's language in the above quotation is, not untypically, careless; that instead of rejecting natural rights as such Burke really rejects only some claims made in the name of natural rights (claims having to do with political rights, especially the rights of popular participation in and control of government).[1] Although the above quotation can, as we shall see, be qualified significantly when placed in the context of Burke's overall position on rights, it suggests at first reading that Burke has offered an exclusive disjunction between natural rights and civil advantages to the marked disadvantage of the former. (But we must remember that Burke says elsewhere that a right 'is' an advantage.) Burke's claim that he must have 'a principle embodied in some manner or other, and the conduct held upon it ascertained' before he can judge its *propriety and practical advantage* points, however, in a somewhat different direction. It serves, apparently, to mark him off from both seventeenth- and eighteenth-century natural rights doctrine and a progressive utilitarianism which repudiates natural rights as socially disruptive and yet often seems willing, at any moment, to start afresh in its calculations and actions on

[1] Under the Test and Corporation Acts the Dissenters were disbarred from membership in corporations and from holding civil and military positions under the Crown. While Burke in 1779 and 1780 had been ready to support the Dissenters' demands for the repeal of these Acts, by 1790 he had changed his mind. He justified this change in part on the grounds that the Dissenters had become 'a faction in the state' and were inspired by subversive political doctrine. Burke had apparently come to believe that what had once been a reasonable plea for religious toleration was now being advanced as part of a systematic attack not only upon the established church but upon a great many long-established powers and prerogatives of the government. 'Principle' and 'right' were in short being used as instruments in a power struggle which involved many issues besides that of religious toleration.

behalf of the social ends it seeks. Burke's insistence that he must see a principle embodied in some manner or other suggests that he will not always be adverse to a principle, even a principle proclaiming a natural right, provided he has, so to speak, seen the principle successfully institutionalized. His belief that a question of a moral and political nature must concern itself with circumstances, with what are often called concrete situations, before it can be satisfactorily answered has in the context of his discussion of rights a decidedly historical quality. Time must have elapsed before we can make the kind of practical test that Burke has in mind. A right must have had a successful historical expression within civil society before Burke will finally pass on its merits. Thus he differs from both seventeenth- and eighteenth-century natural rights theorists, who do not seem concerned with whether a right has become an accepted part of the civil order before deciding on its merits, and the utilitarians, who appear content with the promise, provided it is rationally grounded, of successful *future* results where civil advantages and privileges are concerned. Burke's apparent preference for civil advantages over natural rights in the above quotation seems based upon the fact that civil society has, vulgarly speaking, delivered the goods, i.e., fulfilled the ends naturally desired by man, in a way that natural rights theories have not.

The question for us to answer if we can is whether, granted the differences mentioned above, Burke should be read as being a kind of historically minded utilitarian in the sense of being especially concerned with the past results of advantages and privileges conferred by civil society and with the way in which people have come to have certain feelings and expectations where particular advantages and privileges are concerned, or as a kind of historically minded natural rights theorist who considers past experience within civil society especially relevant to a decision concerning the validity of an alleged natural right. The first alternative, as it is put forth by commentators, may or may not actually refer to Burke as a utilitarian. Sometimes Burke is simply spoken of as being historically oriented and concerned with the feelings and habits of a people, even if these are not rationally justified, in a way that a more 'scientific' utilitarian presumably might not be. But regardless of whether the word 'utilitarian' is accepted or not this reading finally comes round to Burke's emphasis upon the past (with emphasis upon the recent past) utility of advantages and privileges, in terms of their contribution to the stability and growth of the political community in question. Burke may take into account a greater number of variables than the Benthamites, may even deny that he is, strictly speaking, making a calculation at all, but he appears, it is said, to resemble significantly the utilitarians in his deference to the criterion of utility. On this reading, if an advantage or privilege is claimed on the ground that one has a natural right to this advantage or privilege, this argument is either nonsense because man as we know him has left behind the state of nature and those rights which were natural to him in that state (if indeed there ever was such a state) or else it is a clumsy and potentially mischievous way of saying that it is natural or fitting that, given the relationship of the claimant to the civil society in which he lives, he be granted a certain advantage or privilege by that community, i.e., that it is to the general advantage of the community in which he lives to recognize the claimant's right to certain advantages or privileges. This right may be either legal or moral, but it is context-dependent and concerns man as citizen and not man conceived of simply as man.

Given Burke's admittedly peculiar way of weighing the variables that enter into decisions as to whether a claim to this or that advantage or privilege is to be considered a right, it is sometimes argued that in the final analysis Burke will acknowledge a claimant's right to a certain advantage or privilege if he has historically been allowed to enjoy this advantage or privilege. I shall examine this argument at length. A different argument which I shall not consider in any detail is one advanced by critics who see Burke as wholly reactionary and who argue that for Burke the past enjoyment (exercise) of an advantage or privilege is not only a sufficient but *also* a necessary condition for the recognition of a claimant's right to that privilege or advantage. This argument is demonstrably false and arises from an overinterpretation of the fact that Burke appeared to justify at times the rights of the Irish, the American colonists, and the people of India solely on the grounds that they had enjoyed these rights in the past. But there were cases where Burke did not consider such past enjoyment as a necessary condition for the future enjoyment of certain rights. Obviously the people of India, while they may have enjoyed some of the legal rights under native rule which Burke argues (at times in an evidently exaggerated manner) they did, did not enjoy historically the rights and privileges under *English* rule which Burke is arguing they should now be allowed to enjoy. In working for changes within English law that would abolish the cruel and inhumane treatment of homosexuals Burke was clearly arguing for a *new* legal right which homosexuals had not previously enjoyed; also, while Burke has a spotty record on the question of religious toleration (having a consistently good record in the case of Catholics but not in the case of the Protestant Dissenters), he is clearly prepared to argue from the moral point of view for a change in the legal allocation of advantages and privileges that has been historically followed. . . . Therefore, the right question to consider is whether Burke believed that the historic enjoyment or exercise of a right is a sufficient condition to justify the claim that such an enjoyment be allowed to continue.

While Burke believed that a right is (confers) an advantage, he did not believe that all advantages are (confer) rights. Many of the advantages that Hastings and his cohorts enjoyed in India, for example, were not considered by Burke to be rights in either the moral or the legal sense. Hastings was, Burke charged, acting in defiance of both the natural law and the laws of England in conducting himself as though he were the absolute ruler in India. But what about *rights* such as those enjoyed *legally* in India by the East India Company by virtue of a charter and several acts of Parliament? Speaking in defence of a bill introduced by Charles James Fox which would have decreased significantly the independence hitherto enjoyed by the East India Company and would have made it much more responsive to the wishes of the English government, Burke insisted that from the legal point of view he accepted the argument of the East India Company and her friends that the Company governed India legally; by the terms of the monopoly granted to them they were within their rights when they excluded their fellow-countrymen from commerce with India, administered India, commanded an army of sixty thousand men there, and disposed, according to law, of the lives and property of thirty million Indians. Burke denied, however, the charge that Fox's bill was an attack upon 'the chartered rights of men', although there was an ambiguity in this phrase which made the charge seem plausible at first glance. Fox's bill did seek to alter certain rights granted by charter to a company of men. But what 'chartered rights of men' ordinarily refers to, Burke argued, is those natural or original rights of men which are 'further affirmed and declared by express covenants' such as the charters granted by King John and King Henry the Third:

The rights of *men*—that is to say, the natural rights of mankind—are indeed, sacred things; and if any public measure is proved mischievously to affect them, the objection ought to be fatal to that measure, even if no charter at all could be set up against it. If these natural rights are further affirmed and declared by express covenants, if they are clearly defined and secured against chicane, against power and authority, by written instruments and positive engagements, they are in a still better condition: they partake not only of the sanctity of the object so secured, but of that solemn public faith itself which secures an object of such importance. Indeed, this formal recognition by the sovereign power, of an original right in the subject, can never be subverted, but by rooting up the holding radical principles of governments, and even of society itself. The charters which we call by distinction *great* are public instruments of this nature: I mean the charters of King John and King Henry the Third. The things secured by these instruments may, without any deceitful ambiguity, be very fitly called the *chartered rights of man*.[1]

The above passage may occasion surprise to some in view of its confession that the natural rights of mankind are *sacred things*, even in cases where there are no charters or positive laws to uphold them. Critics have often explained it away as being either insincere or else a reflection of what Burke thought prior to the French Revolution—it was written seven years before the condemnation of abstract principles of natural right quoted previously—or as being at variance with the bulk of Burke's utterances on natural rights. I shall offer a different interpretation shortly. Meanwhile, it is clear that Burke's chief intention in the above quotation is to offer a description of the chartered rights of men which he contrasts with the chartered rights of the East India Company, to the disadvantage of the latter. The charter of the East India Company was founded on principles '*the very reverse*' of those of Magna Charta: 'Magna Charta is a charter to restrain power and to destroy monopoly. The East India charter is a charter to establish monopoly and to create power. Political power and commercial monopoly are not the rights of men; and the rights to them from charters it is fallacious and sophistical to call "the chartered rights of men".' These chartered rights 'do at least suspend the natural rights to mankind at large' and may be framed in such a way as to be a direct violation of them.[2]

---

[1] *Speech on Mr. Fox's East India Bill* (1 December 1783), *Works*, II, 437.
[2] Ibid., 438. See also Burke's Notes on Copy-Right Bill and Monopolies Generally, *Correspondence of the Right Honourable Edmund Burke* (London, 1844), IV, 459–60, where Monopoly is spoken of as contrary to Natural Right because ' "Free Trade" is the same thing as "Use of Property" '. The state may, however, grant a monopoly not on 'arbitrary principles, but for the good of the whole'.

Burke writes that 'all political power which is set over men' and 'all privilege claimed or exercised in exclusion of them, being wholly artificial, and for so much a derogation from the natural equality of mankind at large, ought to be some way or other exercised for their benefit'. No species of political dominion or of commercial privilege can be considered as an 'original, self-derived' (natural) right or as a grant merely for the private benefit of the holders. Such 'rights, or privileges, or whatever else you choose to call them, are all in the strictest sense a trust'—and the essence of a trust is that it be rendered accountable and that, in cases where it 'substantially varies' from the purposes for which it was created, it may cease altogether. This is true of 'trusts of power vested in the highest hands, and of such as seem to hold of no human creature'. If it is true of them, who can doubt that it is true of 'subordinate derivative trusts' such as that enjoyed by the East India Company? Burke then argues that the trust bestowed upon this Company by Parliament requires not that Parliament refuse to interfere with the legal rights of this Company but that Parliament acknowledge its duty to interfere, on the ground that the power and authority granted by Parliament have been perverted from their original purposes: 'if the abuse is proved, the contract is broken, and we reenter into all our rights, that is, into the exercise of all our duties'. To replace the alleged 'chartered rights of men' that the East India Company and its friends defend Burke supports Fox's bill as forming a 'Magna Charta of Hindostan'. In this bill, Burke argues, there is provided 'a real chartered security for *the rights of men*, cruelly violated' under the existing charter.

Typically enough, Burke confesses to 'an insuperable reluctance to destroy any established institution of government, upon a theory, however plausible it may be' even when the government in question is controlled by a company of merchants. Therefore, to change the administration of the affairs of the East India Company from mercantile to political hands (Burke's motives, as usual, were said not to be disinterested), Burke specified that the following conditions must be met: '1st, The object affected by the abuse should be great and important. 2nd, The abuse affecting this great object ought to be a great abuse. 3rd, It ought to be habitual and not accidental. 4th, It ought to be utterly incurable in the body as it now stands constituted.'[1] It should perhaps be noted that Burke's conditions for revoking a subordinate (secondary) derivative trust are strongly reminiscent of Locke's conditions for revoking the trust upon which government depends for its existence. Indeed, Burke's entire argument is an application to the trust that the British government had conferred upon the East India Company of Locke's account of the trust that society has conferred upon government as such. Burke's argument that the secondary trust, in this case the monopoly granted to the East India Company, must ultimately benefit the common good as the justification of the special privileges it confers upon a few, or else be altered or revoked is, obviously, Lockian in origin. Burke's claim that the abuses allegedly committed by the East India Company do in fact constitute a great, habitual, and (under the present charter) incurable abuse and mismanagement in public affairs is reminiscent, too, of the conservative qualifications that Locke expressly placed upon the right of revolution (although, of course, Burke is proposing here not a revolution but a *revocation* of legal privileges granted in a secondary derivative trust).

While Burke does not explicitly make a distinction between a right and a privilege and appears indifferent as to whether one speaks of the rights or privileges or 'whatever else you choose to call them' given in trust to the East India Company, it seems he has in mind some such distinction when he marks off original or self-derivative rights from those rights which are given in trust and which are derivative either in the primary sense, as in the case

[1] *Works*, II, 439–42.

of the rights of a government, or in the secondary sense, as in the case of the rights granted by a government to a person, a group, or a corporation. Burke nowhere characterizes original or self-derivative rights as privileges nor, of course, does he characterize all privileges as rights.

There are those who think Burke believed that in civil society *all* rights become derivative and are held in trust, that while man may have had original, self-derivative rights in a state of nature, in civil society he exchanges these rights for privileges for which he is held accountable, just as the East India Company is. Because Burke said that (civil) society is an artificial contrivance and because he emphasized the conventional nature of the arrangements and the rules operative therein commentators have sometimes proceeded as if Burke's discussion of the East India Company and its rights or privileges provides a suitable model for understanding Burke's position concerning the individual member of civil society and his rights or privileges. I shall try to show that this interpretation of rights as being merely privileges is vastly overstated, but for the present the important thing to note is that whether one speaks of the rights or of the privileges of the East India Company Burke acknowledges that these rights or privileges have been enjoyed historically (and were actually *conferred* upon the Company by the English government) but denies that they should be enjoyed in the future. Burke confesses to an 'insuperable reluctance' to destroy any established institution of government on theoretical grounds alone, even the subordinate, derivative institutions of a corporation of merchants, but theory and practice (a long series of grave abuses by the corporation in question) can together make this reluctance superable.

The question now arises, did Burke believe that the past enjoyment of a right or of a privilege is in *any* case a sufficient condition to justify its continuance ? It is important to find a case which provides the best opportunity for an affirmative answer to this question. The rights or privileges of the Irish Catholics or of the people of India will not do because while Burke makes a point of calling attention to those rights and privileges which were historically enjoyed by these people, the enjoyment of these rights had been significantly interrupted by the conquests of the English; and in urging the restoration of these (pre-English) rights within the different context of English dominion Burke in both cases explicitly argues for the rationality of his policy proposals from the perspective of natural law. The rights of the *ancien régime* in France scarcely afford a better case, although Burke certainly uses the historicity of the rights or privileges of the monarchy, the aristocracy, and the Church, as part of his defence of these rights or privileges. The rights of the American colonies are also considered by Burke to be justified in part on the grounds that the colonists had long enjoyed them and that they were confirmed by charters granted to the colonies by the home government, but when called upon to defend his sympathy for a cause that had occasioned such a great loss to the Empire his claim is chiefly that the colonists had been fighting for their rights as Englishmen.[1] In fact, it turns out that the rights of Englishmen provide the best hope for those who would argue that in at least

[1] In his *Address on the King's Speech at the Opening of the Session* (24 November 1767) Burke complained of England's treatment of the American colonies where the 'constitutional rights of Englishmen' have been invaded and 'legislative assemblies have been suspended, for no other reason than their having assented to unalienable rights of their constituents. . . .' *Speeches*, I, 16–17.

In his *Address to the British Colonists in North America* (January 1777) Burke wrote, 'We also reason and feel as you do on the invasion of your charters. Because the charters comprehend the essential forms by which you enjoy your liberties, we regard them as most sacred. . . .' *Works*, VI, 188.

Burke noted in attempting to explain the 'fierce spirit of liberty' prevalent in the American colonies that 'First the people of the colonies are descendants of Englishmen. They are therefore not only devoted to liberty, but to liberty according to English ideas and on English principles.' *Speech on Moving his Resolutions for Conciliation with the Colonies* (22 March 1775), *Works*, II, 120.

Burke's retrospective judgement in his *Appeal from the New to the Old Whigs* (1791) was that the Americans had fought not to 'enlarge' but to 'secure' their liberty in the '*ancient* condition': 'He considered the Americans as standing at that time, and in that controversy, in the same relation to England as England did to King James the Second in 1688.' The Americans had fought for 'English constitutional rights and privileges'. *Works*, IV, 100–2.

one case Burke believed the past enjoyment of a right is sufficient to justify the continued enjoyment of this right. Given Burke's preoccupation with things English and his conviction that rights are enjoyed with more security in England than anywhere else, it is highly significant that this reading of Burke appears more defensible in the case of his treatment of English rights than in the case of his treatments of Irish, Indian, French, or American rights.

The rights of Englishmen that most concerned Burke were those which, like Blackstone, he often called 'liberties' as a means of marking what Blackstone had called their 'political and extensive sense' and which, again like Blackstone, he believed had been secured in the Charters granted by King John and King Henry the Third and in the Bill of Rights.[1] The rights or liberties in question were those which Blackstone had divided into three 'primary' rights and five 'auxiliary' rights. Under primary rights Blackstone listed those of (1) 'personal security' of life and limbs against 'civil death' or 'duress', including the guarantee of 'due process' in the punishment of a crime; (2) 'personal liberty', including the guarantees of habeas corpus and the lawful judgement of equals; and (3) 'private property', including (a) indemnification for expropriation and (b) taxation only by Parliament. Under auxiliary rights Blackstone included (1) the constitution, powers, and privileges of Parliament; (2) the limitations of the King's prerogative; (3) the right of redress in court; (4) the right of petition; and (5) the right to bear arms.[2] Burke's extensive reviews of Blackstone's *Commentaries* shows his familiarity with these classifications, although characteristically he seems most impressed by and quotes mostly from that part of Book II of the *Commentaries* which concerns the origin of property and which begins with the observation that 'there is nothing which so generally strikes the

---

[1] See Sir William Blackstone, *Commentaries on the Laws of England* (Chicago, 1899), Book I, 127–9. All pagination is that of the original edition.

[2] Ibid., 129–45.

imagination, and engages the affections of mankind, as the right of property. . . .' (He includes Blackstone's discussion of whether there is a tacit and implied consent of all mankind according to which occupancy by itself confers the right to permanent title to property or whether the act of occupancy alone is, 'from a principle of natural justice, without any consent or compact, sufficient of itself to gain a title'. Blackstone's conclusion, quoted by Burke, is that this dispute savours too much of scholastic refinement—the important thing is that both sides to this dispute agree that 'occupancy is the thing by which the title was in fact originally gained'.)[1] Although Burke does not in his discussions of English liberties employ much of Blackstone's technical language, does not, for example, speak of 'auxiliary rights' as such, a comprehensive list of the English liberties or rights that Burke defends at various times would include all the actual liberties or rights Blackstone lists and none not listed by Blackstone in the *Commentaries*.

Burke's preoccupation with property is in some respects fortunate for the student of his thought in that his treatment of the liberties or rights of Englishmen concerning property provides what is, for Burke, a fairly clear model for the understanding of his overall position concerning the various rights listed by Blackstone. While it is true that, as has been remarked in another connexion by a modern student of ethics, we must as philosophers attend to distinctions between (1) rights to do certain things or to act in certain ways ('action rights'), (2) rights to receive certain things or to be treated in certain ways ('receivatory' or 'treatment rights'), and (3) rights in or to something ('property rights'),[2] it is necessary to confess that as historians we do not find in Burke explicit distinctions between rights *to do* or *to act*, rights *to receive* or *to be treated*, and rights *in* or *to*. Even such elementary distinctions are

---

[1] Ibid., Book II, 2–9. Burke reviewed Books I and II in the *Annual Register* for 1767 and Book III in the *Annual Register* for 1768.

[2] Marcus G. Singer, 'On Duties to Oneself', *Ethics*, LXIX (April 1959), 202–5.

conspicuous by their absence. To be sure, this threefold classification of rights can be applied *to* Burke's thought, but the fruitfulness of such an application seems limited. First we have to realize that 'property rights' as given in (3)—rights *in* or *to*—might be construed as more inclusive than property rights as understood by Burke; it might remind one of Locke who sometimes spoke of property rights as including the rights *to* life and liberty. Whether we take (3) to include the rights of personal security, personal liberty, and private property or to include only private property, many of the rights we would class under (1) and (2) come to bear in Burke's thought a special relation to those classed under (3). If I have a right in or to property in any sense and if I am to have an effective enjoyment of this right, then I must be allowed to do certain things, to act in certain ways, to receive certain things, and to be treated in certain ways. Burke is far from indifferent to those conditions which must exist if my right to property is to count as an effective right, i.e., if I am to enjoy or exercise this right fully. As a political champion of the rights *of* property, Burke stands second to none, but as an analyst of the right *to* or *in* property on either the legal[1] or the philosophical level he is brief and sketchy. He apparently presupposes the whole of Blackstone on property, but he says nothing in detail or in depth on such key topics as the rights of contract and the rights of inheritance.

Conceptual analysis is not among Burke's conscious intentions, and when he pauses as he sometimes does to analyse concepts such as the *chartered rights of men* he does this only from his conviction that his adversaries have placed a faulty or sophistical construction upon them. For an historical understanding of what Burke is trying to do,

[1] In his first review of the *Commentaries* Burke writes that before Blackstone separated the law from 'the rubbish in which it was buried' the law was generally found to be of 'so dry, disgusting, and heavy a nature, that students of vivacity and genius were deterred from entering upon it'. While Burke's mastery of the history of English law impressed the members of the House of Commons, he did not bore them with its details. His *Essay towards a History of the Laws of England*, *Works*, VII, 475–488, is an unfinished fragment of fourteen pages.

it is important to bear in mind both the primitiveness of his tools of analysis from a modern point of view and the comparatively simple and restricted nature of his interest in the question of rights. It is a political more than a juristic or philosophical motive that leads him to take up his investigations. First, he wants in his capacity as legislator to grade or sort out legitimate claims to rights from illegitimate ones (I am using *claims* here in that sense in which one might say that Jones has filed damage claims against Smith and Webb without in any way committing oneself to the rightness of these claims.) Second, he wants to provide some grounds for showing that the results of this grading or sorting activity are justifiable. What we are dealing with at present is this second question; and it is philosophically, I think, of greater significance than Burke's argument that certain claims to political rights are illegitimate, an argument which I shall not explore in this study. But even when Burke is considering the grounds of rights as a political philosopher his suggested distinctions are often lacking in both subtlety and comprehensiveness just because Burke is more interested in practice than in theory. In mapping the various rights and their relations to one another and to political circumstance, Burke's primary concerns are those of the navigator and not those of the geographer or scholar.

Property rights function as a model for the comprehension of Burke's views on rights. This is so not as a matter of chance but as a reflection of his absorption with the rights of property and their defence. Property rights serve as an especially illuminating model not merely because Burke has more to say about them than about other rights but also because he believed that 'for the protection of property, all governments were instituted', that a respect for property rights is a necessary condition for the recognition of many other rights (even the right to life), and that morality and the arts depend upon property as their basis. The importance that Burke attached to property is clearly shown in the following passage in which he argued that he did not attach the importance to the rights of property that his critics alleged (he is discussing the needs of France):

It was not for any particular system of government that he contended, but for some government. Let it be a pure monarchy, a democracy, or an aristocracy, or all mixed, he cared not, provided a government did exist, the first principle of which must necessarily be security to property, because, for the protection of property, all governments were instituted. First, therefore, restore property, and afterwards let that property find a government for itself. The number of its inhabitants constituted the strength of a nation, but it was property alone on which government was formed. If the formation of government was committed to the no-property people, the first thing they would do, obviously would be to plunder those who had property, and the next thing would be to plunder and massacre each other. After all, if it were asked, did he prefer property to virtue ? his answer would be no. To honour ?—No. To Morals ?—No. To arts and literature ?—No. But he respected property in as much as it was the basis upon which they were all erected—the soul that animated, the genius that protected them.[1]

Burke's judgement that 'it was property alone on which government was formed' is overstated. Burke on rights is strongly reminiscent of Burke on the various parts of the English Constitution where, by his own admission, he tended to speak of the part he was defending at any given moment as if it were the only part that really mattered. Rightly or wrongly, it was the destruction of property rights that Burke believed to be uppermost in the minds of the men who had brought about the French Revolution: hence his exaggerated claim in the above quotation. Burke's belief that his position as a legislator forbade him to interfere with the rights of property was strong and sincerely held: 'As far as my share of a public trust goes, I am in trust religiously to maintain the rights and properties of all descriptions of people in the possessions which they legally hold, and in the rule by which alone they can be secure in any possession. I do not find myself at liberty, either as a man or as a trustee for men, to take a vested

---

[1] Burke on Bill to Enable Subjects of France to Enlist as Soldiers (11 April 1794), *Speeches*, IV, 166.

property from one man and give it to another, because I
think that the portion of one is too great, and that of
another too small.' On this occasion Burke went on to state
that 'the ascertaining and securing of *prescription*' is 'one
principal cause' of the formation of states, thus providing
a more moderate and characteristic estimate of the part
which he believed considerations concerning property had
played in the establishment of civil society and at the same
time justifying his refusal to turn a deaf ear to such considerations after civil society is established:

It is not calling the landed estates, possessed by old *prescriptive* rights,
'The accumulations of ignorance and superstition,' that can support me
in shaking that grand title, and which all my studies of general jurisprudence have taught me to consider as one principal cause of the
formation of states;—I mean the ascertaining and securing of *prescription*. 'But these are donations made in ages of ignorance and superstition.'
Be it so;—it proves that they were made long ago; and this is prescription,
and this gives right and title. It is possible that many estates about you
were obtained by arms; a thing almost as bad as superstition, and not
much short of ignorance;—but it is old violence; and that which might
be wrong in the beginning, is consecrated by time and becomes lawful.
This may be superstition in me, and ignorance; but I had rather remain
in ignorance and superstition, than be enlightened and purified out of
the first principles of law and natural justice.[1]

The zeal of Burke's defence of property rights undoubtedly owed something to his affiliation with the great
landowners who comprised the Rockingham Whigs; as
Sir Philip Magnus has suggested Burke's defence of prescription was deeply rooted in the political circumstances
of his time.[2] It seems likely, however, Burke's studies of

[1] Edmund Burke to Captain Mercer, 26 February 1790, *Correspondence of
the Right Honourable Edmund Burke*, III, 142–5.

[2] See Magnus, op. cit., 37, 69, for an account of Burke's efforts on behalf of
the Duke of Portland against Sir James Lowther, later the Earl of Lonsdale. The
Duke of Portland's ancestor, Count Bentinck, had been given a vast amount of
Crown land in the north of England for his part in helping to bring over William
of Orange during the Glorious Revolution. Lowther, who belonged to the Court
Party, discovered a flaw in Portland's title to certain estates; the disputed lands
were returned to the Crown and the land was leased at a nominal rent to the man
who had discovered the flaw in Portland's title. While Portland's family had held
these estates for nearly a century, it took years of litigation before he was confirmed
in his possession of them.

'general jurisprudence' had inclined him toward an acceptance of prescription years before it became politically
advantageous for him to endorse prescription. While he
does not make use of Blackstone's distinction between
prescription and custom (see the *Commentaries*, Bk. II,
chap. 17, where custom is defined as a local usage not
annexed to any person while prescription is 'merely a
personal usage') and seems at times to use prescription to
cover both personal and local usage, his deference to prescription is in keeping with Blackstone's belief that possession as such confers a right or title to property not merely
according to English law but according to natural law as
well. Burke's application of Blackstone's rule that a person
establishes his prescriptive rights to property by showing
that he 'immemorially used to enjoy it' may have reflected
the exigencies of contemporary politics. Undoubtedly
Burke spoke of immemorial usage when the usage in
question did not extend so far into the past as the word
immemorial suggests; however, while he was probably
guilty of stretching a principle, he was not guilty of an
ignorance of what that principle was and of its vital place
in the history of English jurisprudence. 'Veneration of
antiquity is congenial to the human mind' Burke had noted
in his *Tract on the Popery Laws*;[1] this judgement was true
at least of Burke himself and of the legal profession of
which he had once hoped to become a member.

The doctrine that the rights of Englishmen were immemorial and protected under an ancient constitution was
not a novelty introduced into political discourse by Burke.
The appeal to immemorial usage was a practice long followed in English legal and political discussions; Coke and
Blackstone had used it long before Burke. The elaboration
of the doctrine of an ancient constitution is dated from
about 1600, and the curious history enshrined in this
doctrine was that each great advance in the history of
English law was in reality but a codification of customs

[1] *Works*, VI, 339.

and rights previously (if imperfectly) acknowledged as such in ancient law. Thus, it was held, one could trace Magna Charta back to a charter granted by Henry I, beyond that to a charter granted by William I, and finally to pre-Norman law. Burke in his *Essay towards a History of the Laws of England* commented adversely on one version of this thesis, that given in Chief Justice Sir Matthew Hale's *History of the Common Law*, as reflecting 'national vanity and professional narrowness'. Burke denied the thesis that the history of English law reflected little or no change in the content of that law. Still he was familiar with this way of thinking; and he was, as we shall see, given at a later time to speaking as if this doctrine of the ancient constitution were substantially correct insofar as the more basic laws of England were concerned, provided one did not deny the influence of foreign jurisprudence[1] and other historical factors.

The Revolution of 1688–9 was made, Burke held, 'to preserve our *ancient* indisputable laws and liberties, and that ancient constitution of government which is our only security for law and liberty'.[2] My present concern is with the connexions between Burke on property rights and Burke on those immemorial or ancient rights or liberties protected by the ancient constitution and secured by the

[1] 'The Norman Conquest is the great era of our laws. At this time the English jurisprudence, which had hitherto continued a poor stream, fed from some few, and those scanty sources, was all at once, as from a mighty flood replenished with a vast body of foreign learning, by which, indeed, it might be said rather to have been increased than much improved: for this foreign law, being imposed, not adopted, for a long time bore strong appearances of that violence by which it had been first introduced. All our monuments bear a strong evidence to this change. New courts of justice, new names and powers of officers, in a word, a new tenure of land as well as new possessors of it, took place. Even the language of public proceedings was in a great measure changed.' *Essay towards a History of the Laws of England, Works*, VII, 487–8. Unlike Pocock, I see nothing in the later Burke which in any way implies that the condition of English law in the past cannot be reconstructed and that changes in its content cannot be detected. His use in later years of the doctrine of the ancient constitution seems less literal than Pocock thinks, designed to emphasize basic continuities in the law and not to insist upon a literal equivalance in all respects of all features of the Constitution with immemorial (pre-Norman) custom or usage. But see Pocock, op. cit., 139–43.

[2] *Reflections on the Revolution in France, Works*, III, 271.

Glorious Revolution. Property rights, in addition to figuring prominently in Burke's list of ancient or immemorial rights, form according to Burke the basis of many other rights in that the secure enjoyment of property rights is a necessary condition for the enjoyment of many other rights. Of even greater significance perhaps is the fact that *Burke deliberately invites his audience to conceive of all their rights and of the ancient constitution that protects them in the same manner as they now (according to Burke) conceive of their property rights.* Among the various ways in which property rights might be secured in the eyes of the law and of the community (with law serving as an expression of the reasoned judgement of the community) Burke considered inheritance and prescription as the most relevant to political philosophy.

Burke's use of the concept of inheritance in which 'all that we possess' and not property alone is conceived of as an inheritance is best illustrated in the following passages:

The very idea of the fabrication of a new government is enough to fill us with disgust and horror. We wished at the period of the Revolution, and do now wish, to derive all we possess as an *inheritance from our forefathers.* Upon that body and stock of inheritance we have taken care not to inoculate any scion alien to the nature of the original plant. All the reformations we have hitherto made have proceeded upon the principle of reference to antiquity; and I hope, nay, I am persuaded, that all those which possibly may be made hereafter will be carefully formed upon analogical precedent, authority, and example.

You will observe, that, from Magna Charta to the Declaration of Right, it has been the uniform policy of our Constitution to claim and assert our liberties as an *entailed inheritance* derived to us from our forefathers, and to be transmitted to our posterity,—as an estate specially belonging to the people of this kingdom, without any reference whatever to any other more general or prior right. By this means our Constitution preserves an unity in so great a diversity of its parts. We have an inheritable crown, an inheritable peerage, and a House of Commons and a people inheriting privileges, franchises, and liberties from a long line of ancestors.[1]

While in the first of these passages Burke seems to mix his metaphors and to conceive of inheritance under two

[1] *Reflections on the Revolution in France, Works,* III, 272–4.

aspects, the legal and the physiological, the legal aspect
predominates; and in the second passage the legal aspect
stands alone. Burke's next paragraph shows, however, that
the English laws of inheritance take on new dimensions in
his hands. Not only does he wish to apply them to 'all
that we possess' and to all our liberties but he wishes to
think of them and of the political system which resembles
them as being especially in accord with 'Nature' and with
'the order of the world, and with the mode of existence
decreed to a permanent body composed of transitory
parts. . . .' I have quoted this celebrated eulogy of the
English Constitution *in toto* in Part One, but I shall here
repeat several crucial lines: '. . . the people of England
well know that the idea of inheritance furnishes a sure
principle of conservation, and a sure principle of transmission, without at all excluding a principle of improvement. It leaves acquisition free; but it secures what it
acquires. Whatever advantages are obtained by a state
proceeding on these maxims are locked fast as in a sort of
family settlement, grasped as in a kind of mortmain forever. By a constitutional policy working after the pattern
of Nature, we receive, we hold, we transmit our government and our privileges, in the same manner in which we
enjoy and transmit our property and our lives.'

Liberal critics of Burke have always wondered at the
facile way in which Burke proclaimed that the idea of
inheritance both leaves acquisition free and secures what it
acquires, without considering how free acquisition actually
was in eighteenth-century England; certainly there is some
evidence here of a formalism (in this case, an attention to
the letter of the law apart from the social context in which
the acquisition and inheritance of property in any significant amounts was largely confined to a few landowners
and merchants) which Burke usually professed to despise.
The defects of partisanship are usually evident in Burke
in just those passages which are renowned for their poetic
and even mystical tone. For present purposes, however, it

is less important to note Burke's shying away from possible conflicts between the laws of inheritance and freedom of acquisition than to note the way in which he remarks that 'we hold, we transmit our government and our privileges, in the same manner in which we enjoy and transmit our property and our lives'. If taken literally, this remark would be astonishing; but taken in the spirit of 'philosophical analogy' it shows how struck Burke is by certain resemblances between the transmission of life and of property. Taken either way, it suggests how closed Burke's mind was on the question of the relationship of the right of property to the right of the transmission of property to one's heirs or designees; for him one of the most important marks of property rights *is* the right of inheritance.

While it is extremely difficult to grasp all that Burke may have had in mind in linking the laws of inheritance to 'Nature' and 'the order of the world', the idea of the inheritance of property seems to form a connecting link in Burke's philosophy between two seemingly different things: the continuation of life in its most literal, physical sense and the continued enjoyment of our rights or liberties as members of civil society. If we can pass over the evident difficulties that arise from a literal reading of Burke's claim that we transmit our government and our privileges in the same manner as we transmit our property *and* our lives, and if we can ignore the injustices that seem to have attended the laws of inheritance operative in the England of his day, we can find in Burke a thesis of considerable importance and one in accord at least in some crucial respects with natural law doctrine. The transmission of life is, according to this doctrine, necessary but not sufficient for the realization of the ends implanted in man; other conditions must also be fulfilled if he is to actualize his moral and intellectual potentials. Now Burke (along with many of his American admirers) is certainly mistaken in believing that the natural law tradition is univocal in its support of private property as being among those conditions that are necessary to man's moral and intellectual development; here there is a real difference within the tradition. But granted Burke's belief that private property improves the lot of man (and not just that of a minority of men), then it seems reasonable to take the idea of inheritance and to extend it to cover two phenomena: first, to proceed from the transmission of life to the transmission of property, and second, from the transmission of property to the transmission of those liberties (and of that government which secures those liberties) which contribute to man's moral and intellectual betterment. Throughout this process the conception of the family takes on new dimensions. First, there is the biological family; then there is the family acquiring, sharing, and transmitting property; and finally there is a new kind of family, a civil family consisting of the members of civil society sharing in and transmitting to posterity the rights, liberties, and privileges of civil society.

Thus far, Burke's use of the notion of a family and of the 'family settlement' seems in accord with the natural law; but two things about families in general and the 'family settlements' of Burke's day in particular must be noted: first, there are evident inequalities in responsibilities, rights, rewards, and punishments in them which may or may not be defensible from the moral point of view; second, the details of the structure of families and especially of the laws governing family settlements owe much to history, geography, the temper of a people, &c., in short to just those features that Burke (following Montesquieu) considered so important, while it is not always so clear that they owe as much directly to reason or that they are rationally defensible. Thus, if we take Burke on the family and the family settlement seriously and consider its *political* implications as he would have us do, serious difficulties emerge where the question of Burke's affinities with the natural law is concerned. This is evident in that passage where Burke speaks of 'our liberties as an *entailed inheritance* derived to us from our forefathers, and to be transmitted to our posterity,—as an estate especially belonging to the people of this kingdom, without any reference whatever to any other more general or prior right'. Two things are disturbing about this passage: (1) In the passion of his anti-French tirade he seems to be lapsing into that narrow provincialism he had condemned in Chief Justice Hale and also to be indifferent to those more general considerations which presumably the natural law should never lose sight of. (2) It is not clear whether Burke's insistence that certain liberties belong to the English people 'without any reference whatever to any more general or prior right' is intended as a denial of the thesis that in a state of nature before the establishment of English civil society the individuals who were to become members of that society had certain rights which English civil society was bound (by contract or otherwise) to observe both for the original members and their descendants, or whether it is intended as a denial of the moral priority of certain rights which man possesses *qua* man over the rights he may possess *qua* Englishman. If it is the former, then, as I have suggested, Burke's natural law and natural rights commitments need not be affected by any criticisms or reservations he may have had about the state of nature or the social contract; logically speaking, he could have abandoned them altogether and still believed in the natural law and in natural rights. If, however, he means to deny the moral priority of natural rights over the civil rights or liberties of Englishmen, then his natural law–natural rights commitments are in danger. While the natural law tradition is not as precise as one might wish on this point, the question 'Should John (or the English nation) inherit X ?' is taken by this tradition to be morally prior to the question 'Is John (or the English nation) legally entitled to inherit X ?' The sense in which the former question is morally prior is roughly this, that one may still ask it (and if need be answer it negatively) even when there is no longer any question of the legal rights involved, and that in the event a negative answer is given and in cases where revision or revocation of the law or decision which is responsible for the unjust or immoral allocation of X is at all possible such revision or revocation should be carried out. Surely this is a large part of what the distinction between natural and positive law amounts to. For that matter, it makes perfectly good sense according to the natural law tradition to ask whether from the moral point of view there should be any legal right of inheritance at all. Burke unfortunately seems predisposed at times to treat *legal* property rights (especially English ones) as if they were a kind of ultimate moral datum, which from the point of view of the natural law they simply cannot be, however much they might possibly be expressions in the imperfect language of positive law of the dictates of a 'more general or prior' natural law (or natural right). This difficulty is even more in evidence when Burke speaks of inheritance and possession through prescription.

Burke's first recorded remarks about prescription occur in his *Abridgement of English History*, where in speaking of the inheritance of property in Anglo-Saxon times he contrasts the great estates held by charter (Book-land) with the lesser properties held by prescription (Folk-land) and contrasts them both with the fiefs of the feudal period: 'they were to all purposes allodial. . . .'[1] In 1772, speaking in the Commons against the Church's attempt to press certain long-dormant claims to lands and tithes it once held, Burke sought 'to quiet' the possessions of the subjects against these claims by appealing to the principle of prescription both as a part of positive law and as a principle of natural equity. The end of prescription, he said, is 'to secure the natural well-meaning ignorance of men, and to secure property by the best of all principles, continuance.'[2]

---

[1] *Works*, VII, 324.
[2] *Speech on Dormant Claims of the Church* (17 February 1772), *Works*, VII, 140–2.

It is not clear exactly what Burke sees as the relationship between the means of prescription and the end of securing the natural well-meaning ignorance of men, but in this context he appears to have in mind chiefly the fact that men most often buy and sell property without being fully aware of who its past owners were or what limitations upon such ownership may have existed. Ignorance of these matters must be presumed to be 'natural' and 'well meaning' and not a pretext for fraud and deceit; such ignorance must be protected by a continuance of the familiar and established ways of dealing with the property in question and by an ignoring of long-dormant claims upon such property.

Burke is fearful of the question of the origins and conditions of initial ownership and prefers to employ the criterion of continuous possession where possible; he claims that this modus operandi is sanctioned by positive law, the principles of natural equity, and by man's predisposition to look upon continued possession as creating at least the presumption of rightful ownership. In his later years Burke spoke with pride of having helped 'perfect prescription' (a reference to his part in the passage of Sir George Savile's *Nullum Tempus* Act) and pointed out to his critic the Duke of Bedford that the future of the Duke himself depended upon prescription: 'The Duke of Bedford will stand as long as prescriptive law endures,—as long as the great, stable laws of property, common to us with all civilized nations, are kept in their integrity. . . .' This was part of a warning to the Duke and other friends of the French Revolution that the Revolution was an avowed enemy of prescriptive right: 'The learned professors of the Rights of Man regard prescription not as a title to bar all claim set up against old possession, but they look on prescription as itself a bar against the possessor and proprietor. They hold an immemorial possession to be no more than a long continued and therefore an aggravated injustice.'[1]

---

[1] *Letter to a Noble Lord on the Attacks upon His Pension, Works,* V, 209-10.

Against prescription the French had, Burke alleged, instigated confiscation; against the natural law which, according to Burke, sanctioned prescription they proclaimed the merits of what was to Burke's mind an untenable version of natural rights theory: 'With the National Assembly of France, possession is nothing, law and usage are nothing. I see the National Assembly openly reprobate the doctrine of prescription, which one of the greatest of their own lawyers (Domat) tells us, with great truth, is a part of the law of nature. . . .'[1] Against the 'rights of men' there can be no prescription, according to the French. French peasants are invited to construe the laws of Nature so that the prescriptive rights of the landlord may be set aside in favour of the occupancy and toil of the peasants themselves: on this reading of the natural law 'there is no prescription against Nature. . . .'[2] Burke does not go into detail as to why he considers this to be an improper construction of natural law; nor does he show an explicit awareness of the different ways in which the word *occupancy* is used. It seems clear, however, that there is *occupancy* in Blackstone (in that passage, for example, which Burke quoted with evident approval and which claims that in the origin of property rights occupancy was sufficient to establish such rights), and there is *occupancy* in the philosophy that Burke attributes to his adversaries (where the emphasis falls upon the present occupancy of a piece of property without attending to the conditions attached to this occupancy or to the ownership of the property being occupied). Where Burke uses *occupancy* disapprovingly it is occupancy as contrasted to legal ownership that he has in mind.

Although Burke as a student at Trinity College had apparently favoured a 10 per cent tax on the property of absentee landlords who held large estates in Ireland while living wholly or for the most part in England, he

[1] *Reflections on the Revolution in France, Works*, III, 432–3.
[2] Ibid., 529.

consistently defended, once he had embarked upon a political career, the rights of the landlord or landowner, including the somewhat notorious absentee landlords whom he had criticized in his youth. (Some of his closest political associates, including the Marquis of Rockingham, were among the wealthiest absentee landlords possessing great estates in Ireland.[1]) What justification if any might he have offered for this defence of the owner at the expense of the occupant who actually lived and toiled on the land ? Prescription, he would probably have said, justifies the possessor of property in his possession, and it is often the case that the possessor, the occupant, and the toiler are one and the same person. In some cases, where the history of the property in question is not known or is not known fully, occupancy and toil might by themselves establish a prescriptive right to a particular property both in the eyes of natural and positive law; but in many cases we do know the history of the property well enough to be familiar with the conditions which affect the possession, occupancy, and labour upon a piece of property; and in many of these cases we know that possession, occupancy, and labour are not always united in the same person or persons. Consider, for example, the following case which I have constructed along Burkian lines. Y rents a property P to X who hires Z to till the soil. Y has a legitimate claim against X for his rent and Z has a legitimate claim against X for his wages; X has a right to the use of property P for the length of time specified in his 'agreement' (whether explicit or tacit) with Y under the conditions set forth in that agreement and to the labour that Z has 'agreed' to provide so long as X pays Z what they have agreed upon, and in addition he has a right to whatever price his crops will fetch in the market place. But Z has no right to anything in addition to his wages, has no right to X's profits (if any) or to Y's land, and X has no right to more of Z's labour than was agreed upon and no right to Y's land beyond the use of it as specified in their agreement.

[1] See Mahoney, op. cit., 310, 351–2; Samuels, op. cit., 251.

And if X and Z should be the same party, or should join forces together, they still have no right to acquire ownership of Y's possession by virtue of their toil and occupancy.

Burke's case for prescription might well acknowledge that it does not cover all conceivable cases where ownership is at stake. It is not the only way to show title to property and in some cases (such as might occur if a group of men were to discover a virgin, uninhabited land and wished to determine how this land was to be divided or shared amongst them) it would seem wholly irrelevant. Even in cases where it is relevant it is not always relevant in the same way, its relevancy being determined in large part by what, if anything, is known of the history, especially the fairly recent history, of the property in question. On the one hand, if we go back far enough, we can cast doubt upon the most widely acknowledged titles to property. On the other hand, if we imagine that we can disregard continued possession and start afresh with new or newly emphasized criteria in disregard of traditionally accepted criteria; if we in our moral speculations ignore the fact that, as Burke put it, old violence has become lawful and continuous possession has obscured the question of how possession may have occurred long ago; if we overlook the fact that in many cases conditions of occupancy and labour have been agreed upon for generations and that this agreement ordinarily leaves the right of possession unaffected, then we shall be violating the laws of nature. Agreement or consent are far from being the clearest of concepts in Burke; Burke himself admits that what he would call agreement or consent might in some cases be considered by others to be the results of duress and force (and hence not binding).[1] Burke's point is, however, this: regardless of

---

[1] *Reflections on the Revolution in France, Works*, III, 529. According to Burke, the argument of his adversaries that there can be no prescription against Nature contains this feature: 'that the agreements (where any there are) which have been made with the landlords during the time of slavery are only the effect of duress or force,—and that when the people re-entered into the rights of men, those agreements were made as void as everything else which had been settled under the prevalence of the old feudal and aristocratic tyranny'.

how certain practices began, the continuation of these practices, with their recognition in custom and law (English property laws serving as a model for the articulation of these practices), amounts in effect to an agreement or consent by all the parties participating in these practices to abide by the rules under which the practice is carried on.

In answer to the question, 'Why should I respect Y's property P ?' Burke considers it at times a sufficient stopper to reply, 'Because you, your father, your father's father, and the laws and customs of your country have done so in the past.' I shall examine shortly the sufficiency of this answer in terms of the natural law. Meanwhile, it is clear that the new rulers of France considered it (at least as Burke represents their opinion) to be an answer insufficient to the point of absurdity: 'They have, it seems found out in the academies of the Palais Royal and the Jacobins, that certain men had no right to the possessions which they held under law, usage, the decisions of courts, and the accumulated prescriptions of a thousand years.'

It is important here to note the use to which Burke has put the doctrine of prescription; from the context it emerges that he is speaking in the above quotation of the seizure of *church* property which his enemies have defended as a 'judgment in law' but which he condemns as a confiscation.[1] He reports the French as now professing to believe that 'ecclesiastics are fictitious persons, creatures of the state, whom at pleasure they may destroy, and of course limit and modify in every particular; that the goods they possess are not properly theirs but belong to the state which created the fiction; and we are therefore not to trouble ourselves with what they may suffer in their natural feelings and natural persons. . . .'[2] Burke in this passage has sought to shift attention from the question of whether the Church is a fictitious creature of the state to that of the

---

[1] Burke elsewhere speaks of the French as having resorted 'to *confiscation* to supply the defect of taxation'. Burke to Mons. Dupont, October 1789, *Correspondence of the Right Honourable Edmund Burke*, III, 110.

[2] *Reflections on the Revolution in France, Works*, III, 372.

'natural feelings' of the individuals who comprise the administrative and clerical aspects of the Church, from the question of the rights and privileges of the clergy as a collective body to the question of their natural feelings as individuals. In this passage he has linked together prescription, the Church, and natural feelings, and while he does not explain the exact nature of this linkage the above passage is far from being a fortuitous grouping of concepts. Elsewhere, Burke speaks of prescription and its chain of 'legitimate prejudices' as the mainstay of European religions:

All the principal religions in Europe stand upon one common bottom. The support that the whole or the favored parts may have had in the secret dispensations of Providence it is impossible to tell; but, humanly speaking, they are all *prescriptive* religions. They have all stood long enough to make prescription and its chain of legitimate prejudices their mainstay. The people who compose the four grand divisions of Christianity have now their religion as an habit, and upon authority, and not on disputation,—as all men who have their religion derived from their parents and the fruits of education *must* have it, however the one more than the other may be able to reconcile his faith to his own reason or to that of other men. Depend upon it, they must all be supported, or they must all fall in the crash of a common ruin.[1]

Burke's position, briefly put, is this: all the major European religions are prescriptive and each is justified as a habit and upon authority not upon disputation or demonstration. This seems reasonable as a statement about men who can accurately be described as having derived their religion from their parents, but why it applies to men whose religion is also derived in part from the 'fruits of education' (where presumably *disputation* would count for something) is by no means clear. The import of Burke's argument is, however, unmistakable: what damages one religion damages all religions, and what does much of the damage is disputation or, speaking less pejoratively, the demand for a rational demonstration of the 'truths' of the

---

[1] *Letter to William Smith, Esq. on Catholic Emancipation* (29 January 1795), *Works*, VI, 368.

faith in question and also of a rational justification of the special privileges of the established Church. In speaking in another context of prescriptive right Burke, we have seen, mentions how an old violence may over a period of time grow lawful; here his position seems to be that the old faiths have grown habitual and that the privileges of the various churches can be justified in part by their long duration. (Burke, of course, also defended the established churches of Europe as institutional expressions of man's 'natural feelings' about God, his relations to God and to other men.) While Burke was willing to champion the prescriptive rights of Englishmen against the Church of England's efforts to reactivate long-dormant claims against their possessions, his primary use of prescription in the religious realm was in defence of the established Church and its possessions whether it be Protestant or Catholic.

Burke's employment of prescription becomes increasingly ambitious. From an unexceptional defence of prescriptive rights to property, unexceptional at least from the point of view of the English legal system, he passes to a more ambitious defence of the property and privileges of the Church as prescriptive without attaching any significance, so far as I can determine, to the counter-argument that there is a significant difference between the rights of a natural person and those of a fictitious person such as a Church. (The fact that he himself has acknowledged the importance of the distinction between natural and fictitious persons in his discussion of the rights of a corporation, the East India Company, seems damaging here.) Finally, his ambition is completed when the rights and privileges of government itself are defended on the ground of prescription. What happens in brief is this: various rights and privileges have been defended, usually against governmental action, in the name of prescription; now the rights and privileges of the government (which has been urged to respect the rights and privileges of its citizens and some at least of its corporate bodies as prescriptive) are in turn defended on the grounds of prescription—and once again no attention is paid in this connexion to the distinction between an individual creature and that which is the creation of individuals or groups of individuals.

Burke's use of prescription in defence of the rights and privileges of the English government and his frank acknowledgement that his defence of these rights and privileges serves in part at least as a means of defending the rights of property is evident in some detail in the following passage where prescription is held to be 'the most solid of all titles':

Why, what have you to answer in favor of the prior rights of the crown and peerage but this: Our Constitution is a prescriptive Constitution whose sole authority is, that it has existed time out of mind ? It is settled in these *two* portions against one, legislatively, and in the whole of the judicature, the whole of the federal capacity, of the executive, the prudential, and the financial administration, in one alone. Nor was your House of Lords and the prerogatives of the crown settled on any adjudication in favor of natural rights; for they could never be so partitioned. Your king, your lords, your judges, your juries, grand and little, all are prescriptive; and what proves it is the disputes, not yet concluded, and never near becoming so, when any of them first originated. Prescription is the most solid of all titles, not only to property, but which is to secure that property, to government. They harmonize with each other, and give mutual aid to one another. It is accompanied with another ground of authority in the constitution of the human mind, presumption. It is a presumption in favor of any settled scheme of government against any untried project, that a nation has long existed and flourished under it. It is a better presumption even of the *choice* of a nation,—far better than any sudden and temporary arrangement by actual election. Because a nation is not an idea only of local extent and individual momentary aggregation, but it is an idea of continuity which extends in time as well as in numbers and in space. And this is a choice not of one day or one set of people, not a tumultuary and giddy choice; it is a deliberate election of ages and of generations; it is constitution made by what is ten thousand times better than choice; it is made by the peculiar circumstances, occasions, tempers, dispositions, and more, civil, and social habitudes of the people, which disclose themselves only in a long space of time. It is a vestment which accommodates itself to the natural. Nor is prescription of government formed upon blind, unmeaning prejudices. For man is a most unwise and a most wise being. The individual is foolish; the multitude, for the moment, is foolish, when they act without deliberation; but the species is wise, and when time is given to it, as a species, it almost always acts right.[1]

It is beyond my intentions or resources to do full justice to this celebrated passage. While its 'poetry' is of course renowned, the price that Burke (and his readers) must pay for this poetic dimension has largely gone undetected. Some of Burke's images are relatively harmless and indeed brilliant: the way in which he moves from prescription and the political constitution to presumption and the *constitution* of the human mind is striking and serves to strengthen the parallel Burke is seeking to establish. Serious difficulty emerges, however, with Burke's use of the words *choice* and *election*. When he says that it is a better presumption even of the *choice* of a nation, far better than any sudden and temporary arrangement by actual election, that *any* settled scheme of government under which a nation has long existed and flourished is to be preferred against *any* untried project, it is not clear as to what kind of choice or election is involved. It cannot be an 'actual' election or even an 'actual' choice, for Burke's primary point seems to be to contrast two kinds of election and choice. Undoubtedly, too, *election* may stand for a more or less formal process of voting for men for various offices and for a less formal process of choosing or selecting from among various alternative courses of action (as in 'John elected to go to a film'); and it is clever of Burke to contrast the chaos of political election with the 'deliberate election of ages and generations' to the disadvantage of the former. But what is the nature of this deliberate election? How does this deliberate election become 'a thousand times better than choice' when previously it was used quasi-synonymously with choice? The answer appears easy up to a point: it is a choice that is made and reaffirmed over a period of time and not a momentary or an unthinking

---

[1] *Speech on Reform of Representation of the Commons in Parliament* (7 May 1872), *Works*, VII, 94–95. Burke wrote but did not deliver this speech.

choice. But is either *choice* or *deliberate election* the right description for the process of making a (political) constitution, a constitution which Burke immediately goes on to add 'is made by the peculiar circumstances, occasions, tempers, dispositions, and moral, civil, and social habitudes of the people' ?

Ordinarily, *choice*, in the sense of conscious choice at least, and *deliberate election* in particular, are used to mark off certain ways of behaving or deciding from those that are attributed to circumstances, dispositions, and habits. Now it may be, and probably is the case, that the British Constitution was made by conscious, deliberate choice interacting with non-deliberate circumstances, dispositions, and habits; and the crucial question simply put would seem to be how much does it owe to choice and how much to habit. Burke seems, however, to ignore this question, to act as if there were, for his purposes, no significant differences between choice and deliberate election, circumstances, dispositions, and habits, and as if all the crucial differences lay between choice (of the sort that is repeatedly reaffirmed), deliberate election, circumstances, dispositions, and habits taken together and a kind of hasty, and even silly, choice such as some voters might perhaps make on election day. Moreover, the good kind of choice or deliberate election (good from Burke's point of view) turns out to involve a kind of holism in which, according to Burke, the species in the long run is capable of choosing wisely in a way that the individual and the multitude cannot.

Part of what seems to be involved in Burke's treatment of *choice* and *deliberate election* is something like the notion of a *tacit consent* (on the part of the rational species as a whole if not on the part of the foolish individual members thereof) to those rights and privileges which either an individual or an institution has enjoyed without challenge, or without successful challenge, over a period of time. More than this is needed, however, if the above passage from

Burke is to be rendered intelligible: in the history of mankind there is operative, Burke appears to think, some process for selecting acceptable rights or privileges and for rejecting those founded or supported on 'blind, unmeaning prejudices'. We are left largely in the dark as to how the results of blind, unmeaning prejudices are separated off in time from those that result from or are in accord with 'just prejudices', 'natural feelings', &c. The acceptance of Burke's thesis that we should trust in time and the wisdom of the species would seem to depend upon his being able to tell us something about the dynamics of this process of selection; and yet this matter, and indeed the whole of Burke's philosophy of history, remains especially obscure. If it is not an 'evolutionary' process with a natural selection of fit institutions and practices that Burke envisages as occurring (and here many Burke scholars would demur and point to his Christian beliefs, his acceptance of free will, his emphasis upon choice, deliberate election, &c.), then what is it ? Most likely, Burke himself has no clear picture of this process or its dynamics and is content with something resembling the traditional Christian belief that the workings of God's wisdom and the course of human history are not wholly separate. The ticklish question here is whether Burke was not too content and too satisfied with this belief so that his God finally becomes too involved, too immanent in history from the point of view of most Christian teachings on this matter—but this problem I leave to the theologians.[1]

The long quotation from Burke given above poses serious difficulties for the natural law interpretation of Burke if it is read literally. These difficulties stem largely from two of Burke's claims: (1) that the rights of various parts of the

---

[1] The solution to this problem will depend in part upon whether scholars can provide a clear construction of Burke's conception of 'extraordinary Providence' and 'ordinary Providence' and of the respective parts these two aspects or kinds of Providence play in human affairs according to Burke. The passage that poses perhaps the greatest difficulty in this connexion occurs in Burke's *Second Letter on a Regicide Peace*, *Works*, V, 349, where he remarks that the rules of prudence are 'formed upon the known march of the ordinary providence of God'.

English community were not adjudicated or partitioned 'in favor of' (on the basis of) natural rights; (2) that the 'sole authority' of the English Constitution is that it has existed time out of mind. The seriousness of Burke's seemingly critical approach to natural rights (and hence to natural law) is, however, lessened by the following considerations. Burke's remarks occur in a context where the reform of representation in the House of Commons was under consideration, an undertaking to which Burke was adamantly opposed. The reform under consideration was moreover being urged on the ground that representation was the natural right of the individual. Burke's position on representation will not be discussed in detail, but it is well known that his doctrine of 'virtual representation' was a counter to those who were urging an extension of actual representation by such devices as increasing the electorate, redistributing the seats in the House, or holding annual elections. On this particular occasion Burke's denial that the right of actual representation is a natural right is accompanied by an effort on his part to show that a large number of rights and privileges and 'prerogatives' (especially of the ruling classes) are recognized in England that were not decided or distributed upon the basis of natural rights. It is important to note, too, that the model of natural rights that Burke has in mind in this passage is one that might be called *historical* in that the crucial concern seems to be with the historical origin or genesis of certain rights in civil society and their 'adjudication' or 'partition' (if any) on the basis of 'natural' rights exercised by individuals prior to the establishment of civil society. Burke points to the endless disputes as to when various rights were first recognized or granted by civil society as evidence of the relative fruitlessness of the claims made by those who believed the state of nature and natural rights to be historically prior to civil society. But this rather literal-minded way of looking at natural rights which has plagued practically all contract theories leaves unaffected, as I have noted earlier, the more fundamental question of the moral priority of natural rights, of whether certain rights and privileges acknowledged by civil society coincide with or, under the circumstances, are adequate expressions of those natural rights which belong to man *qua* man (regardless of whether he has ever enjoyed or exercised these rights in the past). Burke, as we shall see, appears as sympathetic to natural rights conceived of in this second light as he is critical of them conceived of as principles upon which the institutions and practices of civil society were actually arranged at some past time. Two things should, however, be noted here: first, Burke's sympathy with natural rights as criteria for evaluating the rights and privileges sanctioned by a particular civil society at a given time is qualified (a) by the restricted number of those rights that Burke would admit to be 'natural' and (b) by his insistence upon the *presumption* of right in *all* cases of rights and privileges sanctioned by civil society over a period of time; second, Burke's criticism of natural rights conceived of as having been the principles upon which civil society was organized at some historic moment is also qualified in part by his reluctance to let go entirely of the concepts of the state of nature and of the social contract.

The more serious difficulty for the natural law reading of Burke is posed by his second claim that the 'sole authority' of the English Constitution is that it has endured time out of mind. Various approaches to this passage may be attempted. The fact that Burke wrote but did not deliver this speech may be used to create doubt as to whether he considered it a satisfactory expression of his own thought in this matter. Or else since Burke was speaking in large part of the history of English legal and political institutions it might be suggested that what he really had in mind was the 'sole authority' recognizable from the strictly *legal* point of view, from the point of view of positive law rather than of the principles of natural equity. Yet the chief point of Burke's homilies about the English Constitution is most often its excellence from the moral point of view. More-over, even from the restricted perspective of positive law, it seems odd for Burke to speak of the Great Charters which specifically acknowledged certain rights and privi-leges at particular times and then to say of the Constitution as a whole (a prominent part of which consists of the Great Charters such as Magna Charta) that its *sole* authority is that it has existed time out of mind. The doctrine of the 'ancient constitution' properly construed would allow at least some supporting authority to be found in the fact that these allegedly immemorial rights and privileges had been *reaffirmed* or *reacknowledged* at particular moments in English history. In any event, from the moral point of view it seems to many persons inconclusive to use the historical existence of a practice or an institution as the sole justification of that practice or institution; indeed from the moral point of view one may question whether this can count even as a partial justification. The problem, therefore, is what exactly did Burke have in mind in speaking of the English Constitution as if its existence over a period of time was a sufficient condition for the *moral* rightness of the legal rights and privileges existing under it and whether this is consistent with his commitment to natural law.[1]

Previously I noted the difficulty of reconciling Burke's natural law commitments with that passage in the *Reflections* where he invites Englishmen to claim and assert their liberties 'as an *entailed inheritance* derived to us from our forefathers, and to be transmitted to our posterity—as an estate specially belonging to the people of this kingdom without any reference whatever to any other more general or prior right'. If anything, Burke's claim that the 'sole authority' of the English Constitution is that it has 'existed time out of mind' poses graver problems for the natural law

---

[1] At least three commentators have stressed the importance of this problem. See Robert M. Hutchins, 'The Theory of Oligarchy: Edmund Burke', *The Thomist*, V (1943), 61–78; Leo Strauss, *Natural Right and History*, 319; Canavan, op. cit., 132–5. To my knowledge, however, none has proposed the solution to this difficulty which I shall now set forth.

reading of Burke. Significantly perhaps, he is speaking in the present context of what may be called the rights of the Establishment, of the government and of the ruling classes; here he has used stronger language in defending these rights than he ordinarily would in the case of those rights that belonged to all Englishmen (those primary and auxiliary rights to be found in Blackstone's *Commentaries* and defended *in toto* by Burke). But in both instances parties who have exercised certain rights over a long period of time are invited by Burke to continue claiming and asserting these rights solely on the grounds of the historicity of the rights in question.

This might do very well for those countries (Burke, as I shall attempt to show, believed England to be the best example of this) where the requirements of natural law had long been fully provided for in the positive laws of the land, but clearly it is irrelevant for countries where this is not the case. Moreover, it is a dangerous doctrine for even England to embrace. If we were to grant Burke's belief that from the point of view of natural law England had long enjoyed a remarkable harmony of natural and positive law, and if we were to acknowledge the doctrine of parliamentary supremacy which Burke (like Blackstone) championed, then it follows that this harmony of natural and positive law need not always endure. Where the Constitution is not a single document or set of documents but is, so to speak, being constantly made anew or added to by laws enacted by Parliament and where the judicial system has no power of judicial review, no power to set aside an act of Parliament which might, for example, run counter to the provisions of Magna Charta, then new positive laws contrary to natural law might become the law of the land, might endure for a terribly long time, and the rights and privileges conferred by them might be defended against criticism from the point of view of the natural law on the grounds that these rights and privileges have after all existed for a very long time. Indeed, this difficulty is the basis, I think, of many of the criticisms directed against Burke by his more progressive or radical contemporaries who regarded Burke himself as defending *unjust* privileges in the name of historic rights.

Certainly the situation does not look very promising for Burke at this point. I shall not discuss the question of whether Burke or his critics had the better case as to the justice, or lack thereof, of the legal, social, and political order of eighteenth-century England; but solely from the logical point of view Burke's commitment to the natural law seems to totter precariously in the presence of the 'general or prior right' and the 'sole authority' passages. Can the natural law commitment be reconciled with the commitment revealed in these passages, and if so how ? If this can be done at all, the best approach is, in my opinion, to look closely at what Burke thinks presumption does (and does not do) for prescriptive rights and to pay some attention to what might be called different levels of discourse in Burke. Much of the difficulty that plagues Burke interpretation stems from a failure to attend to the fact that just as Burke's political philosophy embraces a hierarchy of social and political classes with various degrees of mental and political competence and with an unequal distribution of rights and privileges, so his political philosophy is expressed in a hierarchy of statements which exhibit varying degrees of universality and different levels of justification concerning the distribution of rights and privileges.

One commentator remarks that for Burke 'Prescription means that whatever is old confers a right, and nothing confers a right unless it is old'.[1] But this, I think, is mistaken on three counts: (1) Most obviously, the 'whatever' covers too much ground: old chairs, old paintings, and old loves do not seem to confer, ordinarily, any right at all. (2) Burke certainly nowhere says that every old social or political institution or practice confers a right. His reasons for not saying this are (a) that he recognizes the fact of obsolescence and an accompanying loss of relevance in the history of

[1] Hutchins, op. cit., 73.

some of man's social and political contrivances: '*But when the reason of old establishments is gone, it is absurd to preserve nothing but the burden of them*';[1] and (b) that *one of his chief contributions to political thought lies in his insistence that talk of rights forms but one part of the language of politics and morality*; he would, I think, therefore, be inclined to deny that all old institutions and practices, even those that are still morally relevant, must in every case confer some kind of right. (3) Given Burke's commitment to a natural law with a changing content and his insistence that we must obey the great law of change, he could not very well believe that in new situations new rights or at least newly modified versions of old rights could never emerge. His political conservatism and his actual resistance to the 'new' rights being claimed by his adversaries do not in any way commit him to the claim that nothing confers a right unless it is old; indeed, it would be extremely odd to find a man seated in a legislative capacity and engaged in the making of new laws and the modification of old ones who believed that no new rights (recognized in moral and political deliberation and expressed in positive law) ever came into being.

What then is the relation of the old, the ancient, and the immemorial to the claim to and the justification of a right or rights? Obviously, the relationship is extremely complicated, and Burke for all his emphasis upon the complexity of the social and political fabric nowhere acknowledges how complicated it is. It is, however, possible to discern in Burke's remarks about the presumption that allegedly accompanies the old, the ancient, &c., a key to the relationship he believed to exist between the old and a right or rights. I shall admittedly be arguing for what might be called a 'soft' interpretation of Burke where this relationship is concerned, but it seems to me the only interpretation that can be squared with Burke on presumption.

What is the presumption (the 'ground of authority in the constitution of the human mind') that Burke is speaking

[1] *Speech on the Plan for Economical Reform, Works,* II, 305. My italics.

of ? Presumption has both a descriptive and a normative role in Burke's thought, although he himself makes no effort to distinguish between its two roles. In the above passage Burke seems to have in mind first the descriptive and later the normative part that presumption plays. Man, he believes, is a creature of habit who is psychologically disposed to accept a political constitution and a distribution of rights and privileges that have existed for a long period of time as being a just constitution and a just distribution of rights and privileges. Such a constitution and such a distribution are presumed to have been shorn of their imperfections by gradual changes and piecemeal reforms over a period of time; they have been accompanied by the growth of a host of habits and expectations such as established laws and social arrangements naturally further. Such habits and expectations are widely shared, and so the great bulk of the population is naturally disposed, Burke believes, to look with suspicion upon proposals that would radically alter these habits and shake these expectations. Burke's position here is very much like Hume's; and it shares the same obvious weakness, namely that in periods of great social changes, man may become habituated to presume *against* long-established constitutions and distributions of rights and privileges as being obsolete. For example, to say today of any piece of factory or social legislation that it has endured even for fifty years would only arouse the suspicion that it is no longer adequate to the needs of our time regardless of what it may have been in the not-too-distant past. More generally, man may become distrustful of all habits, especially those of loyalty and obedience to established political and social arrangements, although social anarchy may (as Hume and Burke feared) result from this distrust.

Undoubtedly, presumption has also a normative role in Burke's thought, i.e., he believes that men *ought* to continue to behave as he believes they have behaved in this matter, that the presumption in favour of the established order of things is defensible from the moral point of view. If one is going to make a distinction between traditional and modern natural law theories, it might well be made on just this question of the stance that a natural law theorist takes toward established constitutions and established distributions of rights and privileges. One might suppose that all natural law theory would be committed to a posture of initial neutrality before evaluating the merits of established social and political arrangements. Yet the history of natural law shows that traditional natural law theory (Thomism, for example) usually exhibits that kind of initial sympathy with or presumption in favour of the established order of things which Burke displays, while much of seventeenth- and eighteenth-century natural law theory seems predisposed toward a critical approach, assuming that the social injustices prevalent in these centuries are painfully obvious. Apparently, the initial neutrality required of our 'model' natural law theory is hard to come by in fact; and I submit that so long as no claim of *ultimate* justification or ultimate rejection of a positive human law or arrangement is derived from the mere fact of the existence of this law or arrangement the natural law tradition is not seriously jeopardized whether one takes the sympathetic stance, as Burke did, or the critical one, as Thomas Paine did. It is mainly a question of point of view, so long as one does not insist that the ultimate moral rightness or wrongness of a law or arrangement can be derived (and not simply presumed) solely from the fact of existence over a significant (if unspecified) period of time.

The question remains, however, as to why Burke adopted this point of view rather than the critical alternative; and, although this is usually ignored, a large part of Burke's willingness to presume in favour of the established order of things derives from his vast faith in the reasonableness of law and in the power of positive human law at least to approach the moral ideals of the natural law. I say faith deliberately because much of the ground of this faith in the dynamics of the juristic and political processes remains obscure. It is, I think, no accident, however, that the word *presumption* occupies a significant place in the legal profession for which Burke had at one time prepared. I think, too, that it is no exaggeration to say that English law serves as a significant bridge in Burke's thought between the *is* of human inclinations, needs, and habits and the *ought* of the natural law. We have seen Burke himself speak of 'presumptions of law': a presumption *in* law can be defined as an inference founded on previous experience or 'general knowledge' and a presumption *of* law as a rule or policy of the law which requires that certain inferences be made in certain kinds of cases, in the absence of overwhelming evidence that such inferences should not be made. Presumption appears to function in Burke's thought much as it functions in English law, connecting (either as an inference or a rule of inference) the facts of human inclination, &c., with the norms of the natural law in the manner in which it connects in English law the facts of human inclination, &c., with the legal norms of positive law. Moreover, Burke believed, rightly or wrongly, in a high coincidence between the norms of natural law and the legal norms of positive law, especially of the English variety: 'It has ever been the method of public jurists to draw a great part of the analogies on which they form the law of nations from the principles of law which prevail in civil community. *Civil laws are not all of them merely positive. Those which are rather conclusions of legal reason than [merely] matters of statutable provision belong to universal equity, and are universally applicable.*'[1]

Burke's belief that '*If not the right, the presumption, at least, is ever on the side of possession*'[2] is in his judgement supported by both English civil law and the natural law. It is not merely a belief incorporated in positive law but it is rather a conclusion of legal reason which belongs also to 'universal equity' and is 'universally applicable'. Burke's

---

[1] *Second Letter on a Regicide Peace, Works*, V, 321. My italics.
[2] *Tract on the Popery Laws, Works*, VI, 337. My italics.

distinction in this sentence between right and presumption is important, for if it means that presumption recognizes the probability of right to be on the side of the possessor of a property or a privilege but does not take such possession to be a *conclusive* sign of rightful ownership, then Burke can preserve his allegiance to both the English legal system and its laws of property and to the natural law. What he is saying in his discussion of prescription and presumption is chiefly this: in all cases such actual possession is a sign that confers a probability that the property or privilege in question has been held rightfully from the point of view of both positive and natural law, a probability which becomes higher in direct proportion to the length of time this possession or ownership has continued; it may, however, be true that in some cases there will emerge strong evidence that the right is other than it appears to be; in such cases the inferences we would ordinarily make as to the legitimacy (either legal or moral) of ownership would not be made or, having been made, would be revoked. But prescription and presumption cover the vast majority of cases; that they admit of exceptions is no reflection of the inadequacy of these rules but of an unsophisticated and faulty reading of them as though they were intended to admit of no exceptions. One might quarrel with Burke on the grounds that the idea he has of justifiable exceptions to the decrees of prescription and of presumption is not spelled out and that if it were spelled out it would (so far as we can tell) make no allowances for distributive justice in the way that the natural law might be expected to; but from a more formal point of view Burke's willingness to allow a distinction between the right and the presumption of right helps to salvage, at least formally, his commitment to the natural law.

Our problems are, however, far from over where Burke and the natural law are concerned. There is the problem of reconciling, if we can, Burke's denial in the *Tract on the Popery Laws* that 'laws can derive any [moral] authority from their institution merely, and independent of the quality of the subject-matter. No arguments of policy, reason of state, or preservation of the constitution can be pleaded in favor of such a practice',[1] and the later claim, made while defending the English Constitution, that the Constitution derives its 'sole authority' from the fact that it has existed time out of mind, i.e., from its institution over a long period of time. At this point it would be tempting to conclude with liberal interpreters of Burke such as Robert M. Hutchins that if the early Burke had believed in natural law and natural rights the later Burke certainly did not. The alternative, which I want to explore, is that Burke on the whole did not seriously contradict himself, did not abandon the natural law and natural rights, but rather that he became more subtle both in his conception of them and in his intuitive awareness of the importance of different levels of discourse and of the different kinds of arguments that work most effectively on these various levels.

Before I can make a case for this alternative I must, however, do two things: (1) I must show what would be lost *if* Burke's later position could be reduced to the claim (a) that the mere legal institution (or acknowledgement) of a right or privilege is sufficient to establish the ultimate moral rightness of this right or privilege, and (b) that in the absence of legal recognition of a claim to a right or privilege no claims on behalf of this right or privilege can be considered morally acceptable. (2) I must show that the disjunction between natural law and natural rights on the one hand and English law and the rights of Englishmen on the other, while rooted in the English political and legal tradition, is not so firmly rooted as Barker, for example, believes, and that it certainly is not to be taken as an exclusive disjunction, especially not in the case of Burke. Having made this negative point, I then want to find in this very English way of talking of English law and the rights of Englishmen some clue as to why Burke thought as he did.

[1] *Tract on the Popery Laws, Works*, VI, 322.

What would be lost if either or both (a) and (b) under (1) were accepted as Burke's final position on rights is, as I have suggested, his commitment to natural rights and ultimately to the natural law as well. On my interpretation (1) is incompatible with Burke's protestation in his *Reflections on the Revolution in France* that he did not wish to deny either in theory or practice 'the *real* rights of man', which he took to include the benefits or 'advantages' conferred by civil society, the right to live under a rule of law, the right to justice, the right to the fruits of one's industry, to the acquisitions of one's parents, and to 'equal rights' (though not to equal things).[1] These 'real rights' appear to be in Burke's judgement *bona fide* natural rights: rights which belong to man *qua* man regardless of his nationality and which he does not have to 'earn' or 'merit'. To be sure, they are at the same time civil rights in that they belong to man as a member of civil society, but they are not *merely* civil rights in any sense that would suggest that the recognition or withholding of these rights is to be left entirely to the discretion of civil society which may do as it *pleases* or *wills*. I find it impossible to believe that the later Burke would have spoken in the following vein during the trial of Warren Hastings had he ceased to believe in natural rights:

We have shown you, that if these parties are to be compared together it is not the rights of the people which are nothing, but rather the rights of the sovereign which are so. The rights of the people are everything, as they ought to be in the true and natural order of things. God forbid that these maxims should trench upon sovereignty, and its true, just, and lawful prerogative!—on the contrary, they ought to support and establish them. The sovereign's rights are undoubtedly sacred rights, and ought to be so held in every country of the world, because exercised for the benefit of the people, and in subordination to the great end for which alone God has vested power in any man or any set of men.[2]

While it is easy to find in the later Burke protests against what he considered false or exaggerated claims made on behalf of man's natural rights or illegitimate demands for

[1] *Works*, III, 308.
[2] Speech in General Reply (May and June 1794), *Works*, XI, 232.

political power in the name of man's 'natural right' to representation, I find the later Burke substantially in agreemen with the following passage from his *Tract on the Popery Laws*. (Readers will note that both here and in the *Reflections* emphasis falls upon man's rights to the 'advantages' of civil society.)

Everybody is satisfied that a conservation and secure enjoyment of our natural rights is the great and ultimate purpose of civil society, and that therefore all forms whatsoever of government are only good as they are subservient to that purpose to which they are entirely subordinate. Now to aim at the establishment of any form of government by sacrificing what is the substance of it, to take away or at least to suspend the rights of Nature in order to [secure] an approved system for the protection of them, and for the sake of that about which men must dispute forever to postpone those things about which they have no controversy at all, and this not in minute and subordinate, but large and principal objects, is a procedure as preposterous and absurd in argument as it is oppressive and cruel in its effect. For the Protestant religion, nor (I speak it with reverence, I am sure) the truth of our common Christianity, is not so clear as this proposition,—that all men, at least the majority of men in the society, ought to enjoy the common advantages of it.[1]

Burke's judgement that 'Civil laws are not all of them merely positive' but that some of them belong to 'universal equity' as well must be balanced against his more provincial moments, which become more frequent in his later years, when he stresses the Englishness of the laws and liberties of his adopted country and the uniqueness of her achievements in the fields of politics and jurisprudence. Probably Burke's audience was more familiar with this second line of thought. Why so many of the English and not just those who subscribed to the doctrine of the 'ancient Constitution' have looked upon English law in this way has never been sufficiently explored. Their emphasis upon the uniqueness *and* the antiquity of English law and of the liberties recognized by that law may stem from a determination to deny the importance of the Norman Conquest by insisting that English law was in fundamentals well established before

---

[1] *Works*, VI, 333–4. My italics. The last sentence of this quotation was discussed in Part One in connexion with the question of Burke's religiosity.

the coming of the Normans and the introduction of continental law. Possibly, too, the later creation of the Church of England contributed to a desire to deny English indebtedness to canon law comparable to the wish to deny any indebtedness to continental law. Or perhaps nothing more complicated is involved in the emphasis upon old English laws and old English liberties than this: 'Those rights which people think they ought to have are just those rights which they have been accustomed to have, or which they have a tradition (whether true or false) of having once possessed'.[1] This explanation has a Burkian quality in its emphasis upon the 'accustomed', and probably it provides some help in understanding how Burke's own veneration of antiquity limited the scope or range of his speculations on the question of rights.

The question remains, however, as to the relation of English law to the natural law. As I noted earlier, the test of *reasonableness* in English law is one link to the natural law tradition and a significant one; but what is the importance of the English insistence upon the Englishness of their laws and liberties ? My suggestion is that the English in this way of speaking have, obliquely, been calling attention to achievement as contrasted with aspiration. The achievement is English law which, in the opinion of many of the English, has succeeded better than any other legal system in actually protecting those rights which the natural law says should be protected. So why continue to speak of natural rights, thus suggesting that these rights still stand as an unfulfilled ideal, when one can point to the actual enjoyment of these rights by Englishmen under English laws of long duration ? An American of today might behave in a similar manner when speaking of *American* law, *American* rights, and the *American* Constitution. In neither case is the intention to deny that the principles of these laws belong to those of 'universal equity'; if pressed the Englishman and the American might well acknowledge

[1] David Ritchie, *Natural Rights* (London, 1895), 82.

that both historically and logically the affinities between natural law and their national laws are striking. They are simply indicating that they have achieved (at least in their own eyes) a positive law with a higher ethical content than have other nations.

Even if this explanation does not do full justice to what most Englishmen have had in mind when they speak of ancient or immemorial English law and of the rights of Englishmen, it seems to work in the case of both Blackstone and Burke. Blackstone while admitting that all men by virtue of their humanity have rights to personal security, personal liberty, and private property says of these rights that 'in most other countries of the world, being now more or less debased or destroyed, they at present may be said to remain in a special and emphatic measure, the rights of the people of England' (*Commentaries*, I, 128). Much of Burke's veneration for 'the good old common-law of England, and the principles of the English constitution'[1] seems to stem from his belief that the natural rights of man have remained, since time immemorial, in a special and emphatic measure the rights of the people of England. 'Our Constitution', he writes, 'is like our island, which uses and restrains its subject sea . . . . In that Constitution, I know, and exultingly I feel, both that I am free, and that I am not free dangerously to myself or to others. I know that no power on earth, acting as I ought to do, can touch my life, my liberty, or my property. I have that inward and dignified consciousness of my own security and independence, which constitutes, and is the only thing which does constitute, the proud and comfortable sentiment of freedom in the human breast.'[2]

Burke's belief that the English Constitution provided such excellent protection for his rights to life, liberty, and property (these being, of course, the natural rights championed by John Locke) helps us understand both why he

---

[1] Edmund Burke to Richard Burke, June 1792, *Correspondence of the Right Honourable Edmund Burke*, IV, 15.

[2] *Speech on Reform of Representation of the Commons in Parliament, Works*, VII, 100–1.

usually saw no need to look beyond the English Constitution in his discussion of these rights and why he was angered
by any discussions which presupposed or stated that the
English Constitution did not provide sufficient protection
for life, liberty, and property. The natural law and the
theory of natural rights serve chiefly as criteria for evaluating existing political constitutions; and Burke, having performed this evaluation, was ordinarily content to extol the
virtues of the English Constitution without referring to the
criteria he had used in ascertaining these virtues in the first
place. He was most comfortable in exploring the question
of rights within the limits of the Constitution and of legal
decision:

> If you have a right (continued Mr. Burke)—if you have a right upon
> what maxim of law or equity is it founded: When was this right juridically
> discussed, and finally determined ? On what day was the decision given ?
> In what court are we to look for the record of this decision ? To what
> does this right extend ? To all, or only to some of the territorial acquisi-
> tions [of the East India Company] ? If only to some, of what nature are
> they ? How specified, described, and distinguished from the rest ? If
> you have a right to all the Company's territorial acquisitions, you truly
> begin a redress of their grievances in a peculiar manner; to restore the
> ruined state of their finances, you plunder them of their property; and
> to re-establish the Company's affairs on a permanent basis, you suffer
> not the proprietors to have a foot of land in India which they can call
> their own.[1]

Burke, as we have seen, reversed the position he took in
the above remarks delivered on 5 April, 1773, and went on,
with great reluctance he claimed, to insist that Parliament
did indeed have just the right he had denied it to have in
1773. It was, he later claimed in effect, both a legal right
arising from the peculiarities of the rights of the monopoly
conferred upon this corporation and a moral right arising
from the abuses by this corporation of its powers. *Ordinarily, however, Burke was more preoccupied with questions
of what might be called constitutional law than with those
of natural law*: 'Men justify their acts in two ways,' he

[1] *Speeches*, I, 171–2.

observed during the Hastings' Trial, 'by law and by precedent; the former asserts the right, the latter presumes it
from the example of others;[1] and it is clear from the context
that Burke has in mind primarily positive law and legal
precedent. Yet in the same trial we find some of Burke's
most impassioned tributes to the natural law since the *Tract
on the Popery Laws*. Thus it seems that Burke was ultimately capable of working on three different levels of
justification. Justification could be provided by positive
law, by precedent, or by the natural law; and here, as in
the case of the three parts of the British Constitution, Burke
has the habit of speaking of either of these levels of justification in the heat of the moment as if it were the kind that
mattered most or at times as if it alone mattered.

To speak of three levels of justification in Burke is
undoubtedly to formalize a situation which in Burke's
own mind remained rather more fluid. Burke was not a
very precise philosopher, partly from habit no doubt but
partly from a reluctance on his part to mark distinctions
that might obscure vital resemblances. Positive law and
legal precedent can both, Burke believed, partake of the
natural law; English positive law and legal precedent having
done so to a remarkable degree, Burke is loath to distinguish
among the three of them. Indeed, in Burke's mind there
may be only two levels where he would admit any distinctions worth attending to: on the first level would stand
both positive law and legal precedent, with the presumption that accompanies precedent in the courts of law being
no different in kind from the presumption that accompanies
possession whether possession is being discussed in the
Commons, in the courts, or in the streets[2]; and on the

---

[1] *Works*, XI, 272.

[2] Information on Burke's conception of precedent is extremely sketchy, but
one finds an occasional warning—not restricted solely to legal precedent—against
a rigid application of precedent: 'God forbid that we should attempt to be wise
by precedent.' Edmund Burke to William Windham, 30 December 1794,
Correspondence of the Right Honourable Edmund Burke (London, 1844), IV, 254.
This, however, seems consistent with his declaiming that precedent confers the
presumption (not the certainty) of right.

second level, there would stand the natural law which provides the principles that should in all cases and in many cases do, Burke thinks, inform both positive law and legal precedent.

A comprehensive treatment of Burke's two (or three) levels of discourse seems impossible not only because of the imprecise and fragmentary nature of Burke's reflections on them but, more seriously, because the logic of moral discourse itself remains inadequately explored. One of the distressing features in the history of ideas is the way in which philosophers are sometimes called sharply to task for failing to heed allegedly vital distinctions (analytic–synthetic, is–ought, &c.) which the practising philosopher may suspect have not really been settled upon or accepted in the way that the historian of philosophy seems to assume. Thus, for example, when Hegel, Marx, Mill, and Spencer appear to attach too much ethical significance to 'mere' facts they are accused of committing the most elementary of errors which any schoolboy could detect at once; and the natural law tradition has suffered a similar fate. But, standing off-stage so to speak, there remains a large number of highly puzzling questions about the relation of fact and value, one of which must surely be why so many people (and not just bad philosophers) go around attaching a peculiar moral significance to facts of a certain kind.

I remarked earlier that Burke nowhere explicitly commits the so-called naturalistic fallacy. The closest he comes to doing so perhaps is when he speaks of the English Constitution as deriving its sole authority from the fact that it has existed time out of mind; but when this passage is 'unpacked' the long existence of the English Constitution which justifies this authority (which I take to be a moral authority as well as a legal one) is one in which fact and value are after all interwoven—at least in Burke's eyes it has been the product of a continuing (if in our eyes rather curious) consent and free, rational choice on the part of generations of Englishmen and not simply or even primarily the result of brute force and duress. Burke's opposition to slavery and the slave trade (see his *A Letter to the Right Hon. Henry Dundas with the Sketch of a Negro Code, Works,* VI, 257–89) shows that the historicity of an institution or a practice is not always in his opinion a fact of moral significance in favour of the institution or practice in question let alone a sufficient condition of its moral worth. The question remains, however, as to why in cases where past generations were believed to have consented freely and rationally to certain institutions and practices, Burke spoke of the continuous existence of these institutions and practices as being of peculiar moral significance. Burke claimed modestly that *he* (unlike his adversaries) had made no discoveries in morals; and in speaking as he did of the moral value of certain established institutions and practices he must have believed, rightly or wrongly, that he was in this respect behaving no differently from others who speak the language of morality.

Without pretending to have unravelled all or even most of the logic of moral discourse and without assuming that what I am about to say absolves the natural law tradition and Burke of further criticism, it does appear that in some contexts (which are admittedly hard to specify) the kinds of facts that Burke believed to count heavily from the moral point of view do in fact count heavily. The long duration of an institution or practice that has proved beneficial and to which people (all or most of them) have consented expressly or tacitly does make a *moral* difference to many people who would at least consider themselves to be moral. Moreover, it seems that people do speak of a role, an institution, or a practice as if certain moral imperatives could be seen to 'follow' in some sense from certain facts about such a role, institution, or practice. Consider the following examples: (1) *Q.*: 'Why should I feed the child?' *A.*: 'Because you are the mother.' (2) *Q.*: 'Why should the army fight the enemy?' *A.*: 'Because that's what armies are for.' (3) *Q.*:

'Why should I go to John's filthy party ?' *A*.: 'Because you promised.'

After Hume and Moore some philosophers, I think, have tended to act as if these answers would not count from the strictly moral point of view unless they were accompanied by general moral rules like 'Mothers should feed their children', 'Armies should fight the enemy', and 'Men should keep their promises'. Yet the fact of the matter is that such answers do often appear to count for something without any *mention* of the appropriate rule. One might make any of several moves at this point: one might say that such rules are certainly presupposed (although obscured by the looseness or imprecision of ordinary language); or one might say that the kind of justification afforded by calling attention to the fact of motherhood, the function of armies, or the fact of having made a promise is a partial, incomplete, or low-level justification (which still requires at least logically the general rule in question); or one might say that the difference between a partial and a complete moral justification remains obscure in many respects and that the important thing about mentioning the facts in question is that in some rather important contexts they do serve as a moral justification regardless of what kind of moral justification it may turn out to be (certainly the answers given in the preceding paragraph often serve as 'stoppers' or ends to the inquiry in question). Each of these approaches is, of course, plagued by a myriad of problems; but either the second or third approach would, I think, help us to see that even when Burke does attach moral significance to various roles, institutions, and practices, without explicit mention of *any* general moral rule, this is not necessarily a sign of moral deficiency in Burke or a logical flaw in his argument so much as it is a reflection of the fact that his arguments reflect the complexity (and even imprecision) of what goes on in moral discourse. Between the second and third approaches, I should (tentatively) choose the second, believing, as I do, that Burke and the natural law tradition have generally been more conscious of the importance of general rules (beginning, of course, with the rule, 'Do good and avoid evil') and more aware of a hierarchy both of values *and* of levels of justification than their critics have often recognized.*

With this preamble, I have hopefully established a sympathetic atmosphere for the following claim: Burke's (informal) insight into moral discourse is this, that the kind of justification that occurs on the level (or levels) of positive law and legal precedent should be seen in certain contexts as being acceptable from the moral point of view, although in terms of the natural law it remains a limited and incomplete justification. One of Burke's chief points about the reasoning process, whether it be in morals, religion, politics, or the law, seems to be that most men have not the time, inclination, or training to go back always to first principles and to make the complicated deductions that such operations may sometimes require. Generally speaking they are saved from such labours by being able to fall back upon habit, precedent, established rules and conventions, and even general opinion. More specifically, the majority of men are saved from such inquiries by the fact that there are 'natural' limitations which inhere in the various contexts (usually practical) in which they operate. A mother once reminded of the fact of her motherhood would not ordinarily inquire further and would, perhaps justly, be accused of being cold or unfeeling if she did, and our reluctant party-goer once reminded of his promise would probably go off to the party grumbling rather than appear to be a person who does not keep his promises. This is not to say that these limitations are always inviolable, that the mother

---

* For relevant discussions of the logic of moral discourse see Max Black, 'The Gap between "Is" and "Should" ', *Philosophical Review*, LXXIII (April 1964), 165–81, and John Searle, 'How to Derive "Ought" from "Is" ', *Philosophical Review*, LXXIII (January 1964), 43–58. The arguments put forth by Black and Searle have, of course, been vigorously challenged; and my present concern is less with the question of whether the derivation of *ought* from *is* is logically defensible than with calling attention to the fact that, logically defensible or not, this language game *is* played.

or the party-goer could not persist in asking a whole series of why questions, but that in the ordinary course of events it would be considered improper or bad form to behave in this manner; and this not because of some delicate aesthetic sense of good form but because of the belief that morality to be effective simply cannot permit an incessant going back to first principles, cannot allow the limits of everyday moral discourse and decision making to be stretched or distorted in this way, if any moral business is to be done.

On this way of thinking, there is a *moral* presumption in favour of the established way of doing things including following the established rules and conventions of civil society, obeying its positive laws, and accepting the precedents provided by the laws and the courts, although the probability of rightness in particular cases may vary tremendously from civil society to civil society and even within the same civil society. It is, however, the mark of a *moral* man to obey the positive laws of his society unless he has clear-cut evidence that they work a grave injustice or inconvenience, i.e., unless he has serious reasons to break out of the 'natural limitations' inherent in the contexts in which he operates as citizen. Even in cases where there is a law that is obviously bad, he must remember that (as Burke says) 'laws like books lean on one another' and that disobedience may result in a loss of many moral as well as practical goods which civil society confers or makes possible.

Although Burke does not spell out any of this, it seems reasonable to assume that there are two principal contexts in which justification on the level of positive law and legal precedent is in his opinion acceptable from the moral point of view. First, in situations where the law or precedent in question has already been shown to be in accord with the natural law or where in extremely simple cases it is evident at once that such an accord exists, it is sufficient to point to the long existence of the law or the established nature of the precedent without in all cases running through the list of questions and all the deductions which would reaffirm the agreement of the positive law or legal precedent in question with the natural law. Second, in situations where the law or precedent in question has long stood unchallenged and where the community has prospered, this absence of dissent and distress creates a *presumption* in favour of that law or precedent so strong as to justify the continued acceptance of that law or precedent; even in cases where this law or precedent has not been formally tested according to the criteria of the natural law, the presumption is that, in the absence of overwhelming evidence to the contrary, it would pass such tests. Throughout Burke there are repeated affirmations that a happy, prosperous country is in itself evidence of the justice of the laws of that country and that a people that feel themselves to be free are free.

It is extremely difficult to evaluate the significance of these claims which appear implicit in Burke's argument that the Constitution of England does (in some contexts) derive its sole authority from the fact that it has existed time out of mind. What Burke has to say about the first context in which it is sufficient to point to the long existence of a law or precedent as evidence that this law or precedent is morally acceptable seems to be more a point about the *pragmatics* of language than about the logic of justification; and it poses no serious problem for the natural law reading of Burke to find Burke apparently saying that when a positive law or legal precedent has once passed muster in the eyes of the natural law its full credentials do not have to be repeatedly introduced into every discussion for it to be acceptable to us. From the point of view of pragmatics and of sensitivity to what actually goes on in moral discourse this seems to be a point worth noting, but in any event it poses no challenge to the ultimate authority of the natural law. Burke's handling of the second context is more difficult, for here critics have charged that Burke's use of presumption works so well for the *status quo*, for whatever laws or precedents exist, that appeals to the natural law and against positive law and legal precedent will *always* fail to get beyond this presumption. On the political level one can see some justice in this fear in that sometimes, especially in the case of English domestic policy and of his critique of the French Revolution, Burke did seem to make such a use of his doctrine of presumption against more radical or liberal applications of the natural law such as those suggested by Thomas Paine. But on the philosophical level, if we simply attend to the *meaning* of presumption as having to do with probability and not certainty, and if we remember the limits which Burke has at least formally placed upon its powers (limits in the form of questions concerning the prosperity, the sense of freedom, &c., of a people), it seems difficult to see how his doctrine of presumption, even while it affords strong initial moral sanction to that which is, was ever intended to, or could logically, stand forever in the way of a strong demand that the law or precedent in question be either *fully* justified or repudiated in a more formal test or tests in terms of the natural law.

For that matter I see no political or philosophical aspect of Burke's system which need affect the sincerity of his impassioned protestation that if the smallest rights of the poorest people in England were challenged he would defend these rights to the fullest: 'I have incurred the odium of gentlemen in this House for not paying sufficient regard to men of ample property. When, indeed, the smallest rights of the poorest people in the kingdom are in question, I would set my face against any act of pride and power countenanced by the highest, that are in it; and if it should come to the last extremity [revolution or at least civil disobedience], and to a contest of blood, God forbid! God forbid!— my part is taken: I would take my fate with the poor, and low, and feeble.'[1] On another occasion Burke, speaking of the Indian situation but also referring back to the English

---

[1] *Speech on Mr. Fox's Bill for the Repeal of the Marriage Act* (15 June 1781), *Speeches*, II, 280. (It was usually *outside* the House of Commons that Burke was often accused by various pamphleteers of paying too much regard to men of ample property.)

Revolution of 1688-9, stated 'I can conceive a necessity so urgent as to supersede all laws . . . .';[1] and it is just the superseding of all positive laws and legal precedents that the natural law requires in cases of utmost urgency. I, therefore, see no reason to suppose that Burke as a man of principle would have defended the *status quo* in seventeenth-century England to the degree that he did in eighteenth-century England (but not in eighteenth-century Ireland or India) or that he would not have participated fully in the Revolution of 1688-9 which he believed to have been a justifiable revolution on both the principal levels of justification I have been discussing. Failing to see this, I fail all the more to see any inconsistency (a) between Burke's professed belief in the natural law and his dedication to those (largely English) positive laws and legal precedents which he thought were in accord with or not in violation of the natural law, and (b) between the natural law properly conceived (at least formally) in terms of its moral supremacy over positive law and Burke's own conception of the natural law. Substantively, I find Burke's conception of the natural law inadequate from the point of view of distributive justice, but this is too long and complicated a consideration to be introduced here where my emphasis is largely upon problems of a more formal nature.

Speaking most generally what I want to say is that Burke had reasons for acting as he did and that formally at least these reasons were not in the final analysis incompatible with natural law and natural rights; even substantively, his treatment of life and liberty if not always of property seems acceptable from the point of view of natural law and natural rights. This is not to say that I think his *application of* natural law and natural rights doctrine was always correct; and in the case of the French Revolution there is room for serious doubt. However, given the data available to Burke (which is a somewhat oblique way of recalling that Burke was poorly informed about the conditions of the French

[1] *Works*, XI, 131.

under the *ancien régime*) and given his conservative reading of the natural law, he may well have reasoned at least coherently (instead of emotionally and inconsistently as his enemies charged) about the French Revolution. In any event, this is not the problem I have set out to solve.

I have been concerned rather with showing that Burke in talking of law and rights operates on two principal levels, that of positive law and legal precedent and that of natural law and natural right. I have suggested that, provided one recognizes some kind of distinction between what I have referred to as a lower level and pragmatic justification and a higher level and more formal justification, one can reconcile Burke's commitment to the natural law tradition with his belief that on the lower level of justification legal right, chartered right, ancient right, prescriptive right, and English right all can serve in various contexts as *stoppers*, as ends to inquiry and discussion in *that* context but not in all contexts. From an American point of view, as I have indicated, Burke's preference for talking about *English* liberties, constitutional guarantees and safeguards of these liberties, &c., should seem in some respects familiar. Consider, for example, the field of civil rights where the NAACP has in the past talked about the rights of Negroes as American citizens living under the protection of the Constitution more than it has talked about natural or human rights; it is only in more recent and more desperate contexts that CORE and other organizations have talked more about human rights than about legal rights. The reason for this seems clear: as long as we stand a good chance to justify our claims to rights within an established legal or political framework the less inclined we are to appeal to considerations outside of that context.

What makes Burke seem so conservative is his refusal to admit that the circumstances of the late eighteenth century were such as to justify a change of the framework of discussion from the historical and the legal level to the ultimate moral level where we ask what rights belong to man simply because he is a man. Things, Burke insisted, just were not that desperate in France or in England. Also, in England the past enjoyment of a right would ordinarily be presumed, in the context of political and legal decision making, to count as a sufficient condition for the continued enjoyment of that right in part because, according to Burke (following Blackstone), these rights when examined in the context of philosophical analysis coincide with or are expressions of natural rights. Many historic rights, especially English historic rights, instead of being contrasted with what Burke considered to be bona fide natural rights are either equivalent to them or are adequate expressions of them in civil society. There is then a difference between lower level, pragmatic justification and ultimate moral justification in Burke. If we attend to the context in which he is operating it is usually clear what sort of justification he has in mind. And what seem to be internal difficulties in his system occasioned by his approval of both historic rights and of natural rights tend to disappear if we note the differences in context and in levels of justification that are to be found in Burke's thought.

That Burke himself was fully aware of the limitations of the lower level, pragmatic justification of the sort that often functions so effectively in political and legal discussions is evident in the following passage, in which he appears to recognize the limitations which inhere in appeals to the long existence of an institution or the continuous exercise of a right: 'It is true that to say your Constitution is what it has been is no sufficient defence for those who say it is a bad constitution. It is an answer to those who say that it is a degenerate constitution. To those who say it is a bad one, I answer, Look to its effects. In all moral machinery, the moral results are its test.'[1] Burke's distinction between bad and degenerate is not at all clear, but perhaps he means

---

[1] *Speech on Reform of Representation of the Commons in Parliament, Works,* VII, 96.

to distinguish the question of the ultimate moral goodness or badness of the Constitution from the question of whether it fulfils its functions well and to suggest first that its long existence is evidence that it has been a practical success and second that this success cannot be entirely overlooked from the moral point of view. Finally, he seems to want to suggest that even the morally good and the good (success) from the practical point of view cannot be wholly disentangled when we are considering something so complex as political machinery.

If, however, it could be shown that the English Constitution was morally bad and that the distribution of rights and privileges which it provided for or sanctioned was not in accord with natural law and natural rights properly conceived, then Burke would, apparently, have ceased to talk about historic rights, about what has been, and commence to talk about natural rights, about what ought to be. That he recognized ultimately the need in some contexts to talk about natural rights is nowhere more in evidence than in the following passage: 'You hope, sir, that I think the French deserving of liberty. I certainly do. I certainly think that all men who desire it deserve it. It is not the reward of our merit, or the acquisition of our industry. *It is our inheritance. It is the birthright of our species.*'[1] Characteristically Burke then goes on to discuss the restrictions that must apply to this liberty if civil society is to exist; but it seems especially significant that Burke would employ the vocabulary of *inheritance* and *birthright* and apply these terms not as he and his contemporaries usually did to the *English* inheritance or the *English* birthright of liberty, but would rather insist that liberty is the inheritance and the birth-right of the species as a whole, i.e., that it belongs to man *qua* man regardless of the civil society in which he lives.

---

[1] Burke to Mons. Dupont, October 1789, *Correspondence of the Right Honourable Edmund Burke*, III, 105. My italics.

SUMMARY

The history of ideas may, as I noted earlier, be concerned chiefly with either the problem of correspondence or the problem of coherence. By the problem of correspondence I have in mind the relationship between the ideas of one philosopher and the ideas of another or other philosophers or between the ideas of a philosopher and those of the age or culture in which he lived; by the problem of coherence I have in mind the question of the internal consistency of a philosopher's thoughts. My emphasis in the present study has been upon the second of these problems, but I was led to this emphasis in large part because of the difficulties that one encounters when the problem of correspondence and of Burke's place in the history of ideas is considered. In Part One I have explored the historiography of Burke scholarship and have sought to explain why Burke is said by some commentators to be a utilitarian and an enemy of the natural law and by others to be a natural law theorist and a foe of utilitarianism. Following in the footsteps of those who have recently argued on behalf of the natural law reading of Burke, I have concluded that while Burke speaks the language of expediency, convenience, and utility, he also speaks in terms of justice, natural equity, and natural right. More significantly, while he speaks of equity and utility as the 'two foundations of law', he nowhere attempts to explain justice as a function of utility. I have noted, too, that the natural law tradition has scarcely been indifferent to considerations of utility, and that Burke's emphasis upon prudence, circumstance, and utility is scarcely novel in terms of the natural law tradition.

Then, of course, we face the problems of what *is* the natural law tradition and of whether there is a difference of degree or of kind between the Thomistic natural law and the natural law of the seventeenth and eighteenth centuries. Here I have argued on behalf of an older, pre-Straussian scholarship which admitted only a difference in emphasis between Thomistic natural law and seventeenth- and eighteenth-century natural law in that the former was more concerned with natural duties and the latter more concerned with natural rights. Unlike Strauss, I do not see this as establishing a difference in kind: rather I am struck by the continuities between St. Thomas and, for example, Locke. While recognizing Burke's place in the natural law tradition and accepting the fact that, like St. Thomas, he was preoccupied with duties, I do not interpret this conclusion as suggesting an especially sharp division between Burke and Locke. Part of what it means, I submit, to have a natural law theory is that such a theory allows either explicitly or implicitly for there being *both* natural duties and natural rights. Another part of what it means to have a commitment to the natural law is that one finds it valuable and at times indispensable to talk about human nature or man in general and does not feel restrained or confined to talking about particular men or men as members of some particular culture, class, or nationality.

Another way of putting this is that, on my interpretation of the natural law, it is a necessary condition that to qualify for natural law status a theory must allow for both natural duties and natural rights; it is another necessary condition that we find the concept of human nature useful and not embarrassingly vague or unmanageable. In this study I have not explored in full the relationships between these two necessary conditions, so that Parts Two and Three read in large measure like separate studies. There are, however, reasons to account for this, namely that Burke himself did not undertake such an exploration at any length and that I am extremely reluctant to undertake such an exploration on the basis of suggestions made by Burke and then to foist my conclusions upon the reader in Burke's name. Twentieth-century philosophy is, or imagines itself to be, much more sophisticated than philosophy hitherto, so that the temptation to rewrite both classical and early modern philosophies in the modern idiom and with greater precision has become almost irresistible. We have had, for example, in recent years an apparently serious and ambitious effort to present Hegel as a precursor of Wittgenstein. Such efforts while they may be exciting or helpful from the analytic point of view often place a great strain upon our sense of history; at the risk of appearing at times unduly sympathetic to Burke's frequent lack of precision I have chosen in this study to remain as faithful as possible to historical considerations and to avoid an overinterpretation of the texts in question. Historical accuracy constrains me to admit that only a general picture and not a detailed argument can be offered when it comes to representing Burke on the interconnexions of human nature and those rights which men are said to possess (rather than to earn or merit) by virtue of their humanity. Burke is much impressed by man's threefold dependence upon God, the physical world, and upon other men, and he will recognize no rights (or duties) which ignore or minimize this fact of man's dependent status. Any claim to a right which encourages the alleged possessor of that right to exercise this right as though he were wholly or largely independent of other men and could safely disregard the social context upon which he depends for his very existence was anathema to Burke. On the other hand, however, from the fact of human dependence and of the impossibility of one man's ever gaining total independence from or mastery over other men Burke reasoned that it was folly to disregard the rights of all men to life, liberty, and property. Civil society could be a going concern only if both natural duties and natural rights were recognized, and if on the political level the statesman (the philosopher in action) could see to it that the exercise of these rights and duties was carried on in an atmosphere of mutual trust and accommodation among the different parts of the body politic. While Burke believed in the moral *and* legal equality of men (equality before the law) and while like Hobbes he seems to have drawn the lesson of mutual dependence in part at least from man's approximate physical equality with other men, he did not believe that men were equal in their political or intellectual capabilities. Accordingly, he saw proposals to widen the suffrage or to reduce the qualifications for voting as an assertion of a spurious equality and a denial of the *natural* dependence of the less able, less experienced, and less informed people of a community upon their betters. Were this a critical study of Burke, I think Burke might be severely faulted for his apparent failure in this connexion to note that while *natural* dependence of some sort may be a datum of social experience, the exact sort of dependence that prevails at any given time may sometimes be altered and sometimes for the better by concerted social effort. Specifically it could be argued that as society becomes more complex *express* consent by a more or less formal and elaborate voting procedure must come to do much of the work that tacit consent may have performed in the days of an older, simpler society and that, therefore, the vital task consists not in restricting the suffrage but in seeing that it is better informed. Burke failed to grasp that the popular vote was already well on the way to becoming a necessary means in modern society to securing the ends of life, liberty, and property. It could, however, be argued that Burke's notions of dependence and hierarchy helped save him from the *philosophical* error of treating all rights as though they were on a par with one another, as though the right to vote were on the same level with the rights to life, liberty, and property and not in a means–end relationship with these more fundamental rights.

I wish now to recapitulate briefly the principal points which emerge from this study. In Part Two I have argued that Burke, for all his alleged historical awareness of the changes and differences among men, speaks of human nature as though in its essential characteristics it remains unchanged. Moreover, while Burke emphasizes the importance of habit, the passions, and prejudice to any comprehensive analysis of human nature, he does not make reason out to be wholly a slave of the passions but sees reason as at times guiding and directing the passions and hence human behaviour. Although Burke is often critical of what he calls 'naked' or 'private' reason, he praises habit, custom, and even prejudice in large part because of his respect for the 'latent wisdom' or rationality which, in his opinion, many but not all habits, customs, and prejudices exhibit when examined sympathetically. I find that he does not commend prejudice indiscriminately and that in the final analysis he will endorse only what he calls a 'just prejudice', that is, a prejudice which is in accord with morality and the natural law. Chapter II in Part Two is a long digression into Burke's aesthetic theory which was undertaken chiefly because of the fears expressed in various quarters to the effect that Burke in his *Inquiry* makes some judgements about the weaknesses of reason in relation to the passions which would undercut the claim made in his political writings that reason can often control and direct the passions. I have tried to show that these fears are largely without foundation.

In Part Three I have argued that Burke despite his deference to historic rights, to rights and privileges exercised over a long period of time, does not defer to *all* historic rights any more than he defers to all prejudices. As in the case of prejudice, he is primarily recommending an initial sympathy for historic rights, believing as he does that most of them, at least in England, will be found to be compatible with natural rights properly conceived. But, as noted above, natural rights properly conceived refer to the rights to life, liberty, and property and do not, Burke maintains, include political rights such as the right to increased popular participation in government. Burke found the whole discussion of rights in the England and Europe of the late eighteenth century to be disruptive of the peace and stability of civil society and a menace to past achievements in the securing of man's natural rights. In the final analysis Burke, however, did not lose sight of the distinction between natural law and natural rights on the one hand and positive law and historic rights on the other. Rather he affirmed that in certain contexts, in England especially, most historic rights could safely be *presumed* to satisfy the requirements of natural law and natural rights, in the absence of overwhelming evidence to the contrary. What this adds up to is that Burke's political philosophy was a conservative version of the natural law and not a denial of the natural law in the name of either history or utility.

SELECTED BIBLIOGRAPHY

WORKS BY EDMUND BURKE

The Correspondence of Edmund Burke. General Editor T. W. Copeland. University of Chicago Press and the Cambridge University Press. Chicago, 1958, 1960, 1961, 1963.

J. P. GILSON (ed.), *Correspondence of Edmund Burke and William Windham*. Cambridge University Press, 1910.

Correspondence of the Right Honourable Edmund Burke. Edited by Earl Fitzwilliam and Sir R. Bourke. 4 vols. Rivington, London, 1844.

H. V. F. SOMERSET (ed.), *A Notebook of Edmund Burke*. Cambridge University Press, 1957.

The Speeches of the Right Honourable Edmund Burke. 4 vols. Longman, Hurst, Rees, &c., London, 1816.

The Works of the Right Honorable Edmund Burke. 12 vols. Little, Brown, and Company, Boston, 1865.

WORKS BY OTHERS

ST. THOMAS AQUINAS, *Basic Writings of St. Thomas Aquinas*. 2 vols. Random House, New York, 1945.

SIR WILLIAM BLACKSTONE, *Commentaries on the Laws of England*. 2 vols. Callaghan and Company, Chicago, 1899.

DAVID HUME, *An Inquiry Concerning Human Understanding*. Henry Regnery and Company, New York, 1957.

—— *Political Essays*. Bobbs-Merrill and Company, New York, 1953.

—— *Treatise of Human Nature*. Oxford University Press, 1960.

JOHN LOCKE, *Essays on the Law of Nature*. Oxford University Press, 1960.

—— *Two Treatises of Government*. Cambridge University Press, 1960.

SECONDARY SOURCES

H. B. ACTON, 'Prejudice', *Revue Internationale de Philosophie*, VI (1952), 323–36.

JOHN DALBERG LORD ACTON, *Essays on Church and State*. Hollis and Carter, London, 1952.

GORDON W. ALLPORT, *The Nature of Prejudice*. Addison-Wesley Publishing Company, Boston, 1954.

MORTON AUERBACH, *The Conservative Illusion*. Columbia University Press, New York, 1959.

SIR ERNEST BARKER, *Essays on Government*. Oxford University Press, 1945.

—— *Traditions of Civility*. Cambridge University Press, 1948.

ROBERT BISSET, *Life of Edmund Burke*. George Cawthorn, London, 1800.

MAX BLACK, 'The Gap between "Is" and "Should" ', *Philosophical Review*, LXXIII (April 1964), 165–81.

J. T. BOULTON, Introduction to Burke's *A Philosophical Enquiry into the Origin of Our Ideas of the Sublime and Beautiful*. Routledge and K. Paul, London, 1958.

—— *The Language of Politics in the Age of Wilkes and Burke*. Routledge and K. Paul, London, 1963.

—— 'An Unpublished Letter from Paine to Burke', *Durham University Journal*, XLIII (1951), 49–55.

A. P. BROGAN, 'John Locke and Utilitarianism', *Ethics*, LXIX (January 1959), 79–93.

DONALD CROSS BRYANT, *Edmund Burke and His Literary Friends*. Washington University Press, St. Louis, 1939.

FRANCIS P. CANAVAN, *The Political Reason of Edmund Burke*. Duke University Press, Durham, 1960.

WILSON O. CLOUGH, 'Reason and Genius,—An Eighteenth Century Dilemma', *Philosophical Quarterly*, XXIII (January 1944), 33–54.

ALFRED COBBAN, *Edmund Burke and the Revolt against the Eighteenth Century*. George Allen and Unwin, London, 1960.

JAMES COLLINS, *A History of Modern European Philosophy*. Bruce Publishing Company, Milwaukee, 1956.

CARL B. CONE, *Burke and the Nature of Politics, The Age of the American Revolution*. University of Kentucky Press, Lexington, 1957.

—— 'The Burke Revival', *The Burke Newsletter*, III (1961–2), 72–85.

THOMAS W. COPELAND, 'Edmund Burke and the Book Reviews in Dodsley's *Annual Register*', *PMLA*, XLV (June 1942), 446–68.

—— *Our Eminent Friend Edmund Burke*. Yale University Press, New Haven, 1949.

C. P. COURTNEY, *Montesquieu and Burke*. Blackwell, Oxford, 1963.

RICHARD H. COX, *Locke on War and Peace*. Oxford University Press, 1960.

JAMES F. DAVIDSON, 'Natural Law and International Law in Edmund Burke', *The Review of Politics*, XXI (July 1959), 483–94.

W. A. DUNNING, *A History of Political Theories from Rousseau to Spencer*. Macmillan and Company, New York, 1920.

MARIO EINAUDI, 'The British Background of Burke's Political Thought', *Political Science Quarterly*, XLIX (December 1934), 576–98.

R. R. FENNESSY, *Burke, Paine, and the Rights of Man*. Martin Nijhoff, The Hague, 1963.

OTTO GIERKE, *Political Theories of the Middle Ages*. Cambridge University Press, 1951.

J. W. GOUGH, *John Locke's Political Philosophy*. Oxford University Press, 1950.

G. H. GUTTRIDGE, *English Whiggism and the American Revolution*. University of California Press, Berkeley, 1942.

H. L. A. HART, *The Concept of Law*. Oxford University Press, 1961.

F. J. C. HEARNSHAW, *The Social and Political Ideas of Some Representative Thinkers of the Revolutionary Era*. G. G. Harrap and Company, London, 1931.

W. S. HOLDSWORTH, *A History of English Law*. Methuen, London, 1923.
ROBERT M. HUTCHINS, 'The Theory of Oligarchy: Edmund Burke', *The Thomist*, V (1943), 61–78.
—— 'The Theory of the State: Edmund Burke', *Review of Politics*, V (April 1943), 139–55.
WILLMORE KENDALL, *John Locke and the Doctrine of Majority-Rule*. University of Illinois Press, Urbana, 1941.
RUSSELL KIRK, 'Burke and Natural Rights', *Review of Politics*, XIII (October 1951), 441–56.
—— *The Conservative Mind from Burke to Santayana*. H. Regnery and Company, Chicago, 1953.
J. A. LESTER, 'An Analysis of the Conservative Thought of Edmund Burke'. A Doctoral Thesis, Harvard University, 1942.
EWART LEWIS, 'Natural Law and Expediency in Medieval Political Theory', *Ethics*, L (January 1940), 144–63.
JOHN MACCUNN, *The Political Philosophy of Burke*. Longmans, London, 1913.
C. B. MACPHERSON, 'Edmund Burke', *Transactions of the Royal Society of Canada*, LII (June 1959), 19–26.
—— *The Political Theory of Possessive Individualism, Hobbes to Locke*. Oxford University Press, 1962.
SIR PHILIP MAGNUS, *Edmund Burke: A Life*. John Murray, London, 1939.
THOMAS H. D. MAHONEY, *Edmund Burke and Ireland*. Harvard University Press, Cambridge, 1960.
NORMAN MALCOLM, *Ludwig Wittgenstein, A Memoir*. Oxford University Press, 1958.
JACQUES MARITAIN, *The Rights of Man and Natural Law*. Bles, London, 1944.
CHARLES H. MONSON, 'Locke and His Interpreters', *Political Studies*, VI (1958), 120–33.
J. L. MONTROSE, Review-essay on Stanlis's *Edmund Burke and the Natural Law*, *Natural Law Forum*, VI (1961), 201–25.
SAMUEL ELIOT MORISON and HENRY STEEL COMMAGER, *The Growth of the American Republic*. Oxford University Press, 1956.
JOHN MORLEY, *Burke*. Macmillan, London, 1923.
R. H. MURRAY, *Studies in the English Social and Political Thinkers of the Nineteenth Century*. W. Heffer and Sons, Cambridge, 1929.
SIR LEWIS NAMIER, *Personalities and Powers*. H. Hamilton, London, 1955.
H. V. S. OGDEN, 'The State of Nature and the Decline of Lockian Political Theory in England 1760–1800', *American Historical Review*, XLVI (October 1940), 21–44.
ANNIE MARION OSBORN, *Rousseau and Burke, A Study in the Idea of Liberty in Eighteenth Century Political Thought*. Oxford University Press, 1940.
CHARLES PARKIN, *The Moral Basis of Burke's Political Thought*. Cambridge University Press, 1956.

JOHN PLAMENATZ, *Man and Society*. Longmans, London, 1963.
J. H. PLUMB, *England in the Eighteenth Century*. Penguin Books, London, 1950.
J. G. A. POCOCK, 'Burke and the Ancient Constitution—A Problem in the History of Ideas', *The Historical Journal*, III (1960), 125–43.
SIR FREDERICK POLLOCK, *Essays in the Law*. Macmillan and Company, London, 1922.
JAMES PRIOR, *A Life of Edmund Burke*. Baldwin, Cradock and Joy, London, 1891.
CHARLES R. RITCHESON, *British Politics and the American Revolution*. University of Oklahoma Press, Norman, 1954.
DAVID RITCHIE, *Natural Rights*. George Allen and Unwin, London, 1895.
ARTHUR K. ROGERS, 'Burke's Social Philosophy', *American Journal of Sociology*, XVIII (July 1912), 51–76.
MURRAY ROTHBARD, 'A Note on Burke's Vindication of Natural Society', *Journal of the History of Ideas*, XIX (January 1958), 114–18.
GEORGE SABINE, *A History of Political Theory*. Henry Holt and Company, New York, 1950.
ARTHUR P. I. SAMUELS, *The Early Life Correspondence and Writings of the Right Honourable Edmund Burke*. Cambridge University Press, 1923.
JOHN SEARLE, 'How to Derive "Ought" from "Is" ', *Philosophical Review*, LXXIII (January 1964), 43–58.
MARTIN SELIGER, 'Locke's Natural Law and the Foundation of Politics', *Journal of the History of Ideas*, XXIV (1963), 333–54.
RICHARD SEWALL, 'Rousseau's Second Discourse in England from 1755 to 1762', *Philological Quarterly*, XVII (1938), 97–114.
MARCUS G. SINGER, 'On Duties to Oneself', *Ethics*, LXIX (April 1959), 202–5.
PETER J. STANLIS, *Edmund Burke and the Natural Law*. University of Michigan Press, Ann Arbor, 1958.
LESLIE STEPHEN, *History of English Thought in the Eighteenth Century*. Smith, Elder, and Company, London, 1881.
LEO STRAUSS, *Natural Right and History*. University of Chicago Press, Chicago, 1953.
—— *The Political Philosophy of Hobbes*. Oxford University Press, 1936.
—— *What Is Political Philosophy? and Other Studies*. Free Press, Glencoe, 1959.
J. W. STUBBS, *The History of the University of Dublin from its Foundation to the End of the Eighteenth Century*. Longmans, London, 1890.
G. M. TREVELYAN, *History of England*. Doubleday and Company, New York, 1952.
C. E. VAUGHAN, *Studies in the History of Political Philosophy before and after Rousseau*. University of Manchester Press, Manchester, 1939.
GRAHAM WALLAS, *Human Nature in Politics*. A. Constable and Company, London, 1948.
DIXON WECTER, 'Burke's Theory Concerning Words, Images, and Emotions', *PMLA*, LX (March 1940), 167–81.

J. C. WESTON, JR., 'The Ironic Purpose of Burke's Vindication Vindicated', *Journal of the History of Ideas*, XIX (June 1958), 435-41.
BURLEIGH T. WILKINS, 'The Nature of Rousseau', *The Journal of Politics*, XXI (November 1959), 663–84.
WOODROW WILSON, *Mere Literature*. Houghton, Mifflin, and Company, Boston, 1924.
—— 'Edmund Burke and the French Revolution', *Century Illustrated Monthly Magazine*, LXII (September, 1901), 784–92.
ARTHUR L. WOEHL, 'Burke's Readings'. A Doctoral Thesis, Cornell University, 1928.
JOHN W. YOLTON, 'Locke on the Law of Nature', *Philosophical Review*, LXVII (1958), 477–98.

INDEX OF NAMES

SUBJECT INDEX